PALESTINE UNWRAPPED

PALESTINE UNWRAPPED

Stories from real people and places of the Holy Land

KIRSTY LE GRICE

First published in the UK in May 2025 by
Journey Books, an imprint of Bradt Travel Guides Ltd
31a High Street, Chesham, Buckinghamshire, HP5 1BW, England
www.bradtguides.com

Text copyright © 2025 Kirsty Le Grice
Edited by Gail Simmons
Cover design by Ian Spick with art by Thirusha Abeyewardene
Part openers and section breaks by Thirusha Abeyewardene
All photos © Kirsty Le Grice
Layout and typesetting by Ian Spick
Maps by David McCutcheon FBCart.S
Production managed by Sue Cooper, Bradt & Page Bros

The right of Kirsty Le Grice to be identified as the author of this work has been asserted by her in accordance with the Copyright, Designs & Patents Act 1988.

All rights reserved. All views expressed in this book are the views of the author and not those of the publisher. No part of this publication may be reproduced, stored in a retrieval system, or transmitted in any form or by any means, electronic, mechanical, photocopying, recording or otherwise without the prior consent of the publisher.

ISBN: 9781804693186

British Library Cataloguing in Publication Data
A catalogue record for this book is available from the British Library
Digital conversion by www.dataworks.co.in
Printed in the UK by Page Bros

To find out more about our Journey Books imprint,
visit www.bradtguides.com/journeybooks

Paper used for this product comes from sustainably managed forests, and recycled and controlled sources.

CONTENTS

MAPS ix
Israel and Palestine ix
Jerusalem x
The West Bank xi

PREFACE xiii

**PART 1 – THE PEOPLE
AND PLACES OF JERUSALEM** 1

INTRODUCTION 2
The Roots of Jerusalem 2
Moving to Jerusalem 7

CHAPTER 1 – THE HEART OF THE CITY 13
Old City Treasures 13
Being Jerusalemite 21
The Hometown Tourist 25
Sheikh Jarrah Life 28
Round the Table 31

CHAPTER 2 – THE RELIGIONS 36
Cloaks and Clothes 38
Easter 42
Ramadan 46
Haredi Life 49

CHAPTER 3 – THE POLITICS 56
Yad Vashem 57
Temple Talk 60
No Deal 62
Silwan 65

CHAPTER 4 – THE LOCAL BUSINESSES 71
A Bookshop with Soul 71
More Than a Corner Shop 74
Zalatimo Sweets 76
A Hotel With a History 78

CHAPTER 5 – THE LAND 84
Running in the City 84
The Scrapheap 87
Liquid Gold 90
The Demolition 95

CHAPTER 6 – THE OCCUPATION 100
Palestinian Lives Matter 100
The Battle for Sheikh Jarrah 102
The Eleven-Day War 107
Civil War 112
Shireen 114

FOLLOWING THE STAR 119

PART 2 – THE PEOPLE AND PLACES OF OCCUPIED AND HISTORIC PALESTINE 123

THE CHAMELEON 124

CHAPTER 7 – BETHLEHEM 128
Crossing the Checkpoint 128
Aida Refugee Camp 135
The Old Woman and Her Olives 140
Backstreet Bethlehem 143
Christmas in Bethlehem 148

CHAPTER 8 – SOUTHERN PALESTINE 153
The Abundance of Battir 153
Settler Troubles 156
The Nuns of Artas 160
Enclosed in Wadi Fukin 163
Feeling the Heat in Hebron 167

CHAPTER 9 – DESERT DWELLING 173
Hiking Wadi Qelt 173
Desert Adventures at Nabi Musa 177
Under the Night Sky 180
The Baptism 183
National(ism) Parks 186

CHAPTER 10 – CITIES AND SAINTS 190
Smelling the Air in Nablus 190
A Home Visit in Ramallah 197

The Saints of Aboud 202
Palestinian Breweries 207

CHAPTER 11 – OFF THE BEATEN TRACK 211
Nisf Jubeil 211
Encounters in Sebastiya 214
Swimming at Al-Badhan 217
Spring in Zababdeh 221
Tobacco Picking in Zabuba 224

CHAPTER 12 – HISTORIC PALESTINE 230
The Ghosts of Lifta 231
Mary of Nazareth 235
Juicy Jaffa 238
Coexistence in Haifa 242
Defending Akko 245
Kindness in Umm Al-Fahm 247
Survival in the Negev 250

WRAPPING UP 256

READER'S GUIDE 260

ACKNOWLEDGEMENTS 273

PALESTINE UNWRAPPED

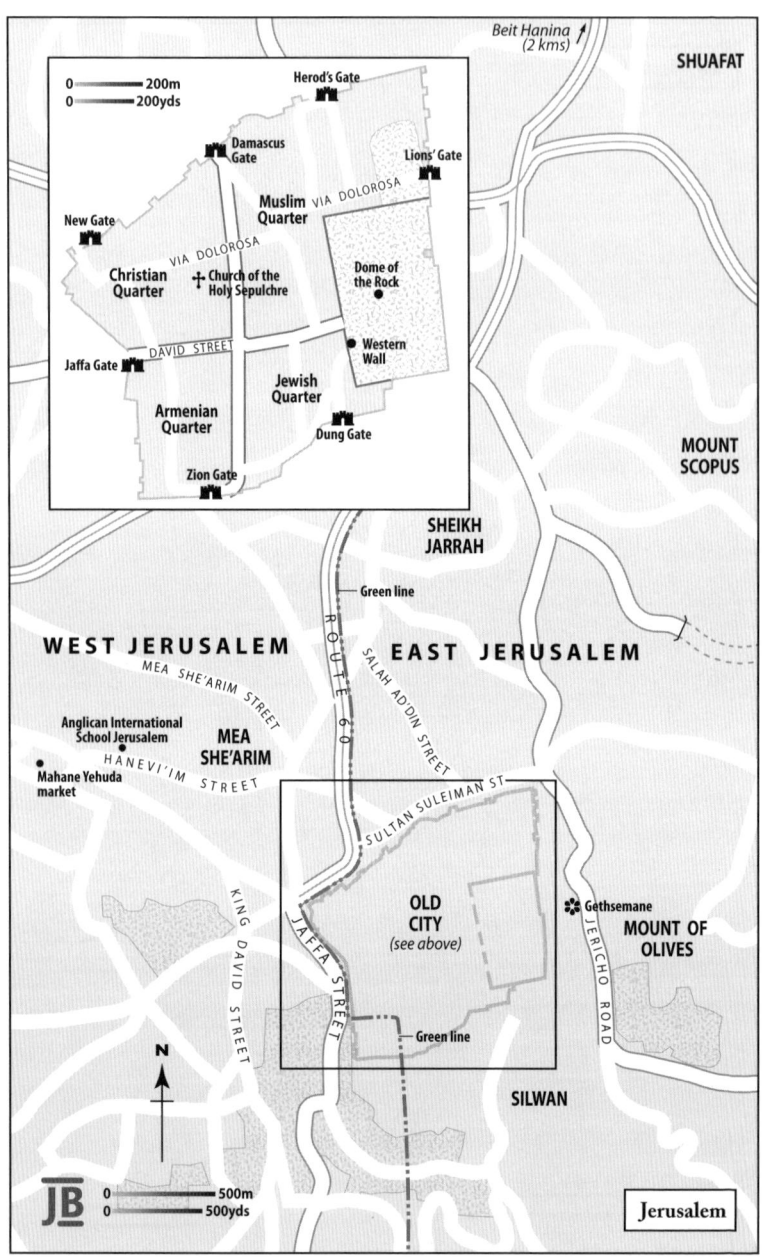

Jerusalem

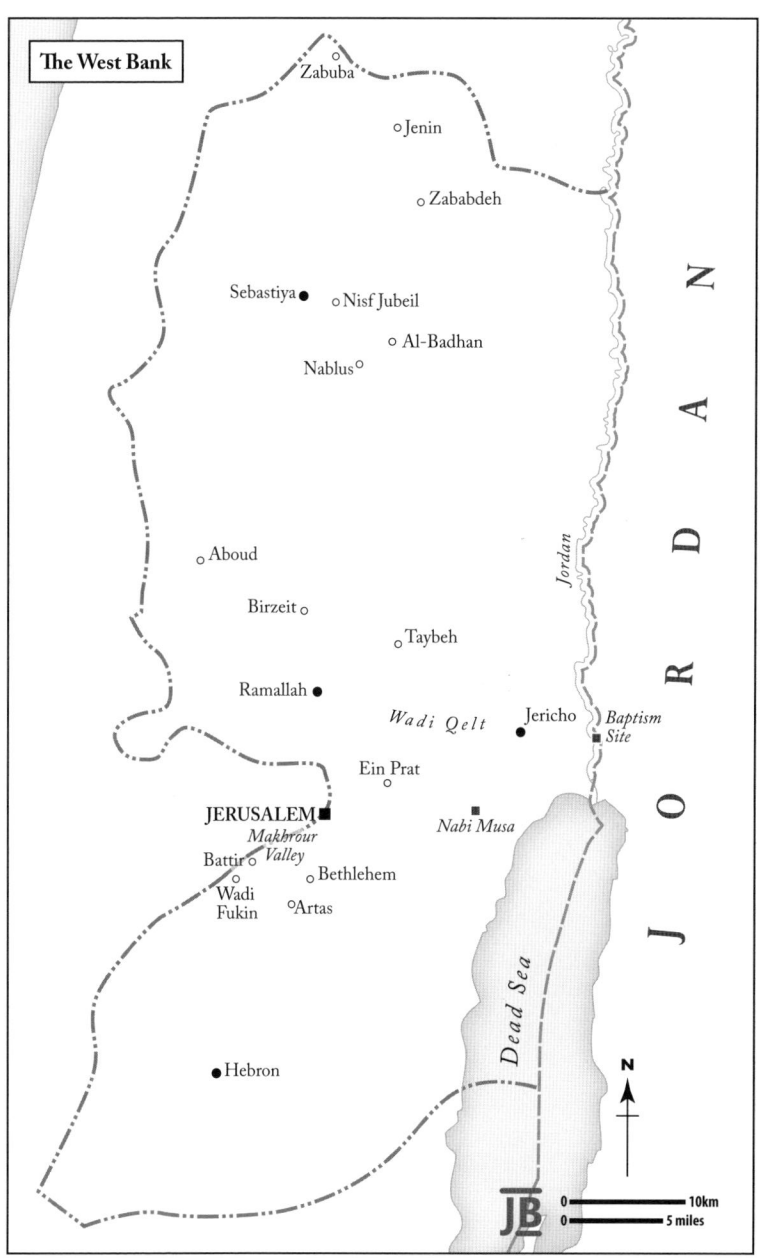

PALESTINE UNWRAPPED

PREFACE

The events in this book took place between 2019 and 2022, during a time when unwrapping Palestine was something that could be savoured if you approached it with a little care, and writing a book to inspire future travellers felt relevant and exciting. Certainly, Palestine had never been an easy destination, but the rewards were more than worth it for the lucky few with the time and opportunity to delve deeper.

During my time in Jerusalem, as part of the international community, I was able to travel extensively across Israel and Palestine and the experience was life-changing. The only area of Israel and Palestine that was not accessible to me was Gaza (or *Raza* as pronounced in the Arabic dialect). Since 7th October 2023 and the devastating events that have followed, the people and places of Gaza have become horrifyingly familiar to people around the world who have been traumatised by the level of brutality which continues to unfold in full view of a global audience.

Although I never saw Gaza with my own eyes, I didn't have to look far to see daily injustices and the layered systems of oppression perpetuated by the Israeli occupying powers against the citizens of the Palestinian West Bank which includes East Jerusalem.

This book is for people around the world who, at the time of writing, are not able to visit Palestine in person. It's for anyone who wants to understand Palestine but doesn't know where to start with a place and a conflict that is age-old, politically evocative and has its own complex lexicon. It's for anyone who wants to see the human face of Palestine and understand some of the realities of life in Israel, Palestine and Jerusalem. Above all, it's for the people of

Palestine, and my own way of saying: we see you and we carry your hope for a better future when you may feel that all is lost.

The characters of the story are the people I encountered while living and travelling in the region, and it is their words and their lives that help to give dimension to what it means to be a Palestinian living in Palestine. Through their stories, I hope you will get to know the place behind the headlines better. In unwrapping Palestine layer by layer, I fell in love with it, and I offer you a share of the wonderful place I discovered in these pages.

December 2024

PART 1
THE PEOPLE AND PLACES OF JERUSALEM

INTRODUCTION

The Roots of Jerusalem

Standing in the Garden of Gethsemane, about to pick olives from the ancient trees where Jesus once sat, with the gold roof of the Dome of the Rock glinting in the background, and with a real-life, brown-robed Monk standing in front of us I thought, *'perhaps this is Jerusalem.'* Fra Diego, the Franciscan monk in charge of proceedings in the garden, scanned his eyes over the group of randomly assorted helpers that had responded to his open call to help pick the Gethsemane harvest. He invited us, in a show of solidarity, to introduce ourselves not by name but by the countries we came from before leading a prayer to kick things off.

I stood with one eye open, and the awkwardly clenched hands of someone not as at ease with prayer as the city expected. I already suspected that the longer I lived in Jerusalem, the more of a stranger it would be to me, and I couldn't think of another place on Earth where such a paradox could be so astonishingly true.

The October sun cast a warm glow over the group. When it finally came, I breathed out the *Amen* with a sigh of relief. If God was present here, I could believe he was in the trees. These ancient oracles, looking every inch like gnarly grandmothers, held me spellbound. Since before Jesus's time, these same trees had given an annual harvest to sustain those who lived under them. For thousands of years their roots had clung to the soil, bearing witness to history as they held their arms open to the world, renewing themselves each year to offer a new crop.

Fra Diego set us loose to choose a tree and find a vantage point to pick from. The children (my own two included) picked

INTRODUCTION

olives from the lower branches as the adults competed for rickety wooden ladders and balanced themselves precariously in the upper reaches. Tarpaulins were placed beneath each tree, and we were told to simply drop the olives on to them. Each olive had to be individually plucked, and it could take an hour or more to clear a single branch. It was satisfyingly repetitive and purposeful. A fun novelty for us as Western adults who were distanced from our food sources.

Within minutes, Diego reappeared, his robes exchanged for khaki-coloured, more practical, working clothes. He moved between the groups, offering ladders and conversation to us as we worked. He told me he had lived in Jerusalem for 10 years already and I asked if he now considered this home.

'Only God knows how long I will stay here,' he responded. I wasn't surprised. Jerusalem was a place that held the person, rather than the person holding the city. Sort of like a beguiling prison of the soul.

Several hours of picking later, Fra Diego ushered us into a small stone room and hit the button which cranked his small olive press machine into action. He invited us to huddle round and watch as the olives were mulched into a thick flow of cloudy green oil. My hair was caked in the dust of the city, and our faces and clothes were streaked with the remnants of a dry summer. A fresh-faced nun offered us a small piece of bread to dip into the oil and the taste was bold and striking. It was the sort of taste that filled our mouths and nose with a rich and silken earthiness that had been squeezed directly from the land. Sure, other places grew olives, but this view, the history, the religions, the cultures: the city had something unique.

Jerusalem is both the jewel in the crown and the thorn in the side. The city is revered by Jews, Muslims and Christians, and is seen by many as the centre of the world. Over thousands of years, so many had sweated, wept and bled on to the earth to build this awe-inspiring city. Even for a cautious believer like me there was a special aura that hung over Jerusalem.

Instead of bringing Jerusalem protection, its holiness has brought centuries of violence and unrest. In 1949, the city was split into an **East** – Palestinian – side and a **West** – Israeli – side. This division continues to be deeply felt, and **Israel's** illegal **occupation** of East Jerusalem in 1967 only served to widen the gap. In theory the occupation reunited Jerusalem under one single municipality but the reality on the ground is very different.

In April 2019, I moved to Jerusalem with my two children (then aged two and four) for my husband's work. We were joining the expat international community for the first time and were happy to be sucked into the close-knit world of those on an overseas posting. People we'd only just met treated us like family and there was a unifying camaraderie. We moved into a new apartment block in **Sheikh Jarrah**, a neighbourhood in East Jerusalem.

There were no absolutes, and the first question I faced was, *'where am I? Do I have an address here?'* The most searched-for term online regarding **Palestine** asked, 'is Palestine a country?' There are different answers to this. While, as of June 2024, 146 out of 193 UN member states recognised Palestine as a state, the US, UK, France, Germany, Canada, Australia, Japan and South Korea did not. It did not have the full functions or authorities of a state such as control over its borders, economy and security, and it was under Israeli military occupation. Palestine had 'non-member observer state' status within the United Nations and most countries referred to it as the **'Occupied Palestinian Territories' (OPTs)**. For brevity, I refer to Palestine when talking about land that falls within the OPTs.

Another complication was that Israel had yet to define all its borders, which made it easier to justify further encroachments into Palestinian land. Some people denied the right of Palestine to exist, others denied the right of Israel to exist, and Jerusalem sat in the middle torn between its overlapping identities. The lines were blurred creating confusion and conflict. So no, I didn't have an agreed address but there wasn't a local postal service anyway so it barely mattered.

Every day I saw glimpses of the city, but it was never enough to piece together an understanding. I wanted to truly know the city and what lay beyond it, but there was a huge gulf between us. I didn't speak Arabic or Hebrew and there was something about *who I was* that would never allow me to unlock *what it was*. From an early stage, I knew that to see Jerusalem was not enough to know it. But how could I ever scratch the surface to gain a deeper understanding?

In this book, I try to make sense of life in Sheikh Jarrah, in Jerusalem and in Palestine. All three were part of my address and yet each of the three was its own world. Israel was inextricably linked to each of these places and there were times when I didn't know if I was in Israel or in Palestine. In exploring Jerusalem and beyond, my day-to-day life was predominantly spent among Palestinians. It is important that everyone has a voice but the greater focus I have given to Palestinian lives directly reflects my experiences. To live in East Jerusalem was to see the effects of the illegal occupation of Israel played out in a thousand different ways each day.

As I saw and understood more, the question, *'how can we let this happen?'* always returned to me. It was hard to live in Jerusalem and not feel complicit in a system of separation and discrimination: an apartheid, for want of a better phrase. Getting under the skin of Israel and Palestine was an uncomfortable experience.

There was an urgency to this. Palestine was disappearing at an alarming rate, and we were all watching it happen. The Israeli occupation of Palestine in 1967 had been normalised and settlement building continued at pace. Israel was not held accountable for its breaches of international law and so they continued to take bolder steps. They started building the **separation wall** in 2002 and locked over two million people into **Gaza** from 2006. Over 40,000 people were killed in Gaza between October 2023–4 and still there was no accountability, so what could **West Bank** Palestinians expect next?

All references to Israel in this book relate to the machinery of the Israeli state (its government, military, police and other authorities). References to the expansion of Israel into Palestine call out the wrongdoings of the Israeli state and not the Israeli or Jewish people themselves. The creation of Israel in **1948** finally gave a recognised home to the Jewish population worldwide and this, along with the unique cultural richness of Israel, also needed to be protected.

The language and terminology applied to Israel and Palestine is confusing for casual readers not familiar with the subject. The reader's guide at the back offers a glossary of the words that have specific meanings in the context of Israel and Palestine, and most of these are included in bold where they first appear in the text.

This book is about the people and the places that I encountered in the **Holy Land**.

INTRODUCTION

By starting in East Jerusalem and then branching outwards to Palestine and **historic Palestine,** I sought to organise the chaos of my experiences into a tangible version of Palestine. I want you to taste and feel the Jerusalem and Palestine that I saw. I want you to be inspired to see it with your own eyes one day but above all, I want you to better understand what is happening in Jerusalem and Palestine and to feel more confident in talking about the issues. Despite the immense challenges faced, Jerusalem and Palestine are spectacular places unlike anywhere else in the world.

Moving to Jerusalem

It was April 2019 in Edinburgh, Scotland. My excitement at the prospect of moving to Jerusalem was only slightly deflated by the response to *telling people* I was moving to Jerusalem.

'Why are you moving to Israel?'

'Isn't there a war there?'

'Will the kids be safe?'

The questions kept coming, and I did my best to answer them based on my own sketchy understanding.

'We'll be living in East Jerusalem, which is the Palestinian bit, but Israel annexed it years ago...' I trailed off. 'Yes, there is a conflict, but we will be completely safe and separate from that. Although we need to dress modestly, and we can't drive in certain areas on Shabbat, or they might throw stones at us, and we'll often need to pass through checkpoints...' My voice caught, confused by the number of contradictions. **Checkpoints** and stone-throwing were indeed a far cry from the neat and clipped lives we had enjoyed in Scotland.

I became very familiar with the look of surprise as eyebrows shot up and a forced smile was pasted on to colleagues' and friends' faces. I had great respect for the few who simply responded, 'fantastic, when can I visit?'

The truth was that I didn't have a clue until I arrived what it would feel like. For me, a move to Jerusalem may as well have been a move to a distant planet. I knew nothing about the geography, the history, the people or the place. My husband Paul, on the other hand, had been eagerly learning and reading about the region since he was a teenager, and the chance to work there was a dream come true for him. In a matter of weeks, we packed up our lives, I took a career break from the job I loved, and we strapped our kids in for the ride.

Would I be free to walk around? To drive? Would a T-shirt be considered revealing?

I approached Jerusalem with an open mind and a curious spirit. I didn't have any preconceptions to pack and that made it easier to take things at face value. The first few months passed by in a blur, and it was only when we returned to the UK over Christmas that I felt that we had left the pressure cooker of Jerusalem behind and could start to reflect on our experiences. I could never find the right words to respond to the recurring question: 'what is it like?' Jerusalem wasn't a place you could summarise in a few lines, and I stuttered and stumbled my way through responses.

In 2019 there was a conflict underway, but it wasn't a war as such. Even the word 'conflict' was dismissed by Palestinians as suggesting a two-way struggle which they had not entered into. I volunteered with people who had refugee status, though they had continued living in their homes since 1948. The countryside and architecture were beautiful, yet it was scarred with ugly walls and violence. I could travel freely, but most Palestinians lived under constant restrictions with curtailed human rights. The situation was so complex and entirely with its own language and jargon that I struggled to simplify it for others.

I wanted our friends and family to see the immense beauty and cultural richness we were tripping over for themselves. In responding to questions from friends and family, I tried to give my enthusiasm the loudest voice and I was still fresh enough to pepper my reflections with hope for the future.

Several days later, on a cold January morning, we left Edinburgh before dawn to return to Jerusalem. It was breakfast time in Brussels as we queued for our second flight of the day. Black hats and beards jostled for position at the departure gate for the flight to Tel Aviv's Ben Gurion Airport – an instant reminder of the religious fervency of our destination. After eight months of living in Jerusalem, the Jewish Haredi (often called the Orthodox or Ultra-Orthodox) way of life remained a complete mystery to me, and I desperately wanted to peek behind the heavy black curtain it seemed that they lived their lives behind.

Boarding the plane, I felt a thrill of excitement that we were returning to Jerusalem as residents. Sitting with our seatbelts on, the aisles were still jammed with activity. Large hat boxes were awkwardly wedged into the overhead luggage racks and there was much fidgeting and fussing. I hoped we wouldn't be delayed. A previous flight we'd taken to Tel Aviv had missed its take-off slot due to a game that could only be described as 'seat chess'. Strong Orthodox Jewish convictions dictated who could sit where and beside whom, and the air hostess had been dismissed out of hand when she tried to insist that everyone took the seats marked on their tickets.

Our first few months in Jerusalem had taught me to always expect the unexpected and to try to avoid making assumptions about people and their circumstances. The blunt style of Israeli communication could come across as abrasive to sensitive British sensibilities. Passers-by on the street felt entitled to give advice on if your kids were dressed warmly enough and how to parent them. It wasn't so much a gentle enquiry but more of a 'STOP, YOU HAVE TO...' and many of the international people I knew bristled in the face of this audacity despite it being well meaning in most cases.

Part of the challenge was that the city pulsed with the rhythm of several different drumbeats, and it was rare that the outcome was melodic. Each **religion** observed not only different holidays but different working days each week.

The Israeli weekend was Friday and Saturday, to accommodate the start of Shabbat (the Sabbath) on Friday evening which brought West Jerusalem and parts of Israel to a standstill for 24 hours. In Jerusalem, many shops, restaurants and even public transport ground to a halt from late afternoon on Friday until after the horn (which sounded like an air raid siren) had signalled the end of Shabbat on Saturday evening.

Shabbat was essentially a day of rest for the observant where operating machinery, or any form of work, was forbidden. This meant not even turning on a light switch. Food had to be pre-prepared and lifts in hotels were programmed to stop at every floor so that they could be used without any buttons having to be pressed. It was recommended that we didn't break any bones on a Saturday as even Israeli hospitals were not exempt from these strict requirements. We were told that although hospitals remained open, they offered a reduced service. Despite Israel being a highly developed tech country, for many people respecting Shabbat was paramount.

INTRODUCTION

East Jerusalem, where we lived, ran to a different schedule. Many Palestinians took Friday and Saturday off, especially if they worked in Israel, but others took Friday and Sunday off. This was to show solidarity between Muslims (whose main prayer day was Friday) and Palestinian Christians. In some families, the children had different days off from their parents. In contrast, the international community generally stuck to a Saturday and Sunday weekend.

Living in East Jerusalem we were not overly affected by Shabbat as there were always Palestinian places open. The main challenge was navigating around road closures if we went out on a Saturday and had to cut through West Jerusalem to get home. We still hadn't had any stones thrown at our car, but this was relatively common, and the threat was ever present. Whole streets were blockaded as 'no drive' areas and that sent a clear message. Our biggest nemesis was Google Maps, which found it hard to keep up with local customs and often tried to lead us into danger.

Figuring out where to go and when was difficult. If it was Saturday, you might struggle to find somewhere open for lunch or a coffee in Israel, but Palestinian places were open. On Sunday, the beaches in Tel Aviv were quiet and Palestine was open unless it was a Christian town. Once you threw a wide range of religious holidays for different religions into the mix, it became thrilling and exasperating in equal measure. It felt like there was always something unexpected going on and this added to the drama of the city. Things were never still and there was never a dull day.

Returning to our journey, after two flights and a long day of travelling, the taxi pulled up outside our modern apartment building on Raghib Nashashibi Street in Sheikh Jarrah. We spent the evening unpacking and breathing life back into the apartment.

We were starting 2020 with a calendar full of planned visits from friends and family and the year stretched ahead like an exciting road to be travelled.

After eight solid months of exploring, Jerusalem and Palestine had only started to reveal themselves to me, and I knew there was much more to see and many more people to meet if I was to begin to scratch the surface of this cryptic, mystic place.

CHAPTER 1
THE HEART OF THE CITY

Jerusalem has its own stone, a milky coloured limestone, which has been used for thousands of years, block by block, to build a stage for the city. The stones have been crafted into some of the most revered places in the world, including the Western Wall, the Dome of the Rock, and the Church of the Holy Sepulchre. The places of Jerusalem undeniably make it valuable, but it is the people who breathe life into the city. It is impossible to separate the people from the places. Many would rather die than leave their city.

This chapter introduces the **Old City** and Sheikh Jarrah, two places that have shaped Jerusalem immeasurably. It then looks at identity in Jerusalem through the lens of several Palestinian voices and an Israeli student to consider how the people and places of Jerusalem interact or if they orbit in different spaces.

Old City Treasures

Turning on to Al-Ya'aqubi Street, just before 9am, I heard the familiar sound, '*Kaaaaaaaaaaaaaaaak, baed, falafel,*' echo down the street. It was sung like a call to prayer. Instead of drawing people to the mosque, however, this was a call to buy fresh Jerusalem bread, eggs and falafel. Every day the word '*ka'ak*' was lengthened and '*baed, falafel*' was shortened to give the call a jauntiness that was lighthearted. I smiled as I walked along the street.

The *ka'ak* man was neither young nor old. His smile and eyes revealed a youthful spirit as he walked, slightly limping, down the middle of the street. Sometimes a young boy of around eight trailed along beside him, but today he was alone. His wares were perched on a wooden board, balanced on his head.

'Good morning,' he greeted me in Arabic.

'*Sabagh an noor*,' I responded, which means 'morning of light'.

'How are you?

'Everything is good, and you?' I asked.

'*Hamdullilah*,' ('Thanks be to God'). The words were comfortable and always the same, yet I sensed that both of us enjoyed this morning ritual. As he walked past me I heard him take a deep breath, ready for his next call.

Ka'ak is a Jerusalem speciality bread in an oblong shape that makes it a popular breakfast and is sold until stocks run out. It is honey-golden in colour and topped with sesame seeds. The taste is slightly sweet and a little bit sour owing to the secret ingredient – dried milk powder. This makes it versatile, and it works well with both sweet and savoury flavours. A personal Jerusalem favourite is to dip *ka'ak* in tahini and grape molasses ('dibs').

I was walking towards the Old City of Jerusalem, and as I got closer, I passed several stalls piled high with *ka'ak*. They also offered fist-sized falafel, both plain and stuffed with red onions and sumac, along with oven-baked eggs. Small paper wraps of *zaatar* were offered as an essential *ka'ak* accompaniment. *Zaatar* is a herby mix of dried oregano, thyme, sumac, sesame seeds and salt. Fresh *ka'ak* dipped into fragrant *zaatar* is one of Jerusalem's signature flavours.

The street running parallel to the Old City between Herod's Gate and Damascus Gate buzzed with commerce on one side but was bare on the side closest to the city wall. City residents promenaded on the shop-free side as Israeli police patrolled the zone.

The shops on the busy side were almost obscured from view by the tumult of pavement life taking place in front of them. Unofficial stalls took up every square inch of ground, forcing pedestrians to step out into the road. Buses hurtled past, tooting their horns. Some stalls consisted of ramshackle carts, others were more basic still, and everything from fruit to cheap jewellery or mobile phone chargers were sold. A few old women in headscarves and long, embroidered Palestinian gowns sat against a wall with sacks of fresh herbs in front of them. Their faces and hands were wrinkled and tanned from working outdoors. They wore black leather sandals with gnarly toes peeking out from below the black gowns. These dresses may have been passed down through the generations and denoted respectability. I weaved my way through the shoppers as I continued on to Damascus Gate.

Damascus Gate leads directly into the Muslim Quarter of the Old City, and it is perhaps the most imposing and iconic of the seven Old City gates still in use. It was built in 1537 directly on top of the Roman gate that is still visible below it. The old Roman Cardo street, running from north to south of the Old City had started at Damascus Gate and some of the ancient flagstones, worn smooth like marble, along with an avenue of stone columns, are still visible along the route.

The gate, which looks like a turreted fortress, had served as a strong fortification and a symbol of power to welcome Suleiman and other notables on their arrival into Jerusalem from Damascus. Older Palestinians remembered when it was possible to take a bus from Damascus Gate to Damascus (little more than 200 kilometres away) but the closed border between Israel and Syria had prevented that for many years.

A semicircle of steps leads down to the entrance of Damascus Gate, creating an amphitheatre-like feel and a natural place of congregation for Palestinians in East Jerusalem. It is an important symbol linking Palestinians to their historic roots and their ongoing right to live in Jerusalem.

There was always a heavy Israeli police presence in front of the gate, and I counted six armed police officers in combat gear chatting in the small police box at the top of the steps. Regardless of the heat, they always wore heavy black boots which laced up past the ankle. Their only reprieve from the weather was that the uniform allowed a cap and pair of sunglasses to be worn. From this vantage point, they observed the area in front of the gate, coming out as their whim suited them to haul Palestinians in for ID checks and questioning as they tried to go about their daily business.

The Old City walls of Jerusalem only encompass an area of one square kilometre, but each gate leads into such different realms that it was as if the laws of physics are being defied to fit so much into such a small geographic space.

Five of the Old City gates were built by the **Ottoman** ruler Suleiman the Great from 1535–42. As well as massively expanding the Ottoman Empire into the Middle East and North Africa, he chalked up an impressive list of building projects. These included building Jerusalem's Old City walls and restoring the Dome of the Rock while also transforming Constantinople (modern-day Istanbul) into a great capital city of the world.

I walked through the huge stone arch of the gate and into the bustling sanctity of the Muslim Quarter, at the heart of the Old City. The smell of coffee, spices, fresh bread, sun-ripened fruit and flowers combined in the air. Automated loudspeakers competed with stallholders in shouting out the daily prices. *'Telate bi ashara!'*, 'three for ten!' Both sides of the street were doing a busy trade, and between them the steps that led down were occupied by fresh fruit stalls, and another set of older women selling fresh fruits, vegetables and herbs from their land. They sat sagely in their long Palestinian hand-embroidered dresses with poise and dignity as they watched people flowing past on either side.

The Old City was a warren of discoveries. There were little alleyways leading off from the main streets, steps going up, tiny doors set into bigger doors and you never knew what you would find by peeking around a corner.

A little green and red cart with big bicycle wheels barged through the crowd, looking like a runaway train. Carts like this were an iconic Jerusalem sight, and they delivered *ka'ak* through the Old City streets. Many streets are steep with ancient stone steps, and ramps have been chiselled into the rock to allow access for the carts and other vehicles.

Determined to explore a new section of the Old City I turned left, heading towards Herod's Gate, or 'Flowers Gate' as the Arabic name translates. This is also part of the Muslim Quarter, but the shops quickly fall away to make way for schools, various religious institutions, and family homes.

Several mangy looking cats picked their way through a torn bin bag and the debris of everyday life spilled out on to the street, creating a less pleasant smell in the air. A group of immaculately dressed schoolgirls in white shirts under navy dresses ambled along on their way home from their morning classes. They giggled as a cat they frightened bolted across my path. I paused on the street corner deciding whether to go left or right, and a lady interrupted my thoughts.

'Are you looking for the tahini factory?' Suddenly I was.

'Oh…yes, is it open?'

This was a stroke of luck as the small and unassuming corner shop, with no name above it, would not have drawn me in otherwise. The shop sold drinks and groceries but an open door at the back led directly to the room that was being used as a tahini factory. Behind the traditional-looking milling equipment, millions of golden sesame seeds lay exposed on the stone floor, arranged in rows like sand tracks. The 200-year-old grinding equipment whirred away and as the large wheel spun, dry-roasted seeds were ground into a smooth and silky tahini paste. The process was simple and yet amazingly effective.

There were several different types of tahini on offer, ranging from the pale-looking variety I knew of, a golden one, a red one which had been extra-roasted in the *taboon* oven and an alarming-looking black version. I was offered a few samples and the taste was creamy and smoky, velvety and with huge depth.

I selected a white plastic container, and the shopkeeper filled it straight from a tap on the wall which was attached to the tahini barrel. There was no label on the pot, and it felt like a secret society where if you knew, you knew. It turned out that the small family business that makes Jebrini tahini was not such a secret after all and the famous chef Yotam Ottolenghi is a self-confessed fan. From that point onwards I was hooked, and no other tahini even closely compared.

No trip to the Old City was complete without a visit to the Church of the Holy Sepulchre and my feet started carrying me in the direction of the Christian Quarter. It is thought to be the site of Jesus's crucifixion as well as his final resting place. Built in 335CE it is one of the oldest churches in the world. The modest exterior of the church belies its significance. It is reminiscent of a time where wisdom advised hiding your treasures rather than making a grand display. As soon as you step over the threshold, however, a special aura surrounds the space.

The church seemed to defy every architectural law expected of a building. It didn't appear to have walls or edges, there were bits patched on through centuries of additions and renovations, and every time it looked like a dead end there was often a hatch or a stairway leading elsewhere. Despite this patchwork evolution, the church felt harmonious. It was dark but not gloomy; ornate but not gaudy.

Mosaics throughout the church depicted scenes from the Bible, including Christ being taken down from the cross. Pilgrims knelt and prayed in front of the slab of stone that was used to anoint his body. The domed roof over the tomb of Christ seemed entirely constructed of light. It streamed in sunlight in golden beams, creating a beautiful and breathtaking space.

Outside I sat on the ancient stone steps that had been worn smooth by thousands of years of worshipping feet. I looked up to check if the little ladder on the second floor was still there and of course it was. Each ledge and corner of the church was owned by one of the 13 recognised Christian denominations and a 'status quo' agreement had been drawn up in 1757 to preserve the arrangement. The ladder and ledge belonged to the Armenians and had been there for hundreds of years already. The status quo agreement made it immovable.

I idled back through the streets of the Christian Quarter and towards the Jewish Quarter. From a vantage point, I looked down over the spacious plaza that led to the Western Wall. This area used to be home to the Moroccan Quarter, but it had been cleared by Israel during the 1967 war, and the residents expelled, to expand the Jewish Quarter and improve access to the Western Wall.

The Western Wall, also referred to as the Wailing Wall or the Kotel, is thought to be the last remaining part of the Jewish Second Temple. When the Temple was destroyed by the Romans in 70CE, Jews started coming to the wall to pray and weep. Access to the Western Wall was open to anyone and a steady stream of people flowed in to pray, separated by gender and partitioned into small, orderly groups. Often people posted written prayers into the cracks of the wall.

To the right of the plaza is Dung Gate, built in 1540 by Suleiman and named after its role as a refuse dumping site. The gate provides the main entry route to the wall, and smartly dressed Ultra-Orthodox family groups streamed in at all times of day along with tour groups. The gate itself was unremarkable apart from some inscriptions marked into the rock and a heavy police presence.

The golden roof of the Dome of the Rock peeks over the Western Wall. This iconic building was built around 692CE and is the oldest surviving Islamic structure in the city. The octagonal base is intricately decorated with blue mosaics, Arabic calligraphy and small windows. The famous domed roof is gold-plated, and sparkles in the Jerusalem sunlight. It stands in the middle of the Al-Haram Al-Sharif site (or Al-Aqsa Mosque), as it is known to Muslims, or Temple Mount as Jews call it. This was the site of the Jewish First and Second Temples, and along with the Western Wall is the holiest site in Judaism. The existence of the Dome is so contentious that some of the art available in the Jewish Quarter blanks the Dome out of city landscape depictions altogether.

I started ambling back towards Damascus Gate. This was a gauntlet run of trying to dodge past fervent religious tour groups. Often, they would be chanting and sometimes even dancing through the streets with joy. At the very least, it was normal to encounter a gaggle of respectfully clad middle-aged tourists wearing matching baseball caps and trying to keep up with their guide, while simultaneously attempting to strike a deal over ceramic bowls.

Less than six months later, there would be no tourists and most of the brightly coloured shop doors would be bolted shut due to the Covid-19 restrictions. On that day, however, the city bustled with an energy that was contagious, and I was hooked by its charms.

Being Jerusalemite

Our friend Rana came over for coffee one morning. She lived around the corner with her extended family. There were four grown-up children and they all lived at home with their parents in typical Palestinian style. We had been to their house several times and they always welcomed visitors with warmth and generosity.

Rana was extremely kind and always turned up with elaborate cakes and presents for the kids. Today she came laden with the freshest breads stuffed with white cheese and *zaatar*. This is another Jerusalem speciality and very tasty.

Rana had recently got engaged and we were thrilled to have the chance to grill her about the wedding arrangements and the Palestinian traditions for getting married. To complicate matters her fiancé was living abroad, so it would be even harder for him to get a work visa for Israel.

It was clear that this uncertainty was proving difficult for both Rana and her close-knit family, who were devastated at the thought that they might lose her to another country. This spiralled into an interesting conversation about identity and if Rana, who had grown up in Jerusalem, felt like a Jerusalemite. She responded in her customary thoughtful way.

'Originating from, or living in, or being in Jerusalem does not necessarily mean we automatically identify as Jerusalemites,' she told me. 'It's a label rather than an identity and unless one chooses to adopt it as an aspect of their personality, it remains a label. For example, I was born in Jerusalem – my family hails from Jerusalem and our historical presence in Jerusalem goes back centuries. This means that I am Jerusalemite by label. If I choose to adopt that description as part of who I am, then it crosses over to being an identity'.

Rana went on to say that identity was 'like a recipe without measurements' and that different ingredients could change their strength over time. The difference with being Palestinian, she explained, was that the system of occupation had created a set of rules and boundaries to treat Palestinians differently, depending on where they lived.

I had observed that people's identities were often defined by the level of freedom they had been granted by the occupying Israeli state. Palestinians living in Jerusalem had 'Jerusalemite' status. This meant they were permanent residents of Jerusalem who had a claim to the land. If they moved out of the city, they lost it. And Palestinians couldn't move in and get it: it was not a fluid thing.

The system to divide and separate people was entirely manmade and created a sliding scale of oppression depending on someone's circumstances and the freedoms they were permitted.

Having Jerusalemite status came with valuable benefits. It meant that people could travel freely within Israel and could therefore access the sea. They could fly out of Ben Gurion Airport in Tel Aviv, but many Palestinians (even with Jerusalemite status) would receive extra hassle if they didn't also have an Israeli passport. Many Palestinians in East Jerusalem held a Jordanian travel document which allowed them to travel internationally. This was a hangover from when East Jerusalem and the West Bank were under Jordanian control (until 1967). It was also easier for Jerusalemites to access work opportunities, and they were close to all the wonderful historic and religious sites such as the Dome of the Rock and the Old City.

But of course there were downsides too. It was difficult for Jerusalemite Palestinians to access the West Bank as they would have to cross checkpoints where they were routinely harassed by the Israeli guards. In East Jerusalem there were also many **Israeli settlements** which were points of friction on top of the other daily struggles of living in such a militarised place. In some cases, a husband or wife had Jerusalemite status, but their spouse did not.

Most of the state bureaucracy was conducted in Hebrew. Many Palestinian families also lived under the constant threat of their houses being demolished for spurious reasons. Things were slightly better for those who were offered, and accepted, Israeli citizenship, but many saw this as selling out on their dream of a future independent state. Palestinians living in Jerusalem who were not eligible for, or rejected, Israeli citizenship were legally defined as Jerusalem residents (not citizens), and regardless of how long their family had lived there this came with a 'second-class citizen' set of rights.

Great efforts were taken to ensure that life was not easy for Palestinians living in Jerusalem. I hoped that Rana would find a way around these obstacles so that she could live together with her future husband.

I wanted to know how typical Rana's thoughts on identity were and so I asked several other Palestinian friends living in Jerusalem what Jerusalemite status meant to them.

My neighbour Wafa grew up in Jerusalem and her family were still there. She had lived abroad but had recently returned with her family to work in Jerusalem.

'I always identify myself as a Palestinian from Jerusalem,' she told me. 'It's a political statement to show that there are still around half a million Palestinians living in Jerusalem. Palestinians, depending on the place they live and the ID they hold, have different kinds of struggle but we all share a common occupation.'

Wafa went on to explain that occupation tries to fuel those differences to divide Palestinians. She said that you see this clearly at checkpoints and with permits given to some but not others. In her view, the most important thing is to be aware of this and to keep unity between Palestinians wherever they are, no matter where they come from or where they live.

My friend Mahmoud was lyrical yet critical in his response.

'I am culturally Palestinian, ethnically Arab, and bureaucratically Jerusalemite,' he said. 'I will not subscribe to the Israeli definition of Jerusalemite – and I don't see myself sharing this identity with an Israeli "Jerusalemite".'

I realised that while many people were proud of their family roots to Jerusalem, the political situation made questions of identity very personal. As with every nationality in the world, there was no single answer that defined what it meant to come from a place as everyone formed their own identity based on a complex mix of lived experience, family histories and values. The difference for Palestinians was that many of the choices about how and where to live their lives had been removed from them.

The Hometown Tourist

As time went on, and we rolled into our second year of living in Jerusalem, it had become increasingly apparent that most people I knew were afraid to speak out about the injustices they saw every day. Most of the international community were bound by their jobs to the formal positions of their home governments or organisations, leaving little scope to publicly voice their true opinions. Many local people feared for their freedoms and livelihood if they spoke out. The result was that expression was curtailed by fear and there was little space for open debate or comment.

I understood the fear of drawing attention to yourself. No-one wanted to be kicked out of the country, and any criticism of how the State of Israel was run could be interpreted by Israel as being antisemitic, and you'd be 'blacklisted' and face difficulties trying to re-enter the country. For Palestinians, the cost of speaking out was much higher and might mean jail, having permits revoked, houses demolished or worse, and the necessity of survival and protecting their family was paramount. This acted as a gagging clause and a lot went unsaid.

In January 2020, I launched a weekly blog. I intended for it to provide small details on both the wonderful aspects and harsh realities of life in East Jerusalem. Each blog post was intended to colour in another small detail about the people, the culture, the history and the uniqueness of the place.

The blog invited people to submit their own diary entries, and during the first few weeks I was thrilled to receive an entry from an Israeli student. Many Israelis had little reason to venture into East Jerusalem, and I'd heard that some were unaware even of the existence of Palestinian neighbourhoods. For most Israelis, Jerusalem was viewed as a single undivided city. A consequence of this was that the only Israelis that Palestinians in East Jerusalem routinely encountered were usually armed police and military or the more extreme **settlers**.

The student's diary entry, submitted to my blog in February 2020, gave a unique perspective on what East Jerusalem looked like for this Israeli (West Jerusalemite) who was seeing it for the first time. The entry read:

> In many ways, my thoughts about East Jerusalem are practically non-existent. This is a problem. I've lived most of my life in West Jerusalem and really, never had any type of reason to travel beyond. If I spare any thought about East Jerusalem, it is, unfortunately, connected to terrorism. And yet, as I've started university and am now living in East Jerusalem, I've been feeling this curiosity for the neighbourhoods around me that are unfamiliar to me. In a desperate attempt to avoid studying, I took a long walk today in East Jerusalem. I won't lie, as an Israeli, it was scary. It's always a little intimidating to walk into a place where you don't speak the

language. Arabic, especially, has been so vilified for most of my life that I am still unlearning not to fear it. Suddenly being surrounded by it made me feel like I'm inherently in danger, even though I was not.

As I walked through the winding streets of East Jerusalem, I felt like I'd stepped into an alternative universe. I always feel at home when I see white Jerusalem stones and the hills and mountains that give this city so much depth. I was struck by the sheer foreignness of it all. I felt like a tourist in my hometown. It's jolting and shocking, I quickly lost all fear as I became overwhelmed with this version of Jerusalem. Curiosity and excitement struck me, this is so new, this is fascinating, so familiar and yet so, so different.

I suddenly felt like my lack of hijab set me apart from everyone I saw around me. I realised that I'm not sure how comfortable I'd be to speak Hebrew. It struck me that this might be similar to how Muslims feel in Jewish dominated spaces. I've never thought about feeling like an outsider in my own hometown, to be a tourist in your home.

I want to get to know these Jerusalem stones as intimately as I know the ones in my old neighbourhood. To feel as comfortable as I do in the streets of West Jerusalem. To be able to hang out with friends in the hipster coffee shops of East Jerusalem and not feel like a foreigner or scared.

I've always loved Jerusalem. I didn't think I could love it more but today I learned that there is much more to love, and I look forward to venturing into the areas that are new to me.

I was impressed with the writer's honesty and the fresh perspective it gave me on what it felt like to walk the same streets in another person's shoes. It gave me hope that if other young people felt the same that Jerusalem's future may be brighter than its past.

Sheikh Jarrah Life

The neighbourhood of Sheikh Jarrah was named after the personal physician of **Salah Ad-Din**, who recaptured Jerusalem from the Crusaders in the 12th century. It was one kilometre from the Old City, and it gained popularity with elite Palestinian families in the latter half of the 19th century after the Husseini family built a large property there. During the 20th century, foreign missions, consulates and NGOs had moved in and it was a strategic neighbourhood in both the Palestinian and Israeli bids for Jerusalem.

The original properties were large Arab-style stone houses with high archways and hand-painted tiling. In recent years large apartment blocks had been built to accommodate the influx of internationals (like our family) and this had played a role in pushing up rent and pricing some local families out of the area. This risked stripping the neighbourhood of its original character.

Sheikh Jarrah was also under threat from the expansion of Israeli settlements, and hundreds of Palestinian families in Sheikh Jarrah were embroiled in legal battles to retain the right to stay on their land. Problems centred around the area of the Jewish prayer site, Shimon Hatzadik, where many Orthodox families had moved in and sought to take over houses forcibly from Palestinian families. The site of Shimon Hatzadik is believed to mark the tomb of Simeon the Just, a Jewish High Priest from the Second Temple period. The tomb is tucked away, in among residential streets in the heart of Sheikh Jarrah. From the outside the site is underwhelming, and consists of a small section of wall where Haredi families stream in to pray.

THE HEART OF THE CITY

During 2021, the streets surrounding Shimon Hatzadik became the focal point of tensions that escalated to a crisis level, and this is discussed in Chapter 6. Before that point, and even after, the streets normally felt very quiet in the neighbourhood and strolling around always led to one discovery or another. One afternoon, I headed out with the kids with no aim other than to take in the life on the streets.

Our street was named after the prominent Palestinian landowner who served as Mayor of Jerusalem between 1920 and 1934: Raghib Nashashibi. As you walk up the street, the British consulate is prominent on one side, with the EU residence on the other. There were CCTV cameras and security guards present, but it didn't feel like a fortress. Most of the time the street felt quite sleepy, especially during the long summer days when the Arab schools and nurseries were on holiday.

On the corner stood the skip where all manner of household waste was placed, guarded and overseen by an army of skip cats. Further along, at the end of our street, we came to St Joseph Hospital. Often there would be parking tickets on the cars that had neatly parked on the narrow kerb outside of the hospital and it seemed a low blow to heap on top of the other problems these hospital visitors were no doubt facing. Sometimes there were excited visitors carrying helium balloons and baskets of gifts for newborn babies.

As we rounded the corner, the Israeli police headquarters loomed large in one direction, with huge blue and white flags billowing in the breeze like the sails of a ship. We had still only gone about 200 metres from home, but the mood had changed. Cars zoomed along the busy road which divided East and West

Jerusalem and the familiar *'ting, ting'* of the tram rang out as it hurtled past.

The Sheikh Jarrah park, with its AstroTurf football pitches, also sat on this border between east and west. Apart from the tram, which was used as a shared space, it was the one place where Palestinians and Israelis would sometimes mix over a game of football. This was a rare sight, but when it happened Orthodox Jews would remove their dark coats and play in their white tasselled shirts with their kippahs on, proving that football really was a shared language around the world.

We turned down the hill to stay in Sheikh Jarrah. The flags of the different consulates peppered the streets here. It was early afternoon and the old couple who ran the *ka'ak* stall on the corner of Mujir Ad-Din street were packing up for the day. They covered their rickety wooden cart with a green tarpaulin and chained it to the tree trunk on the street corner, ready for business to resume the following morning. We walked down past the Ambassador Hotel where business meetings were held over a coffee and something stronger as the sun went down. Further down, we passed Abu Rimon's corner shop which did excellent olive oil from the Palestinian village of Aboud, and Sunbula, the lovely little Palestinian Fairtrade shop was on the right. Every shop had a different family and a different story to tell.

As we walked, I wondered how welcome we – the international community – were in Sheikh Jarrah. The Palestinians I knew were too polite to say it, but did they think we were benefitting from their hardships by living a comfortable life while failing to deliver a lasting solution on the ground? On the one hand the presence of the international community showed that the world had not forgotten about Palestine, but it could also be argued that the international presence did more to slow a resolution than it did to expedite it. Although foreign aid had been steadily decreasing in recent years, it continued to plug the gap and sustain a 'just about managing' situation which stripped away the incentives for a resolution from the Israeli side at least.

Our final stop was to see Ilyas, the Palestinian-Christian man who ran a tiny corner shop beside the roundabout. He was big and burly but spoke in a whisper due to a problem with his throat, which may or may not have been brought on by decades of chain smoking. His shop was no bigger than a small garage and yet he filled it with conveniences from floor to ceiling. As a Christian, he was able to sell alcohol and with so many internationals around he did a busy trade. We bought ice lollies and sat on the benches opposite the shop, taking shade under the flowing bougainvillea flowers which cascaded down the wall like a hot pink waterfall. The sun beat down, and it was a race for the kids to eat their lollies before they became a sticky puddle. I watched the traffic go past. A man stopped his moped in the middle of the roundabout to make a phone call. The cars swerved around him, but nobody beeped. They were used to this. It was East Jerusalem after all, and the rules were a bit looser here. These streets were so familiar and comfortable to me, but they could never be home. We were simply witnesses to a time and a place.

Round the Table

One summer's evening we were invited along with a few others for dinner at our friends Mahmoud and Ahmad's house. They were a large Palestinian family, well known for their bookshops across

East Jerusalem. It was a real privilege to see Palestinian family life in action and to have the chance to delve into a deeper pool of conversations.

The family lived in the Ras Al'Amud area of East Jerusalem, and to call it a house is modest as it was more like a housing complex. The building had multiple apartments to accommodate four generations of the family, including the grandparents, their children and their grandchildren's families. This amounted to a total of 34 people at the time.

This type of interconnected family living is very popular in Palestine and is testimony to the integral close-knit society that still prevails, where family units provide the building blocks of society. Generally, Palestinians live with their families until they marry and often then arrangements are made for renovations or extensions in order to build an apartment in the grounds of the family home. We had seen this several times already with other Palestinian friends and colleagues.

The lounge area was spacious with lots of seating and the conversation flowed easily as we discussed our impressions of Jerusalem and Palestine. The family was well travelled and engaged in international affairs. They took an interest in our homelands as well as discussing Palestinian history and current affairs. Still deep in conversation, we were invited to take our seats for dinner around a table liberally adorned with small salads, olives, stuffed pastries, small, pickled aubergines called *makdous,* and other delicacies.

These were just accompaniments to the main event which was a steaming chicken *maqloubeh*. This was one of Palestine's favourite celebratory dishes and was more than the sum of its parts: rice, chicken, vegetables and spices. The special feature of *maqloubeh* is that it's a one-pot dish which is layered up within a huge pan and then turned upside down on to a large serving plate in front of you, adding anticipation and a dramatic flair to the start of the meal.

Across Palestine, gender stereotypes are more entrenched than they are in the West. Many women work, yet the burden of the household, cooking and caring for children appears to fall more heavily on the women. There were too many people present in the apartment to all be seated around the table, so I didn't read too much into the fact that the women ate in the kitchen with the kids at their feet.

The hospitality of Mahmoud and Ahmad's family stemmed from the warm nest they had made for themselves. There was a feeling of love and connectedness which blurred the lines between the generations. During the evening, uncles, cousins and others appeared at the door, sometimes popping in to say hello or staying to enjoy a plate of food. There was a feeling of respect for each other and the good-natured bantering that came from living alongside one other.

After dinner, we retired outside and were impressed to see that the family had built a swimming pool in the courtyard. The air was still warm, and we sat around on white plastic chairs sipping our mint tea as I fretted about whether the plum and pistachio cake I had made would pass muster with the different generations of the family.

The old grandmother and grandfather had joined the party by this point and were welcomed like VIPs into the fold. Ahmad busied himself pouring tea for them and making them comfortable. At length, my cake was sliced and passed out in dainty portions around the assembled group. There were general murmurings that it was good, and I breathed a sigh of relief. In Arabic, the grandmother asked what spices I had used in it.

'*Mahlab*,' I replied. Ahmad passed the message on, and a further discussion ensued. 'She was just explaining to me what *mahlab* is,' Ahmad said.

'Why, don't you know?' I asked.

'Of course I know,' he replied, 'but I didn't expect you to know.' I was pleased to have passed this unofficial spice test. That hurdle cleared, I started worrying about what I would cook for the family when we returned the invitation, and if we would be expected to host all 34 of them.

It was heartwarming to spend time with an extended family who lived and worked together as a single unit. This was so different from the way most people lived in the West. Time and time again it was proven to us that families were the building blocks of Palestinian society. Perhaps this was driven by choice and traditional values, or perhaps by necessity given the absence of governmental support nets to cover even basic provisions like safety and welfare. Whatever the reason, the family homes we visited always offered a warmth and security that pulled closer the harder that external living conditions became.

Jerusalem meant so much to so many people, and it was hard to comprehend that the Israeli Jerusalem and the Palestinian Jerusalem occupied an overlapping space where people went about their daily business with as little interaction or regard for the other as possible. That was how it appeared to me, and with the exception of the tram and sometimes the football pitches it was difficult to find many spaces where the two overlapped.

It was obvious from the start that Jerusalem was a city with different sides, but it was more subtle and complicated than a simple East/West or Muslim/Jewish/Christian divide. The more I spoke to people, the more questions I had about the role that religion, politics and history had played in shaping the Jerusalem that I saw before me. I wanted to explore if any common purpose and understanding could be found within the city and wondered if religion was at the heart of unlocking Jerusalem's secrets.

CHAPTER 2
THE RELIGIONS

Religion in Jerusalem is not something reserved for one day of the week or behind closed doors: it is an all-encompassing way of life for many people. Jerusalem attracts the most devout, and prayer times set the rhythm of the day with religion providing the driving force behind the way people eat, dress, speak, work, study and live. This chapter delves into the main religions of the city in search of common ground and an understanding of what Jerusalem means to each of these faiths.

Jerusalem is the holiest city in Judaism and Christianity and the third holiest in Islam after Mecca and Medina. All three faiths share a belief that God asked the first Patriarch Abraham to sacrifice his son on Mount Moriah. The first and second Jewish Temples were built on the site and Jews refer to the area as 'Temple Mount'. Muslims believe it is the site where the Prophet Muhammad travelled from Mecca on a journey to the 'furthest mosque' and ascended to heaven. The Haram al-Sharif or Al-Aqsa Mosque compound stands on the Mount Moriah site and is famous for the jaw-droppingly beautiful Dome of the Rock. A few hundred metres away Jesus completed his final journey carrying the cross to his site of crucifixion and burial.

The three faiths were literally piled on top of the same stones, especially in the case of Islam and Judaism, which both centre around the Mount Moriah site. It is a savage real-estate battle that draws on the highest and holiest of justifications. Each stone is steeped in divinity and the people who tread them do everything in their power to reinforce their religion's stake in the city.

The city frequently grinds to a halt in celebration of the many religious festivals that punctuate the year. Spring is especially busy as Passover ('Pesach') and Easter are usually close together, and in April 2022 they coincided with Ramadan. These events all change the rhythm of the city and there were many surprises the first time we passed through the annual cycle of events.

One morning when we had not long arrived in the city, we were baffled to smell burned toast in our apartment when we weren't making any. We came outside to see black smoke billowing everywhere. A bit of research revealed that it was the annual burning of the *chametz* (flour-based products), a requirement of Jewish people before Passover started. The Jerusalem municipality (local council) set up huge fire pits, like skip-sized troughs, across the city where people could dispose of all bread, cakes and biscuits before sunset fell on the eve of Passover. The contents smoked steadily throughout the day as houses were scrupulously cleaned so as not to leave a single crumb in a toaster. It was a bizarre spectacle, somewhat akin to a bonfire night.

Meanwhile, Israeli supermarkets blocked off the bakery aisle with red tape and blinds to forbid the purchase of any bread or yeast-related products during the eight days of Passover. Shoppers were barely afforded a glance at the bread and if Jews weren't allowed it, then no-one was having it. Even cafés and restaurants in West Jerusalem changed their menus and sandwiches were served with unleavened bread or with matzo, the traditional Pesach dry crackers. Something we repeatedly found in Jerusalem, which was both heartening and inconvenient, was that religion often trumped any commercial interests. The fact that non-devout people may wish to buy bread wasn't a consideration; the requirements of the festival were imposed on everyone.

Cloaks and Clothes

Every weekday, I left early to do the short drive from Sheikh Jarrah to HaNevi'im Street where my kids went to school. It was uphill on busy and narrow streets, and it was too far for my younger daughter to walk.

On the journey one day my then five-year-old son innocently asked, 'mum, why can't that lady see?' Looking out, I saw a darkly clothed apparition coming towards us. She was covered from head to toe in a black cloak with thick black lace covering her face. The clothing was loose and gave her whole body a triangular shape. She must have worn shoes, but it appeared from the car like she was floating along the street. I quickly felt out of my depth as I struggled to explain the concept of modesty to my son.

'She doesn't want people to see her,' I said, 'because of her beliefs in God.' It didn't make sense to me so I didn't know what he would make of this, but he just nodded and later compared the costume to his spiderman suit which revealed only his eyes. Was she dressing modestly to please God or was it to prevent others from temptation? And what did each of these say about the role of women in society?

I made a mental note to find out more, and several weeks later I found myself at the Veiled Women of the Holy Land exhibition at the Israel Museum. The exhibition compared Christian nuns, Haredi veiled women and Muslims who wore the *niqab* to show the similarities rather than the differences between these religious women.

Different clothing was on display, but the most interesting part of the exhibition was a video exhibit which showed an actor dressing and undressing in each of the religious outfits. She started in underwear and built each outfit up layer by layer. It was entrancing and theatrical, like peeking into a private changing room. The process was laborious because the veiled women of each religion were often wearing up to eight layers of fabric. Like an onion skin, each layer provided protection from the outside world until the cloth resembled a bullet-like shell and the shape of the person underneath was entirely obscured.

As well as the personal discomfort of wearing so much clothing, often in scorching heat, there was the scorn of others to deal with. Short interviews with the veiled women revealed that many of them faced regular harassment on the streets of Jerusalem for their choices which some people couldn't understand and perhaps felt threatened by.

On arriving in Jerusalem, I knew I was coming to a religious and conservative place where modesty was expected. My own clothes were fairly conservative, so I didn't think it would be too much of an issue. What took me by surprise, however, was how much my clothes would speak a language of identity that I'd never considered before.

In a city full of divisions, clothes were a billboard that revealed a lot about a person's identity, and it was almost impossible not to be judged for what you were wearing. My clothes shouted out clues from which people felt entitled to assume my religion, language, political views and much more.

I was interested to learn that in traditional Palestinian dress, women's best dresses, called *thobes,* were intricately embroidered with symbols representing their village, their marital status, the number of children they had, their faith and much more. This culture of sharing a history through embroidery is called *tatreez* and in 2021 it was added to the UNESCO list of the Intangible Cultural Heritage of Humanity. Dresses were often passed down through the generations and although younger women tended to reserve them for special occasions, many older Palestinians would not be seen out in public in anything other than a *thobe*.

It wasn't just clothes that came under close scrutiny but also hair. Since moving to Jerusalem, I had spent an unexpectedly large amount of time pondering hair. There were no hard-and-fast rules, but observant Muslim women generally wore a headscarf to fully cover their hair, only taking it off in the privacy of their own homes with their families or when among other women. Married Orthodox Jewish women were meant to cover their hair at all times, and they could do so with either a hat, a headscarf or a wig. There was a slightly ironic loophole in the interpretation of the religious text that forbade the showing of one's own hair yet permitted the wearing of a real-hair wig. I could definitely see the appeal in the glossy perfectly set curls which were common among Jewish women and never grew or greyed. Many less devout Jewish women would cover the top of their heads with a small hat or scarf but would allow their hair to be visible. Christian women tended to leave their hair uncovered.

All of this meant that the judgements about who you were started from the top of your head. I had never thought of hair as being powerful before. The most interesting explanation that I'd stumbled across on the Jewish requirement for covering hair is quoted in the Jewish text the Talmud: 'Your hair is like a flock of goats.' This was intended to imply the beauty and power of the hair should be reserved for one's husband.

Particularly in the Old City, it was wise to always carry a scarf that could be flung over your hair if you unexpectedly stumbled into a religious building, which was easily done. I had not tried it myself, but I heard that you could get a better price in the *souq* if you covered your head.

My friend Dina was a young, feminist Palestinian. One day she told me that she was thinking about stopping wearing her headscarf. She had studied the Quran closely and didn't find anything to suggest that women needed to cover themselves. I asked her if her family would mind her not wearing it.

'They will not like it,' she said. 'I will think about it for a while before I decide.' We repeated this conversation a few times over several months and a year later she was still wearing her headscarf. Clearly, it was not easy to break out of family and community traditions and expectations.

Even after some time living in Jerusalem, I was often in a fluster trying to make sure that my clothes were appropriate. I would worry, *'is it disrespectful to wear skinny jeans going through a Haredi neighbourhood?'* (answer: yes, but I did it anyway), or *'does my dress look Jewish and I'm in a Palestinian neighbourhood?'* (again yes). It was not unusual for Westerners to be publicly reprimanded for their clothing, especially in the staunchly Haredi neighbourhood of Mea She'arim, and worse still, you could be spat at. Our staunchly independent friend, who insisted on taking the train from the airport into the city and then Google Mapping a short cut through Mea She'arim, before we'd had a chance to give her the etiquette briefing, found out the hard way that her trendy exercise/travelling clothes were not considered kosher. It was impossible to always get it right when what was considered appropriate didn't just change from city to city, but in Jerusalem's case from street to street depending on the religious majority and fervency.

I concluded that it was impossible to please everyone, and resolved to try and dress conservatively out of a general respect for all religions and the local customs of the city. One day at the Jericho AquaPark (a Palestinian area) a young boy asked me why I didn't wear the *hijab*. I replied that I was international, and he nodded as if that answered things. A quirk of the Arabic language was that the word for the 'West' also meant 'strange', and I was very aware that my 'normal' was foreign and 'other' to many people. Regardless of what I wore, my appearance continued to scream out that I was a foreigner, and no amount of clothing could conceal that.

Easter

Jerusalem is the heart and home of Easter. It is here that the action happens. The city is steeped in the story of Jesus carrying his cross through the Old City streets to the point of his crucifixion and death. His journey along the Via Dolorosa is marked with nine stations of the cross, which indicate significant events that occurred along the route. The final five stations are situated within the Church of the Holy Sepulchre.

Every year thousands of people from around the world flock to Jerusalem over Easter, where they retrace Jesus's journey on Good Friday and recall the miracle of his resurrection. Each Christian denomination brings their own traditions, and for Orthodox Christians this includes observing a different calendar and celebrating Easter a week later.

In 2020, owing to Covid-19 restrictions, the Church of the Holy Sepulchre was closed over Easter for the first time since the plague hit Jerusalem in 1349. Not only was this devastating for the many thousands of people wanting to worship there, but it was also a hard blow for the many businesses that depend on visitors to make their income.

I spoke to a Christian friend, Tala, who had grown up in Jerusalem, to see how Easter in 2020 would be different. She said that Easter for her family was a 'time of prayer and reflection.' I asked her what her favourite Easter traditions were.

'During Easter I really enjoy attending the various services: Maundy Thursday and washing of the feet, which symbolically happens during the service where the Bishop washes people's feet.' Tala also usually attended services on Good Friday where the congregation retraced Jesus's final walk along the Via Dolorosa in the Old City, as well as services on Saturday and Easter Sunday.

Easter for her family represented combining religious duties with family customs.

'My favourite tradition is making Easter cookies,' Tala went on to say. 'Usually, my mother-in-law makes the best cookies and she makes a lot! She uses nine kilos of semolina. You need many people to work on this as each individual cookie is made by hand and filled with dates, pistachio or walnuts and then "pinched" with special tongs to make patterns. We gather at my mother-in-law's house and enjoy making cookies together for several hours,' Tala continued. 'Colouring eggs is another nice tradition that I enjoy. Usually, my sisters and I colour the eggs together. Sometimes we go to my parents' house in Jericho and have a picnic as well as colour the eggs. Easter lunch is also a special time for friends and family.'

I asked how Easter would be different in 2020. 'Unfortunately, none of the things I described above will take place this year,' she responded. 'Services will be broadcast via Facebook and that is it. I feel sad, but I remind myself that this is happening across the whole world, and we have to stay at home to help contain the virus and save lives,' she went on to tell me. 'I am also reminded of many people who live under severe access and movement restrictions like people in Gaza and other people in the world who do not enjoy freedom of religion.'

In 2021, Easter services and processions took place in Jerusalem but it was only in 2022 that pilgrims from abroad were allowed into Israel and the event resumed its full programme. On Palm Sunday we sat on the street outside Lions' Gate waiting for the procession to pass.

The Ottoman ruler Suleiman the Magnificent built Lions' Gate in 1539 to honour the wishes of his father and predecessor. He had dreamed he would be eaten by lions if he destroyed Jerusalem, and so instead he promised to build walls to protect it. Suleiman had four lions carved into the gate, which were still visible albeit well-worn. Lions' Gate has immense significance for Christians (who call it St Stephen's Gate) as it marks the spot where Jesus was brought into the Old City after his arrest in the Garden of Gethsemane.

It was a hot day, and we wilted as we waited for the procession to arrive. Israeli police were stationed at various access points and their guns were poised from vantage points above. Periodically, they would pull over a young Palestinian male for an ID check and we watched as one guy was roughly pushed against the wall.

Suddenly, there was a burst of noise and a group of boy scouts marched past with bagpipes and drums. Both the tradition of scouts and the bagpipes were a legacy from the Scottish soldiers posted in Palestine during the 1920s at the start of the **British Mandate** period. They passed through Lions' Gate and the commotion faded. We waited some more until, finally, the religious leaders at the head of the procession were spotted at the end of the street and began their approach towards New Gate. As they got closer the din increased. They were trailed by thousands of worshippers, singing, dancing and clapping. Some played instruments and many waved tall palm leaves in the air. A few people threw grains of rice over the crowd. There was a carnival spirit, and the event had an energy that was joyous and celebratory. As the waves of people passed we saw that there were many different nationalities, church groups and denominations. Sometimes they sang together as one, and at other times they clattered and clanged along to their own beats.

Christians in Jerusalem are very diverse, and there are churches and communities for Armenian, Greek, Syriac and Ethiopian Christians, as well as the range of Protestant denominations and, of course, the Catholic Church. Despite Christianity leaving a heavy footprint in and around the Old City, the number of Christians living in Jerusalem and the Holy Land has declined rapidly. Estimates suggest that local indigenous Christians make up less than 1% of the population of Jerusalem and less than 2% of the population of the Holy Land. This is down to a number of political, social and economic factors which make life challenging for Christians. As well as facing the same discrimination that all Palestinians face from the Israeli authorities, Christians are also marginalised by the **Palestinian Authority**. Unless steps are taken to preserve them, the indigenous Christian population risks disappearing altogether.

Ramadan

The majority of Palestinians in East Jerusalem and across Palestine are Muslim. There are only two official holidays – Eid Al-Fitr and Eid Al-Adha – and the dates of both change each year. By far the biggest event in the Muslim calendar is Ramadan which takes place in the month preceding Eid Al-Fitr. In 2020, Ramadan kicked off several weeks after Easter, at the end of April. Across the Islamic world it was a time of both celebration and sacrifice.

Ramadan is one of the five core pillars of Islam which requires healthy Muslim adults to go without all food and water from sunrise to sunset for a month-long period. It is a time of increased prayer and reflection, with the aim of getting closer to God and understanding the plight of others in poverty. Despite the daily sacrifices, Ramadan is a celebration, and the evenings are marked with large family gatherings and feasts.

In Jerusalem, the Grand Mufti of Jerusalem and Palestine is responsible for sighting the new moon and declaring the start and end dates of Ramadan. The lunar calendar means that the start occurs around 11 days earlier each year. This was good news for many when we were living there, as it gradually inched back towards the shorter and cooler days of winter. Some people continued their work outdoors during Ramadan, which made it especially tough if the weather was hot.

My neighbours were both Palestinian Muslims who had lived in different countries around the world. I spoke to them about what Ramadan was like for them. They both grew up in families that had always observed Ramadan, so it was a tradition for them to fast. They explained that it was for each family member to decide how strict they wanted to be, and the most religious members of their families observed all prayer times and aimed to read the entire Quran during Ramadan.

They told me that as children they would look forward to the special foods, the decorations, the relatives visiting, and the buzz of excitement around their neighbourhoods. Eid Al-Fitr, which marked the end of Ramadan, was similar to Christmas with presents for children and traditional sweets.

Surprisingly, it was tiredness rather than hunger they cited as the hardest aspect of Ramadan. They both told me that Ramadan 'messes up your sleep schedule.' Normally there were many relatives to visit, and gatherings could go on into the early hours. Sleep was short-lived, with many people waking for a pre-dawn meal called *'sahoor'* before the first prayers started at around 4.30am.

In 2020, things felt very different because of the Covid-19 restrictions. An evening curfew had been imposed on Muslim neighbourhoods to prevent people from visiting friends and relatives and accelerating the spread of infection. They were sad about this and said it didn't feel the same to celebrate Ramadan alone.

'The only thing I miss is coffee,' Ahmad said when I asked him about surviving a long day without food and water. He said that drinking a lot of liquids the night before staved off thirst during the day and it was not too bad if you were lucky enough to work indoors. There are many special drinks prepared during Ramadan to help with evening rehydration, and these include date, carob and apricot juices which are high in energy.

My neighbours were enthusiastic about the benefits of observing Ramadan, telling me that it was 'good for the soul' and 'helps you to break your habits.' It was also a time to appreciate what you had, and they had been talking to their kids about 'how lucky they were.'

Usually, people flocked in vast numbers to worship at the Al-Aqsa Mosque compound which included the Dome of the Rock. In 2019 the city was packed, on Fridays in particular, with coachloads of worshippers pouring in from across Palestine. Covid-19 prevented this during 2020 and 2021, but the crowds were able to return in 2022.

Normally, Israel issues additional permits during Ramadan which allow more Palestinians than usual to enter Jerusalem. For many people, it is an annual chance to visit the Al-Aqsa compound and to pray at this sacred site. It was a special sight to see crowds of people, chattering excitedly, as they passed through the Old City walls and towards the mosques.

Going around East Jerusalem or the West Bank during Ramadan there were a few unwritten rules to be aware of. The first was to try not to eat or drink in view of others. Shopkeepers tended to be a bit shorter with their tempers and driving became more perilous as the day went on. It is a known fact that accidents increase as hungry, thirsty and tired drivers rush to get home for the end of the fasting time.

There is a cultural aspect to Ramadan that means that many Palestinians who are not particularly religious still observe Ramadan and reluctantly relinquish their coffee, cigarettes and other snacks. This gives a sense of solidarity which unifies people. Offices close early to take account of missed lunch and coffee breaks. In addition to the usual five daily calls to prayer, there is a pre-dawn and dusk firing of a cannon from a Muslim cemetery just outside the Old City walls to signify the start and end of fasting times. It feels as if East Jerusalem breathes a collective sigh of relief when the dusk cannon is eventually fired and families, colleagues and friends sit down together for large celebratory *iftar* meals. The continuity of these rituals over many years is part of the fabric of Jerusalem which continues to renew the city's holiness.

Haredi Life

Jerusalem's Mea She'arim neighbourhood is home to one of the largest Haredi (Ultra-Orthodox Jewish) communities in the world, and turning off the main road into the neighbourhood was like travelling back in time. The Haredi are the most easily recognisable religious population in Jerusalem because of their strict dress code. This harks back to an earlier time and a colder climate. Without exception, men wear black suits, white shirts and wide-brimmed formal hats unless it is Shabbat or a special occasion when they dress in a long, silk, golden robe and a round, fur hat. It is traditional for men to grow the front of their hair into long ringlets called *payot*. Trousers are forbidden for women and skirts have to be below the knee and worn with thick tights, even in summer. Short sleeves are not permitted, and married women have to cover their hair.

Despite passing through Mea She'arim daily to collect the kids from school, I didn't actually know any Haredi Jews and I could only recall having one conversation with a Haredi person during our first year of living in Jerusalem. He was a tour guide, so it was his job to speak. Part of the Haredi culture is to avoid non-Jewish people (gentiles) and especially Western influences, and for this reason they live predominantly in separate neighbourhoods.

For internationals like me, and I suspect even for the modern-day secular Israeli, this made the Haredi population something of an enigma. I was desperate to learn more and was intrigued to discover that it was possible to do a tour of Mea She'arim with a resident.

We met our tour guide at the HaDavidka tram stop in West Jerusalem on a Wednesday evening in autumn. The small group shuffled around, surreptitiously eyeing each other up to check if our clothing met the strict requirements that had been stipulated.

The tour guide introduced himself as David and he wore a *kippah* (skullcap) but no hat or suit jacket. I wondered if he remained part of the Orthodox community, or if this tour and his slightly more casual attire were evidence of his departure. He said we could ask any questions we wanted, and I later kicked myself for not having probed more into his background.

It was starting to get dark as we set off down a side street heading deeper into the community. I had seen some of the residential streets before, but nothing prepared me for the buzz and bustle of the main shopping street at this hour. Despite being only a short walk away from where my children went to school, a new world revealed itself and the beating heart of Mea She'arim was completely different from anywhere I had been before.

Men walked briskly along with determination and purpose. Their eyes cast straight ahead or downwards at a pocket-sized Torah. Women pushed babies in prams, with several smartly dressed children trailing behind. The streets were packed with people collecting groceries, or bread from the bakery, and running other errands. Aside from the food and groceries, most shops sold items I didn't recognise and I was astonished that a whole world existed beyond my awareness and what I thought I knew of Jerusalem.

David zipped quickly between the throngs of people, and we raced to keep up, afraid of being left behind in this other world.

Over the next few hours he took us into a hat shop, a clothes shop, a religious bookstore and a Judaica shop, all the while using the props around him to explain the Haredi lifestyle.

In the hat store he explained that although the hats might look similar to the untrained eye, there were a variety of shapes and fabrics which as well as denoting wealth and status were often a nod to the specific traditions of the different homelands people had come from. Few Jews lived in Israel before 1948, so many still dressed in line with their Eastern European (or other) heritage.

Next, David took us into a café, and as we pulled chairs around a small table the seats behind us screeched back and the occupants abruptly left. Did our presence upset them? Or had they simply finished their food? David exchanged a few words with them, but he refused to let us in on the exchange.

In keeping with their strict culture, the food we were offered also placed tradition before taste. David insisted we each try gefilte fish, and he made clear he would be offended if we didn't finish our portion. This was a small ball of fish, mixed with bread to make a cold dumpling, and it looked (and tasted) like a wartime necessity rather than a delicacy. I eyed the dumpling in front of me with suspicion but resolved to approach it graciously despite the slightly grey colour and unappealing look.

The complete absence of the outside world was the most striking aspect. The bookstore only stocked books with religious morals, and this was also true in the children's section. I asked David if television was censored.

'Jews do not have time for TV, our lives are far too busy with study and other commitments,' he replied.

In the bookstore he showed us a simple slide and projector toy for entertaining children. There were some DVDs, and they all came with a stamp of approval to show they had been deemed appropriate for Jewish audiences. This included heavy censoring of seemingly benign content, such as National Geographic animal documentaries. David told us that Haredi parents wanted to shelter their children from all violence and inappropriate content, and that this extended to the animal world.

David went on to explain that, in the Haredi community, it was only permissible to own a mobile phone if it didn't have any internet capabilities. We were told that access to the internet was only allowed for work requirements, and specific websites were checked and approved for individuals rather than access being made freely available. This censorship of fully grown adults was far more restrictive than I had imagined possible. David justified this as being a way to preserve a delicate culture from things that might corrupt or dilute it.

I found the tour staggering, and I came home feeling like I'd had the sort of culture shock one normally has to travel thousands of miles or back several hundred years in history for. I would have loved the chance to speak with the women about their experiences of living in a Haredi community, and what they felt about the expectations their community placed on them. Despite living in close proximity to one of the biggest Haredi neighbourhoods in the world, I could think of no way to make this interaction a reality.

The Haredi detachment from the rest of society poses interesting questions for the future of Israel. The Haredi population stood at around 13% of Israeli citizens in 2020, and was growing twice as fast as the general Israeli population. Despite a decline in the birth rate, each woman still had on average 6.5 live births. This alone was staggering, but more than being their choice, seemed to be the natural consequence of a society where sex for married people is written in as a Friday night requirement and contraception is only available if conception is a threat to the woman's health or life. The rising Haredi population is a problem for the state as many don't work, pay taxes or undertake military service.

As the numbers grow, so too does their political influence and Haredi politicians play an ever-greater role in determining the future of Jerusalem and Israel. For many secular Israelis, this is of more immediate concern than the issue of Palestine.

Not all Jewish people observe the strict Orthodox traditions, but Israel as a whole comes to a stop during September and October for the annual 'High Holiday' season. Over three weeks the festivals of Rosh Hashanah, Yom Kippur and Sukkot are all celebrated.

As with the other religions, the High Holidays in 2020 were conducted under the cloud of a national lockdown. The second lockdown of the year started on the eve of Rosh Hashanah, and Covid-19 regulations restricted the size of prayer groups and family gatherings. One person I asked said, 'everything will change. Only the prayers and *mitzvot* (Jewish commandments) remain the same.'

Yom Kippur, which followed a week later, was a much more austere occasion. This is the Day of Atonement and is the holiest day of the year in the Jewish calendar. It involves fasting from several hours before sunset on the first day to after nightfall on the second day. During this time observers avoid all food and drink and are not permitted to wash themselves or wear leather shoes. The day should be spent in prayer and reflection, in the belief that this purifies someone of their sins. There were no cars or public transport on the roads on Yom Kippur and it had gained traction as a popular day for secular children and families to cycle down the middle of the main highways.

The most noticeable Jewish festival we observed on the streets of Jerusalem was Sukkot. This ran for eight days and required each Jewish household to make a temporary shelter called a *sukkah* with a roof of palms and other foliage. The festival commemorates the time when the Jews escaped slavery in Egypt and spent 40 years travelling across the desert to the Holy Land. Families prayed, ate and sometimes slept in the *sukkah* which is required to have two and a half walls and an open view of the sky.

Many of the apartment buildings in West Jerusalem have been constructed so that the balconies are not directly above each other. This enables each household to meet the requirement of being directly under the sky. During the eight-day national holiday, it was common to see Haredi men dashing around with palm leaves which were used to patch up the *sukkah*'s roof. Restaurants and cafés in West Jerusalem constructed their own *sukkahs* for customers, and it was quite a spectacle to see these competing for space on the pavement.

It was yet another example of Jerusalem providing the stage for centuries-old rituals to be played out, reinforced and renewed, year after year.

Religion is everywhere in Jerusalem, and it plays an integral role in how daily life is organised. Seeing the customs and traditions of each religious festival played out in the city taught me more about faith in one year than in the rest of my life combined. The array of festivals added a layer of performance which brought colour and character to the different seasons. On the face of it, it appeared that Islam, Christianity and Judaism shared the common purpose of promoting a modest life, in the service of God and others and in line with ancient traditions and values. The form those duties and customs took varied hugely between religions but the thread of love and respect for God was the same.

It seemed to me that the devout of different faiths had more similarities than differences between them, yet religion provided a way to widen divisions and reinforce a feeling of different tribes. There wasn't much evidence of religious groups mixing, except among Christian and Muslim communities who shared Palestinian identity. The strict dress codes attached to each religion served as an outward badge of identity that promoted division. Older Palestinians we met talked of times before 1948, when all religions had coexisted peacefully in Jerusalem, and I wondered if religion really was at the root of Jerusalem's problems, or if politics was to blame for fuelling the segregation and fear of the other which pervaded the city.

CHAPTER 3
THE POLITICS

During my first few months in Jerusalem I was told, 'everything is politics here.' To start with I couldn't see it, but the longer I lived in the city more and more issues seemed to link back to politics. Why did the new traffic lights in Sheikh Jarrah change so quickly for cars coming from the Palestinian side and give much longer to drivers heading towards the large Israeli settlement of Ma'ale Adumim? Politics. Why couldn't we buy fresh fish at the supermarket? Politics. Why was there no postal service, or recycling bins, or… it all came back to politics.

Politics in Israel and Palestine wasn't simply about the government of the day. It had been shaped thousands of years ago with the emergence of the Abrahamic religions. Arriving in Jerusalem, I was surprised that so many Palestinians spoke about 1948 as if it were yesterday. Compared to King David, Jesus or the Prophet Muhammad's time, it was. Many Palestinians had first-hand memories and experiences of 1948, or their parents and grandparents did. Politics was the past and the future as much as the present. For both Israelis and Palestinians, it meant the right to exist.

Since Israel came into existence in 1948, it has defined itself as a Jewish state. This means that politics and religion can never be separated, and people from other faiths are not treated equally in law. This challenges democratic values. This chapter explores the meeting point between politics and religion, and how this shapes everyday life in Jerusalem.

Yad Vashem

Visiting the world's main Holocaust Museum, Yad Vashem, felt much like attending a funeral: a necessary, yet dreaded responsibility. There never seemed to be a good time to delve into such a world of horror. I chose a wintry Tuesday morning when the sky was suitably grey and morose, and set off with my friend Mohammad.

Mohammad was from Aida **Refugee Camp**, and he was partway through his first month-long permit to come into Israel in over ten years. This permitted him to cross the separation wall and walk through the checkpoint at the edge of Bethlehem where I collected him in my car on the other side.

Given that he had waited almost all of his adult life for this permit, I was impressed that the museum was on his list of priorities. His view was that no-one could deny the atrocities of the Holocaust, and that people should know about that suffering and pay their respects to the victims. The six million people who died were not responsible for the political course that Israel was choosing now.

Yad Vashem was established in 1953 as the World Holocaust Remembrance Center. It is much more than a museum and undertakes a vast amount of education and research as well as providing a world-class site for documentation and remembrance.

Set in a 45-acre campus surrounded by forest on the outskirts of Jerusalem, Yad Vashem combines a modern and engaging visitor centre with a wider memorial site that is peaceful and felt somehow appropriate.

The collection of buildings and memorials is sculpted from the purest Jerusalem stone, with lots of glass to showcase the beauty of the natural landscape. There is one route through the main exhibition in the visitor centre, and this removes the need for any decisions to be made along the way. The displays are highly visual, with a range of videos, photographs, letters and personal artefacts to take visitors on a journey from the pre-war years through to the sheer horror that unfolded as Hitler's grip over Europe tightened.

Display cabinets included threadbare children's toys, broken spectacles and articles of clothing along with treasured family photographs and small personal items. Discarded shoes were displayed beneath the glass flooring. It was hard to believe that each had belonged to someone whose life had been taken.

The museum was quiet on the day I visited, apart from several large groups of young people in military clothing that we passed. They jostled and chatted like schoolchildren. It was interesting to see that learning about the Holocaust was deemed a necessary part of the curriculum for young Israelis, who would be given large rifles and asked to sit on checkpoints or perform other military duties.

I was also aware of them looking at us, trying to use the visual cues to gauge our identity. We looked like a couple, so where were we from? Certainly, they would not expect a West Bank Palestinian to be present. Was the sweet older Israeli woman at the information desk who gave us a map more courteous because she assumed we were both European?

One of Yad Vashem's missions is to collect the names and stories of each and every Holocaust victim. In the final part of the meticulously curated museum, there is a spiral room with shelves containing encyclopaedic-sized volumes reaching up to the roof. These contain the names of the deceased. They currently hold over 4.8 million names, and work continues to complete the volumes. A mountain of names stretches up to the heavens. The display was striking, and left a deep impression that was both harrowing and tragic.

We were sombre and engrossed as we walked around, and didn't exchange more than a nod until we emerged at the end of the exhibition some two hours later. The time had passed in the blink of an eye. We stared wide-eyed at each other, unsure what words to use to express what we had seen. The final rooms had focussed on securing the land of Israel for the Jewish people, and my only disappointment was that this felt like it tipped into a particular strain of political propaganda that was disrespectful to the dead.

The horrors of the Holocaust represent the gravest human suffering in history. These events didn't occur thousands of years back, but less than one hundred years ago and some of its survivors are still alive. There is no doubt that Israel needs to provide a safe home for the Jewish people and also that Jewish people should be protected in every country where they live around the world. It is our collective responsibility to ensure that the words 'Never Again' are honoured.

Visiting Yad Vashem provided a small insight into the trauma the Jewish people had suffered, and the overriding importance of Israel providing a place of safety and a defence against all threats. As a mission and a narrative, it was strong and unwavering.

Unfortunately, I suspected this meant that Mohammad would not have been welcomed if his Palestinian identity had been clear. Completely at odds with his warm character, he represented a threat because of his place of birth and the political circumstances that had befallen him since. It was this harsh reality that left me saddened that humanity still had some way to go to learn the lessons from the Holocaust.

Temple Talk

One morning in January, my friend and I were catching up in a café just off Jaffa Street in Israeli West Jerusalem. Despite being the main thoroughfare in the city centre, the shops contained an odd collection of sun-faded fabric, mobile phones and cheap clothes. The area lacked warmth somehow, and it was difficult to find a café that was welcoming and relaxing. As we settled into an upstairs café, leaving our coats on because of the cold, an older woman approached our table.

'I heard you speaking English and wanted to ask where you are from?' She was primly dressed in a conservative Jewish style with a long skirt, long blouse, thick beige tights and sturdy, black-laced shoes. She wore a hat that covered her hair. We explained that we weren't tourists but were living in Jerusalem.

'Have you visited the Temple Institute yet?' she asked. We apologised that we'd never heard of it, let alone been. 'Oh, it's the best place in Jerusalem, I take all of my visitors there, you simply have to see it.' There was an awkward pause as she lingered beside our table. We nodded to placate her and said that we would check it out, before resuming our conversation. I sensed that any hesitation could lead to a full sermon on the matter.

My interest was piqued, however, and eager to explore all sides of Jerusalem I wanted to find out more. I was intrigued by the psychology behind the institute, and that weekend we set off to visit it. The small building was situated in the heart of the Jewish Quarter of the Old City, close to the Western Wall. We were asked to pay a small entrance fee before being ushered into the first room where a briefing film was played. The building was modern, and laid out like a small museum with various religious paintings and artefacts on show. Some of these were intended to be displayed in a future Third Temple.

The history of the Temple is at the heart of the Jewish attachment to Jerusalem. Judaism holds that the Holy Temple is such a sacred site that it provides direct access to God. The First Temple was built over 3,000 years ago (1000BCE) and was destroyed by invading armies in 586BCE. The Second Temple was completed in 516BCE but was destroyed by the Romans in 70CE. Some Jewish people feel that God can only be honoured, and the wishes of the Torah carried out, if a Third Temple is built on the same site.

The sentiment was understandable, but the problem was that since the 7th century the site has been occupied by the Al-Aqsa Mosque compound which includes the Dome of the Rock. This is the third holiest site in Islam, said to be where the Prophet Muhammad ascended to heaven from. This makes it the most contested religious property in the world, and since 1967, when Israel took over control of the Old City, it has increasingly become the prize jewel at the heart of the Israeli-Palestinian conflict.

There were only a few other visitors, and the guards kept an eye on us throughout to ensure we didn't get too close to the displays or take any photographs. The final room contained another promotional video, and when it ended I realised I had been clenching my teeth throughout as a deep feeling of unease crept over me. The organisation promoted clearing the site of the Muslim places of worship and rebuilding the Temple during 'our lifetime' – a vague yet sinister timeline. The film showed young children building a sandcastle on the beach in the shape of the intended Third Temple. The caption read 'the children are ready, what about you?'

The underlying tone was that everything would be well once the Temple had been restored. For some people, this yearning was at the core of the Jewish faith. The practical questions of how and at what cost this could ever be achieved troubled me. The organisation's website included short interview clips with people on the streets of Jerusalem, some of whom noted that building the Temple could unleash a third world war, while others said it would bring all religions together.

I didn't know how popular these beliefs were among the Jewish community, but the institute's prominent location and the range of high-powered donors listed on the website pointed towards pretty strong endorsement.

Not for the first time, a darker side of the city was revealed. Once we were back out in the late afternoon sunshine, Paul and I shared our reflections.

'Imagine if there was an institute in the Muslim Quarter dedicated to dismantling the Western Wall,' he said. 'Would that be given a prominent location and a visitor centre?' We both knew the answer to this and left our experience of the institute hanging in the air between us. I wondered what message the woman in the café had wanted to impart, and whether she went around promoting it regularly.

Imagining a future where both religions could share the site seemed like a futile pipe dream in the face of such strong convictions. Politics and religion went hand in hand in Jerusalem, and self-preservation often came at a dangerous cost to others.

No Deal

At the end of January 2020, we huddled around our TV on a Tuesday evening avidly awaiting US President Donald Trump's

'Deal of the Century' speech. This had been talked about since we had arrived in Jerusalem and there was a tentative expectation that it represented a pivotal moment in both the politics of the Middle East and the future of Israel and Palestine.

When it finally came, the officially titled 'Peace to Prosperity: A Vision to Improve the Lives of the Palestinian and Israeli People' was a bitter disappointment. With the Israeli prime minister, Benjamin Netanyahu, standing by his side, Trump delivered his over-hyped speech from the White House with the smugness of someone who was pulling a rabbit out of a hat.

The plan called for an additional 30% of Palestinian land to be transferred to Israel. This was land which had been conquered by Israel during the 1967 **Six-Day War** and where illegal Israeli settlements had been built over the previous decades, despite the **Oslo Accords** which in 1993 had earmarked it for a future Palestinian state. The Israeli occupation of the land had not been recognised by the international community, and to do so now would seal the death warrant on any hopes for the creation of a two-state solution and an independent Palestine.

Trump's proposal reinforced and augmented Israel's dominant position, and left the Palestinians with a few disconnected scraps of land that could never be gelled into a state. There was nothing to signal that any consultation with the Palestinians had taken place in developing the plan, and there was nothing of interest now being offered to bring them to the negotiating table. Trump and Netanyahu slapped each other on the back as they beamed with pride. It appeared to be a moment of theatre and self-promotion rather than a genuine attempt at diplomacy, and this set an ominous tone for the future.

The people I spoke to in the days and weeks after the speech felt powerless and let down that this was what leadership looked like in 2020 – old men in suits massaging their inflated egos instead of working to create the conditions for peace and prosperity.

Any opportunity for progress had been squandered. There were zero incentives for Israel to offer anything to Palestine, and with the unwavering support of the US by its side Israel could continue to carve off slices of Palestine without any fear of rocking the boat.

This shouldn't have been a surprise as the approach had already been set when the US government announced in 2017 that they would move their embassy from Tel Aviv to Jerusalem. This caused a furore as it recognised Jerusalem as the undisputed capital of Israel, dashing Palestinian hopes for a future Palestinian state with East Jerusalem as its capital. In doing so, the US was accused of normalising the occupation.

Some members of the international community rejected the deal outright, while others used diplomatic wording to fudge their position. The lack of a strong and unified international position led many Palestinians to feel let down and abandoned.

I was not naïve enough to think that a solution would be easy, but it seemed impossible with these actors on the stage. It was as if the wheels of progress had become stuck and civilisation was now spinning in reverse rather than moving forwards. How could the world think that this situation was acceptable? Why was the abuse of human rights not met with a stronger international response? Was this really the best that the world's superpowers could come up with? I desperately hoped that change would unstick the cogs of progress before it was too late for Palestine. I couldn't see the path towards it, however, and the fogginess depressed me.

Silwan

The following weekend we took a walk in the Palestinian East Jerusalem neighbourhood of Silwan. Before I moved to Jerusalem, I had watched a Louis Theroux documentary about Israeli settlers living in Silwan and it painted an alarming picture of daily violence and aggression. This had left me feeling both intrigued and apprehensive to visit.

Of all the diverse groups of people that lived in Israel and Palestine when I was there, settlers were one of the most feared. The word 'settler' and 'settlement' had a very particular meaning in Israel and Palestine. Settlers were Israelis who chose to take, and to live on, Palestinian land.

There were different motives for this. Sometimes their actions were driven by a desire to live near sites of Jewish significance, such as the Shimon Hatzadik tomb only a few streets away from us in Sheikh Jarrah, or the City of David in Silwan. In these areas, settlements sometimes comprised only a few houses within a Palestinian neighbourhood.

In the Palestinian West Bank, whole hilltops were taken to establish new communities. Some of the biggest of these housed tens of thousands of people and had been planned and orchestrated by the Israeli government for strategic defence reasons. They offered bigger, cheaper housing to Israeli families, and some settlers were no doubt driven by these practical considerations rather than by politics. Ma'ale Adumin on the outskirts of Jerusalem housed 40,000 settlers, Beitar Illit near Bethlehem had over 60,000, and they continued to expand.

All Israeli settlements established on land designated as Palestinian are illegal under international law. Israel forges on with settlement building despite this, however, and has created a huge infrastructure to support them including water and electricity, motorways, parks and other services. New checkpoints were established to prevent Palestinians from using certain roads, as Palestinian cars had different number plates and weren't allowed through. This also meant that Palestinian drivers of Israeli yellow-plated cars were given a lot of hassle. Road signs and billboards in Hebrew all helped to give the impression that the land was in Israel. Once people were 'settled' it became hard to imagine they would be moved unless by repeating the mistakes of forcible displacement made in 1948.

Because settlers planted themselves in Palestinian areas, they needed high levels of security to protect themselves. When new settlements were established, settlers were often armed, and violent confrontations between the new arrivals and the Palestinian landowners were commonplace. As settlements bedded in and grew, security was often outsourced to private security guards or the Israeli military. Once settlements were fully established, the territory was often fully enclosed with yellow gates to control all access in and out of the settlement.

It was commonly understood that Israeli settlers were 'above the law', and any actions they took, including using their weapons, would always be viewed by the Israeli state as self-defence. This was a terrifying prospect for Palestinians living, farming or even travelling near settlements who had no-one to call on for help if they were attacked. In fact, in some cases Israeli soldiers were seen to support settlers in attacking Palestinians.

The neighbourhood of Silwan sits just outside the Old City walls near the Jewish Quarter and is said to have been continuously inhabited for over 3,000 years. There are Jewish, Islamic and Christian ties to the area, and it contains the ruins of the City of David, the origins of which later became Jerusalem.

A private company called Ir David, or 'Elad' for short, had managed the City of David site for over 20 years and was known to be a far-right Israeli settler organisation. They had been heavily criticised, including by the European Union, for undertaking extensive archaeological excavations which damaged the foundations of Palestinian homes, and for facilitating the increase of Israeli settlers living in Silwan. The Jerusalem municipality and the authorities generally sided with the Jewish minority in rulings over local issues and this had further entrenched divisions in the community.

Hundreds of Palestinian families faced eviction and during the three years I spent in Jerusalem 66 structures were demolished in Silwan alone, displacing more than 250 people. These were the thoughts that occupied us as we explored the neighbourhood.

The Kidron Valley which runs through Silwan is a beauty spot, known for its spring flowers and framed on two sides by steep, rocky cliffs. This isn't enough to give it a 'quaint' feel, and the houses are cramped together, many in a state of disrepair. Building materials, chunks of old cars and other waste cascade down the cliffs in several places, creating the impression of an unloved scrapheap. Similar to other Palestinian neighbourhoods, Silwan has poor infrastructure and the local population are denied many of the basic services that the Jerusalem municipality provides for its West Jerusalem (Jewish/Israeli) residents.

The streets were quiet as we walked through the town that day. Kids played on bikes and trotted in and out of the corner shops for bags of crisps and on errands for their parents. We exchanged a few words of Arabic with several shopkeepers, who were courteous though our limited language skills prevented anything more than a transactional exchange. Israeli flags flew from several gated houses identifying them as settler homes. There were very visible signs that the neighbourhood lived in conflict.

Graffiti was being used by Palestinians in Silwan as a means of peaceful opposition to the occupation. Across the neighbourhood, 150 walls and other areas had been used to paint murals of eyes. Each had its own style, with varying sizes and emotions gazing out. These were visible from across the valley and taken together, the murals were striking and impactful. They all contributed towards the message: 'we see you and you should see us.'

Silwan during the day was not threatening but it was a very central example of the occupation and its divisive politics in action, only a few hundred metres from the Old City walls. Unfortunately, it had been impossible without a guide to get a true sense of the place. Graffiti that probably revealed political slogans and grievances was just art to us. We didn't understand the billboards, the shop signs or snippets of overheard conversation and this meant that the true character of the place eluded us.

The political systems in Israel and Palestine were broken. The Oslo Accords, signed in 1993, had created a transient situation where the Palestinian people were left to perpetually dangle between occupation and independence. Israel took what it wanted from East Jerusalem and the Palestinian Territories, and attempted to justify its actions internationally (with relative success) on the grounds of security and defending the home of the Jewish people and the rights of the Jewish people to live in safety.

The Israeli government was under pressure domestically. Five sets of elections were held in three and a half years between April 2019 and November 2022. Benjamin Netanyahu was ousted from power in June 2021 in the midst of a corruption trial that had already spanned several years, only to be re-elected in 2022. Progress did not feel forthcoming.

Meanwhile, presidential elections had not been held in the Palestinian Authority since 2006. Mahmoud Abbas had ruled the West Bank as president since that time, but he was not allowed to exercise any control over East Jerusalem. Many Palestinians were annoyed that the Palestinian Authority was not run more democratically, and it was regularly accused of being a puppet to Israel or absent where it mattered.

It was during these same elections in 2006 that Hamas was voted into power in Gaza, leading to the full Israeli blockade of Gaza from 2007 onwards.

During my time in Jerusalem, most of the international community stuck to the official position that they were there to promote the move towards a two-state solution, where Palestine could become an independent state. There was absolutely zero progress in this direction, and the evidence on the ground suggested it became less realistic with every passing year. To admit this, however, would leave a void that no-one wanted to face as a one-state solution that would grant Palestinians equal rights within a greater State of Israel was also unacceptable to Israel, and therefore deemed unviable. It was clear that the agreement reached in the

Oslo Accords was dead but there was no political will to launch fresh negotiations.

The Russian invasion of Ukraine in 2022 demonstrated to Palestinians that the international community did have muscles to flex when it chose to use them. Many were left with the sad conclusion that their human rights were not considered equal to others. It appeared as if the world was happy to sit by and watch the situation in Palestine continue to deteriorate and politics offered no hope or prospect of change.

The war in Gaza in 2023 brought this into sharp focus, and many people around the world were horrified that dominant Western powers found it so difficult to push for a ceasefire despite the heavy loss of civilian life in Gaza.

In July 2024, the UN International Court of Justice (ICJ) issued an advisory ruling that Israel's continued presence in the Occupied Palestinian Territories was unlawful, and that all states are under an obligation not to recognise the decades-long occupation.

Surely this time the damage was so devastating that the time for wholescale change had arrived. What that would look like and who had the capability to deliver it, remained to be seen and may well be the greatest global political challenge of the decade ahead.

CHAPTER 4
THE LOCAL BUSINESSES

Jerusalem was not an easy place for businesses to operate, especially Palestinian businesses. This meant that there were not the endless coffee shops and pop-up shops in East Jerusalem as you might find in Ramallah or Bethlehem. The businesses that survived had usually been there for generations. This chapter looks at the stories behind three Palestinian and one international business in East Jerusalem to explore the challenges of surviving in the city and what each of these local institutions meant to the communities they served.

A Bookshop with Soul

There were several places in East Jerusalem that had become little havens for the international community and the Educational Bookshop on Salah Ad-Din street was one such gem where people from all walks of life were welcomed.

I met Mahmoud Muna in our first year in Jerusalem when he taught my Arabic course at the bookshop. One morning, I dropped in for a chat to find out more about the history of the bookshop and the challenges of running a business in East Jerusalem.

Nowhere was the phrase that the pen is mightier than the sword more apt than in describing the bookshop and its sister shop across the road which sold stationery and Arabic books. Not only did the shops offer a treasure trove of interesting and thought-provoking literature but to visit them was to step inside the warm familiarity of a family-run business in its third generation.

Mahmoud's father, Ahmad, founded the bookshop in 1984 on the same premises that had hosted an earlier Palestinian Educational Bookshop. This was run by Edward Said's family but was shut down in 1948 during the '**Nakba**'. When Ahmad came along in 1984, he adopted the name as a mark of respect but was not allowed to include the term 'Palestinian' as it was illegal at the time.

In its early days, the bookshop included a range of Arabic titles with some English books, but Mahmoud explained that this changed in 1989 with the start of the **First Intifada**. Journalists flocked to East Jerusalem and the demand for English literature about the occupation grew. This increased further in 1994 after the signing of the Oslo Accords and the bookshop had continued to grow in popularity ever since.

This was a family business in the true sense of the word. Four of the six Muna brothers were employed full time across their bookshops (which also included the shop located at the American Colony Hotel). The founding father was still involved, and the younger generation were also regulars behind the counter. Mahmoud summed this up by saying 'our board meeting is our dinner time every night. That is when we sit round and discuss new ideas.'

One of these ideas was the expansion of the business in 2009 into its current premises. This allowed for a separation of the English and Arabic bookshops, and the increased space to start a small café serving coffee and cakes. When the grandson of the founder, Ahmad, came in balancing two large and delicious looking cakes, I asked where they bought them from. 'We make them,' he responded with a raised eyebrow, as if it was blasphemous of me to have suggested otherwise.

The café now carried its own reputation, and this gave people a reason to linger. Two girls walked in and ordered coffees as they enquired about the new edition of the *Walking Palestine* book written by Stefan Szepesi. Word had spread that the second volume of this useful handbook of local hikes would soon hit the shelves and as we were discussing it, the door swung open, and the author walked in. This was community! And it was this that made the bookshop special.

I was intrigued to discover how the shop navigated the challenging political context and avoided drawing unwanted attention to itself. Mahmoud acknowledged the lack of avenues for discussion in East Jerusalem and how books often provided an opening for these conversations. The shop had worked hard to fill some of this void. They regularly organised social and cultural events which brought authors and readers together. These were never overtly political and with a shrug and a wry smile Mahmoud said, 'we're just talking about books.'

A fundamental part of the shop's ethos was that everyone was welcome. Mahmoud proudly showed me an email he had received the previous day from a Jewish man who had visited the shop. He praised the atmosphere and collection of books but lamented the abuse he had received on his way to the shop for wearing a *kippah*. We discussed that the inclusive approach of the shop was still far from being the norm in the wider environment due to the deep divisions within the city.

Mahmoud hoped that places like the bookshop would start to create the foundation for a society where people could live beside each other. Commenting on the shop's presence on the street he said, 'we are the first to open and the last to close. We take pride in that. When the bookshop has that role, it's a city that presents hope.'

More Than a Corner Shop

Another well-loved institution among the international community was the small and unassuming Automatic Grocery shop which was another family business run on heart and soul. It had stood on its prominent location on the roundabout of Shimon Hatzadik Street in the heart of Sheikh Jarrah in East Jerusalem for over 100 years.

Stepping into the modestly sized shop you realised that it was an Aladdin's cave of treasures, designed to delight its international customers. It was packed from floor to ceiling with all manner of products, many imported from abroad. If you fancied some French cheese, Italian salami, a bottle of whisky – you would find it there.

The Automatic Grocery was established in 1909 by Mohammad Khawashki. It had stayed in the same family ever since, being passed down first to Mohammad's son Yahya and then on to his son Nidal. Nidal ran the shop with his two sons, Yahya and Yaser, until his death in early 2023.

The shop was named Automatic Grocery since they were the first in Jerusalem to do deliveries. Yahya explained that 'at that time, we were doing deliveries on bicycles, and we had a couple of people working for us. We are always unique in the sense of the products we get and the service we offer.'

Over the years, the shop had adapted as the neighbourhood had changed. Yahya said that from the 1960s, the neighbourhood became a popular location for diplomatic missions and consulates. 'Therefore, our main clientele is the international community, where the clients are often changing.'

THE LOCAL BUSINESSES

One of the first things you noticed walking into the shop was the impressive alcohol selection which had no doubt grown over the years to meet the demands of the international community. There was also a wide array of European and American products that weren't available elsewhere.

There had only been one period over the years when the shop had been closed and that was during the **Second Intifada** in 2000. As Yahya told me, 'my father decided to move to the United States for a few years for us, his kids, to get a better education and live a better life. This was a time when there were many strikes and schools were closing.' Following the 9/11 events in 2001, it became much harder to apply for residency in the US, and the family returned in 2003. Yahya was 13 years old at that point and he started working alongside his father in the shop.

Despite being a popular and seemingly thriving hub in the community, keeping the business going had not been without its challenges.

'For the past four years, since the Trump administration came in place, we have seen a dramatic change in business,' Yahya explained. 'Many of our clients have left their posts due to the lack of funding.'

During 2020 with long periods of Covid-19-related lockdown and quarantine, the shop had been a lifeline for many people. The business responded quickly by initiating a home delivery service and blocking the shop entrance with a wooden broom pole and passing items across the divide. A week later this was replaced with a Perspex screen.

When it became possible to return in person, the customers often lingered for a chat with the family. More than once I heard people say, 'we thought of you when we were abroad' or 'places like this make us feel at home.' It could be hard for the expat to break out of their home to office bubble and meet real people. Local businesses provided a space for that interaction to happen, and that need for connection only grew stronger during the pandemic.

Zalatimo Sweets

Most families had secret recipes but very few could claim to have been as successful as the Zalatimo family's *mutabaq*. After visiting this small family business, I added this sweet and savoury dessert to my shortlist of 'best food in Palestine'.

With several branches across East Jerusalem and beyond, the Zalatimo name was associated with their legendary sweets which had been sold in Jerusalem since the first branch opened in the Old City in 1860. My friend and neighbour grew up a Zalatimo girl and her brother and uncles ran the branches in Shuafat and Beit Hanina. She told me that as a young girl she would often help out in her uncle's shop in the nearby Palestinian neighbourhood of Wadi Joz. The family business had always been part of their family heritage, and this remained important.

One morning she took me to meet her brother who ran the Shuafat branch of the business. This was a Palestinian neighbourhood, only a few minutes' drive away from Sheikh Jarrah. I had been to this area many times before but had never noticed the small doorway tucked around a corner with a few tables outside.

Inside, the bakery was cosy and stylish with nice décor and interesting artefacts. Great care had been taken to make it a welcoming space where people were happy to linger over their coffee and made-to-order *mutabaq*.

There were a range of baklava-type 'oriental' sweets on display, but the main speciality was the *mutabaq*. This recipe was developed by the founder Mohammad Zalatimo back in 1860 and had been passed down through the generations ever since. It consisted of incredibly thin pastry which was folded over salty white cheese before being covered in syrup and dusted with icing. It had some similarities to the popular Palestinian dessert, *knafeh*, but it was much lighter, flakier and more attractive on the plate.

The proprietor Mohammad welcomed us in and invited me to watch him preparing the *mutabaq*. He explained that the dough needed to rest for six hours before it was ready to use and that he made 100 fresh *mutabaq* each day. As we talked, he started squashing out the white circles of dough that he had made that morning on to the large counter. He then used a rolling pin to create a thin circle of dough before picking it up and spinning it quickly to create a huge wafer-thin white sheet that he stretched across the whole counter. This was then folded repeatedly into a square shape and filled with the white cheese before being made into a parcel and put in the oven for exactly seven minutes. This process was to be repeated 100 times over the day. To watch Mohammad at work was to witness a skilled artisan.

A few minutes later, he delivered a hot and perfectly puffed up plate of *mutabaq* to us. The pastry was crispy on the outside and as thin as the most delicate of French pastries. A light syrup was drizzled on top, and it was dusted with icing sugar. Mohammad explained he had modified the syrup over time so that it struck just the right note of being sweet but not sickly. This lightness of touch gave the dish an elegance not usually found in Palestinian sweets. It was a perfect mix of sweet and savoury and we ate it with pleasure.

Clearly this recipe was a labour of love, and although others had tried to replicate it, Mohammad said with a modest confidence that 'others don't have the patience that is needed and ours are the best.' Sadly, the Old City branch of the business had closed in 2019 and the future of the premises was unclear. He said it was a shame, as 'the oven there was really good, and the oven plays a role in the quality.'

The Covid-19 lockdowns were tough on the business and like others they had been forced to close for weeks on end. Sweets had been classified as 'non-essential' and Mohammad would have faced a hefty fine if he had breached the strict regulations. With a young family to support this wasn't an easy time for him.

Now that business had resumed, Mohammad explained that he worked in the shop from 9am till 11pm every day except Friday. Ramadan was the busiest time of the year with the sweets forming an important part of an *iftar* dinner and they were a popular gift. Mohammad found it hard not seeing much of his young children, but it was clear that despite these anti-social hours his passion lay in continuing the Zalatimo craft for sweet making.

A Hotel With a History

One of the most well-known and iconic institutions in Sheikh Jarrah was the American Colony Hotel. It was elegant and exclusive without being flashy, and most prominent visitors to East Jerusalem stayed there. I wanted to get a behind the scenes look at the business and I was delighted when the manager agreed to talk with me.

Jeremy had worked at the hotel for 39 years and was a solid part of the institution. When he called me he apologised for not speaking to me sooner, but explained that he was recovering from an operation, was on strong painkillers and had been slipping in and out of consciousness. But he would be 'delighted' to chat. My offers to postpone the call until he felt better were dismissed and he needed little encouragement to launch into the fascinating tale that followed.

The hotel exuded a high-end quality that was soothing and built on impeccable service. Stepping into the reception area was like stepping back in time to the days when Lawrence of Arabia might have been found sipping a black coffee on the terrace – he had in fact been a regular guest. The courtyards were immaculately tended, and the gardens offered a calm oasis for people to meet and relax.

The hotel complex was situated near the **Green Line** between East and West Jerusalem and considered itself part of the 'no man's land' where everyone was welcome. Jeremy explained that the hotel strove to create an 'air of neutrality,' which 'gives it a feeling that you are coming into an area that isn't Israel or Palestine.'

He explained his own long service at the hotel by saying that 'no-one leaves.' There was something special about the hotel, and the feeling that the staff were a big family evoked sentiments from their colonial roots. Jeremy told me that 'the guests also feel that and within a few minutes of arrival the staff know their names.' This had been the foundation upon which the hotel had built its reputation for excellence.

The families who founded the hotel were still represented on the board. The international board's committee had members in the US, UK and Sweden and the management company was Swiss. Despite being geographically scattered, Jeremy said that the board was deeply involved in all decisions that affected the employees.

This had been tested to the max during the Covid-19 crisis. Before the pandemic, the hotel was employing 135 people. It was with great sadness that the doors were closed in March 2020, and when we spoke, only the restaurant and leisure facilities were open. Jeremy was planning that the hotel would not welcome overnight visitors for at least a year. He explained that only 5% of the usual occupancy came from domestic tourists. It was not a kosher hotel and instead targeted itself at the international traveller.

I knew the hotel had hosted a string of illustrious guests over the years, including prime ministers, presidents and other VIPs, but I wasn't prepared for quite how fascinating the history of the hotel was.

It all started in 1881 when Anna and Horatio Spafford left their home in Chicago and set sail for Jerusalem, in search of a Christian life in the Holy Land. They had suffered repeated tragedies over the years leading up to their departure. Four of their daughters were drowned in a shipwreck (which Anna survived), and a further son subsequently died of scarlet fever. They were devout Christians and Anna felt she had survived the shipwreck for a divine purpose. Instead of finding solace in their church they were cast out as being cursed. This caused a division in their community which resulted in 16 other members of the congregation leaving with them for Jerusalem.

The group took over a property in the Old City and began a life of prayer and charitable works. By the time Horatio passed away in 1888, the group had mounting debts. This forced Anna to return to Chicago in 1894 to free up some capital. Here she joined forces with members of a Swedish commune and they, along with a group from Sweden, decided to join her in Jerusalem. The American colony community grew significantly as a result, with 96 new members coming from America and Sweden.

The group needed larger premises and it was then that they moved into the hotel's current location. They took over the grand site built by Husseini-Effendi as a palace for himself and his four wives. When he died in 1895, with no heir, the site became vacant.

The Swedes brought a new industrial spirit to the commune along with many artisanal skills and they set about ensuring that the colony would be self-sustaining. They grew vegetables, kept animals, baked bread and were renowned for their sewing and weaving skills. It was also around this time, in 1897, that the photography department was launched. This became a major source of activity and income for the colony, along with the American Colony Stores that they also established across the city.

Over the coming years, the pilgrims would go on to amass an enormous collection of photographs documenting the last years of Ottoman rule in Jerusalem, World War I and the start of the British Mandate period. This collection, along with many personal and business-related documents and diaries, is split between the Library of Congress in Washington and an archive within the hotel grounds.

A dedicated historian and curator had worked for around a decade archiving, organising and researching the vast collection and the hotel's archive was available to view by appointment. History continued to be woven into the fabric of the building, and many original photos and artefacts were still available to view in the reception and shared areas of the hotel.

After 1903 the commune gained a reputation as a good lodging house for international visitors and the hotel was born. To supplement their income, the commune rented out rooms, sold photos and souvenirs and offered tours of the city. The onset of World War I brought this to an abrupt halt. During the war, and with the additional food shortages caused by a plague of locusts in 1915, the hotel played an important humanitarian role. Each day over 2,000 people in the local community were fed from soup kitchens which the hotel established to provide frontline support.

Under the careful management of Anna Spafford, the hotel maintained its political neutrality and was witness to many significant events. In 1917 the Turkish Governor of Jerusalem, with whom Anna had maintained good relations, borrowed a bedsheet from the hotel to use as the white flag to initiate the truce that led to the end of Ottoman rule in Jerusalem. The sheet is on display at the Imperial War Museum in London.

During the period of the British Mandate, the city was flooded with diplomats and the hotel provided a safe haven for them to meet. It was at the hotel that Lawrence of Arabia met the *New York Times* correspondent, who wrote the first book about him, and General Allenby was also a frequent visitor. Anna died in 1923, and management passed to the next generation.

In 1925 the family founded the Spafford Children's Centre in the Old City which originally served as an orphanage before becoming a hospital. The centre still operates today, providing special educational support to children in East Jerusalem. Both the hotel and children's centre continue to be led by the descendants of the original founding families.

The hotel's iconic status and fascinating history made it a treasure in the community, and it was a favourite venue for a drink in the secluded summer garden or in winter in the cosy cave of the cellar bar. Above all, it served as an example of how a business or organisation could achieve political neutrality in the heart of Jerusalem.

Looking inside these different businesses in East Jerusalem reinforced my awe that every building and family had a story to tell. Speaking of the American Colony Hotel, Jeremy had said that it was places like the hotel that made up the 'fabric of Jerusalem' and they must be preserved and supported to prosper. Running a business was not easy in any country, but the bitter twists in Jerusalem's history and the added complexities of the occupation meant that only the best survived.

All the businesses I spoke to had involved three or more generations of the same family. Like olive trees, they had put down roots over many years and had fostered a resilience that could weather many storms. It was these institutions that gave continuity of character to the city of Jerusalem, and I hoped they wouldn't be pushed out by the bitter politics.

CHAPTER 5
THE LAND

Time and time again Palestinians told us that no matter how bad things got in Jerusalem, they would stay. They described it as if the land ran in their blood, and being able to remain on the land was what connected them with the generations that went before them. Once a Palestinian farmer asked me where I was from. After I told him Edinburgh, his next question was, 'and how much land does your family have there?'

'Um, they have a house.' It was obvious that my answer disappointed him. Despite the difficult circumstances and the hardships of the occupation, I could tell that he felt far richer for being able to hold on to a plot of land that his grandparents and those before them had lovingly tended.

Over the past 70 years, the occupation had increased the value of land immeasurably. Staying on the land had become an act of defiance and a necessity for existence. In this chapter, I look at different ways in which the land has shaped people's experiences in and around Jerusalem.

Running in the City

I forced myself to get up early one Saturday morning to go jogging with a friendly and informal local Palestinian running club. I had been trying to dust off my trainers more regularly during January and February while the weather was still cooler. I knew it would be almost impossible from March to October to find time to run when it wasn't 30 degrees outside. The Palestine Marathon was scheduled for the end of March in Bethlehem, and I wanted to do a decent time in the 10-kilometre race even if I was shying away from committing to a longer distance.

I had been an on and off runner for years and the efficiency of running appealed to me. It didn't require any equipment or skills. So long as you had a pair of trainers you could do it. Of the many words I associated with running, 'privilege' had never been one of them. Yet that was the lasting impression I got when I met with the leader of the Right to Movement club in Jerusalem later that week.

Mahmoud was young and energetic with a full, yet carefully trimmed, dark beard. He met me in a café on Azahra Street in East Jerusalem to discuss the club and what it meant to him. Straight away he explained that in other countries, if someone wanted to go running, they 'have only to put on their shoes and go.'

Across Palestine a run required careful planning. The route must stick to designated areas and not stray into Israeli-managed zones. Then there was the need to avoid areas near checkpoints, the separation wall, Israeli settlements and other hotspots where clashes could flare up quickly and unpredictably. In fact, when a group of runners trying to train for a marathon in 2012 failed to find a suitable 40-kilometre circuit, it led to the founding of the Right to Movement group.

Right to Movement (RTM) was a community of local runners who simply wanted to exercise their right to move. The group was active in nine cities across Palestine and Israel and continued to attract both serious runners as well as social members. Mahmoud said that he only took up running in 2018 and he was now the leader of the Jerusalem RTM branch.

I was interested in his experience of sports as a child and how much physical activity was mainstreamed in everyday life. Mahmoud explained that sports at his school were very limited. Boys would sometimes be given a football to kick around but there was no training and no investment in sports. He didn't think this experience was uncommon, and he said that even if people were into sports, they generally gave them up once they started working and had a family.

East Jerusalem didn't have many open recreational spaces, and I'd certainly felt self-conscious going out running during daylight hours. Partly this was down to cultural and religious norms where it was uncommon for women to exercise in public.

In 2013 Right to Movement organised its first Palestine Marathon and this annual event had helped to embed the idea of running as a hobby. Mahmoud noted the societal shift that was underway and said, 'girls in Ramallah couldn't go out in the streets and run by themselves before. Now they can.'

It was a trip to the UK which caused Mahmoud to reflect on the privilege of running. Palestinian runners took part in races in Edinburgh and Wales, and they also ran in London. He explained that the sense of freedom they felt from being able to go as far as they wanted in any direction shone a light on the limitations of movement in Palestine.

The Jerusalem running group comprised several younger guys training for a marathon and many more 'shorter distance' men and women who came along for a jog and a chat, or sometimes just the chat. They met several times a week and were welcoming to internationals and anyone who wanted to join in. It was a great sight to see a large group of young people running together, with 'right to movement' on their T-shirts, showing their solidarity with the Palestinian cause in a peaceful way.

In 2020 and 2021 the Palestine Marathon was cancelled due to Covid-19 but in 2022 the event was back with full vigour. Thousands of runners took to the streets in Bethlehem to participate in the marathon and shorter races. There was a carnival atmosphere along the route with lots of music, dancing, eight-foot-tall puppets and other entertainment. Spectators cheered on the runners and offered drinks, snacks and in one case (which I turned down) cigarettes. The route ran along sections of the separation wall and through Aida Refugee Camp to highlight the Palestinian reality.

It was fun to participate in the race, but more than that, the event strongly conveyed the message that Palestinians deserved freedom of movement. I vowed never again to take my own freedom of movement for granted and hoped the day would come when Palestinians could also simply put on their shoes and go, without fear and restrictions.

The Scrapheap

Despite every corner of East Jerusalem and Palestine being hotly contested land, there was a disregard for the environment that wasn't aligned with the love of the land that Palestinians conveyed so deeply to us. On the face of it, there was litter everywhere.

I was interested in why this was the case, and the more people I asked, the more the answer came back to politics. Despite Jerusalem being served by one municipality, there was a completely different system of waste disposal in place in East Jerusalem. In West Jerusalem the streets were regularly cleaned, and rubbish was stored out of view and collected regularly to prevent it from accumulating on the streets. In East Jerusalem there were communal skips on the street where everything was thrown in together.

In all parts of Jerusalem, recycling was problematic and the plastic recycling bins that were present in West Jerusalem were removed in 2020 and not replaced. In 2021, the city was failing to meet its legal recycling commitments and was under investigation. The climate crisis that the rest of the world was painfully aware of had barely registered.

I found it staggering that the municipality could collect taxes from all residents and not offer the East Jerusalem residents a comparable waste collection service. This was even worse in the suburb areas of Abu Dis, Kafr Aqab and Anata which were part of Jerusalem but beyond the separation wall and received no services from the municipality.

Most people in East Jerusalem had no choice but to use the skips on the street for their general rubbish and this resulted in a very visual display of waste. It also led to the tendency that everything could be thrown in together. The contents of skips ranged from furniture to building materials, food scraps to tins and bottles. As a new arrival, I took a macabre interest in the contents of the skip and taking the rubbish up the road became something of a small outing, especially during Covid times.

Our local skip was also known as the 'cat hotel' and there would always be three, five or more stray cats sifting through the waste for scraps. One kitty achieved such notoriety that it even had its own Instagram account: *@theskipking*. Surprisingly, the smell wasn't the worst issue. Instead, the skips acted as ecosystems in their own right, with the cats competing for the best morsels. These were not cute domestic pets but altogether more feral beasts, used to eking out an existence from whatever came their way. I soon learned that the smell only became a problem if a stray cat died. The smell of a rotting cat carcass in 30-degree heat assaulted your nostrils long before you spotted the poor animal. Sometimes it was there for days before being moved.

If rubbish was a problem on the streets, it was not difficult to see where it was coming from. Both Israeli and Palestinian supermarkets generally dedicated an entire aisle to single-use plates and cutlery. Whether it was for a Shabbat dinner or a wedding ceremony, all religions were used to gathering people for shared meals that sometimes tipped into the thousands. Similarly, lots of cafés and lower-end restaurants depended on serving customers using an array of single-use plastic items as it was quicker and more convenient for them. There didn't seem to be any concern among the general population about the volume of plastic consumption, and refusing a bag or turning up with your own coffee cup was a clear indication to the shopkeeper that you were a foreigner. These eco-behaviours were tolerated as a Western quirk.

The problem seemed to be a lack of infrastructure, a lack of awareness and a lack of alternatives. Those who had spent time abroad were generally more alive to the issues and there were a few people who were trying to change the culture. Najla was a Swedish-Palestinian who lived in East Jerusalem and led a Zero Waste lifestyle. In doing so, she refused all items that came wrapped in single-use packaging. As an alternative, she made her own soap, toothpaste, deodorant and cleaning products as well as sourcing loose or packaging-free food. Najla led by example and regularly visited schools and appeared in local media to raise awareness of the issues.

The wide range of fresh produce that was available in Palestine meant it was easier to shop locally, buying loose unpackaged foods and eating food that was seasonal and had a low carbon footprint. Throughout the year fresh fruit, vegetables, herbs, spices, olives, nuts and dried fruits were readily available. Each crop had a season and once it was gone then *khallas* – no more. There was a local Arabic phrase, '*bokra fil mish-mish*', which meant 'tomorrow there will be apricots' owing to the short season of the apricot and how quickly you had to eat them. It was used in a '*manana*' fashion to describe anything that might never happen. For many Palestinians eating seasonally was an approach that came naturally.

It was understandable that plastic consumption featured low on people's list of priorities when faced with much greater existential challenges, but I hoped that awareness would continue to grow and that the environment would be protected for future generations.

Liquid Gold

It was Halloween, the final day of October, and we had been invited to lend a hand picking olives at a family friend's place. Ali was a salt-of-the-earth character who smiled genuinely in spite of everything that life threw at him. He worked as a receptionist and also had a side job cleaning the office. It was a family affair, and his brother also worked at the same organisation as had his father before them.

Life changed dramatically for Ali in 2002 when construction of the separation wall started, dividing his town Al-Sawahrah Al-Sharqiyah from Jerusalem. This, and the neighbouring towns of Al-Ezariyah and Abu Dis, were all cut off by the wall.

The wall meant that anyone travelling from the southern West Bank (e.g. Bethlehem or Hebron) to Ramallah, Nablus or Jenin in the north, had to pass through these towns on the old Jericho road which resembled a clogged artery and was always heaving with slow moving cars and trucks. The journey to work which used to take Ali only 15 minutes now took 90 minutes on a good day.

Drivers regularly got so frustrated that they drove on the wrong side of the road, and Ali had warned us to be alert for this. It was a Saturday morning when we visited and unusually the traffic flowed steadily along like a river.

The town of Al-Ezariyah is a historic spot, identified as Bethany in the Bible. The Arabic name is derived from Lazarus, and it was here that Jesus was said to have raised Lazarus from the dead four days after his burial. It was one of the holiest sites in Christianity, and also had the house of Simon the Leper where Jesus was thought to have stayed. Despite such prominent biblical references, the town didn't deck itself in riches and was modest in appearance.

We were only a few miles from Jerusalem, and still technically in the municipality, but we felt deep in Palestine. Along the roadside not an inch of space was unaccounted for. The shops lining the streets ranged from new, fancy ice cream and crêpe parlours to greasy mechanics' workshops, likely unchanged in 50 years of service. There were bright lights and a myriad of toy shops and small convenience stores. In front of the shops came the street vendors and wooden stalls and carts, most of which could be packed up and moved on at a moment's notice. Some sold piles of fresh fruit and vegetables while others offered fresh coffee poured from a large Arabic pot which could be delivered to passing drivers. Litter poked into the other available corners and was sniffed around by the odd stray cat or dog.

We followed the road up a gentle hill until it reached an abrupt stop. Tall vertical slabs of brutal grey concrete had been planted here. There had been no effort by the Palestinian Authority to smooth over the fact that this road, which once connected the town with the rest of Jerusalem, had been crudely blocked off. Here the wall was brightened up with paintings of the yellow Fatah flag (the leading Palestinian political party in the West Bank), a portrait of one of its popular detained leaders, and black pen portraits of *shaheed*. This translates as martyrs, and refers to Palestinians killed in the resistance.

Further up the hill, and passing through a labyrinth of small turns, we came to Ali's front gate. Inside there were several houses hosting his family, his mother, his brothers and sisters. In typical Palestinian style everyone lived clustered together. We had visited a few similar homes, and they always exuded a warmth and generosity as if you were entering into a family nest.

A few family members were already picking the olives from the five or six trees on the bank. Huge tarpaulins had been placed on the ground and we were given the instruction to simply throw the olives down once picked.

We rolled up our sleeves and assumed positions around one of the bushiest-looking trees. After 20 minutes of stripping one branch I turned my head to see the next section equally endowed with ripe olives. Then there were the higher sections, the lower sections, in towards the trunk, round the back. The scale of the task revealed itself and we picked up the pace. By now we had abandoned the kids, and were pleased to see them walking hand in hand with Ali's small nephews and nieces as they went to visit the new kittens and made endless trips into the house.

Olive picking was a deep-rooted part of Palestinian society that had featured in the annual calendar for thousands of years. It was a lucrative business, and with just a few trees a family could reap enough olive oil to last them throughout the year. With larger plots of land, people could sell the oil and have the basis of a decent income. It was estimated that over 80,000 Palestinian families depended on the olive harvest for their income.

The trees were well adapted to the landscape and didn't need much care beyond pruning, a little pest control and an occasional watering to thrive. Traditionally, the olive harvest was a time when families came together to help each other out and spend long days in the field. Most of the picking was done by hand and it was a time-consuming task but a rewarding one. It would be idyllic if it weren't for the harsh conditions imposed by the illegal Israeli occupation that prevented many farmers from accessing and harvesting their lands.

As well as worrying about physical violence from Israeli settlers and the threat of trees being burned or damaged, many Palestinians were refused access to their land by the Israeli state. The separation wall had cut some farmers off from their land and they now had to apply for permits to access their plots. This was often refused or restricted to a few days a year, which gave insufficient time to tend for and harvest their trees properly.

The gloves Ali had given me to protect my hands soon became ripped at the fingers and finally tore into shreds. The task was laborious but therapeutic. The picking tools Ali offered us seemed largely ineffective as they brought down so much of the leaves and twigs that it made the sifting harder. The best way to do the harvest was the way that it had been done for thousands of years: by hand.

Ali told us that he both looked forward to the olive harvest and also dreaded it. The novelty of a morning spent picking was fun for us, but for his relatives it meant several weeks of work. In true Arab style there were regular coffee breaks accompanied by platters of fresh fruit and homemade cakes which his wife dispatched from the kitchen. We still hadn't met his wife, and it was only when '*khallas*' was declared that we reluctantly clambered down and ambled in for lunch. We were sweaty and dusty, our clothes and faces streaked with the dust from the trees.

Samaheh gave us a warm and genuine welcome. The table had been set for lunch in the garden and from inside the kitchen the warmly spiced scent of a *maqloubeh* drifted out. The two sons, both with a striking resemblance to their father, had wide grins and affable natures as they helped set the table and bantered with the kids.

The lunch was fit for a king and our compliments to the chef were genuine. There was a friendly banter during lunch as Samaheh tried to sneak extra bits of chicken or another spoon of rice on to our plates. Another relative, a brother or uncle of some sort, dropped in with his granddaughter and, catching the scent, was convinced to stay for lunch. Chairs were pulled up as a plate of food was served to him.

By the time we had finished dessert, which included a jelly- and cream-layered pudding as well as another cake, we were feeling embarrassed that our 'day of service' had created far more work and effort for the family than we had put in. We were hooked on the picking ritual and offered to return the next day to finish off the job. Ali politely declined, probably thinking that his wife would have strong words to offer if he committed her to yet more hospitality.

The olive harvest was a period of intense activity for many Palestinians. Whether you had one tree or hundreds, the race was on to pick them before the rains started. The ritual of olive picking went so much deeper than the practical task. It was an economic requirement and a backbone of the Palestinian agricultural economy. A bad crop meant a high price per litre of oil and not much surplus for families. But more than that, it was a way to renew one's authority over one's land and to connect with a heritage which was bound up in family, nationalistic duty and custom. It reflected the Palestinian right to tend their land, and for some was an act of resistance.

Several days later, we were presented with a glass bottle of green oil. Ali had taken the harvest to be pressed the day after we visited, and when the cap was unsealed an earthy, petrol-like smell wafted out from the bottle. The pedigree of this liquid gold gave it a price much higher than its monetary value.

The Demolition

It was an icy-cold, yet sunny, Monday morning in January 2022 when the Israeli forces turned up to evict a Palestinian family from their home and demolish the house and garden centre business which the family ran. Demolitions happened most weeks, but this one happened only a few hundred metres from where we lived, and that made it feel personal.

Normally the official reason given for a demolition was that the family had extended their property without building permission from the Jerusalem municipality. It was reported that the municipality rejected over 93% of building permit applications from Palestinian residents. As families expanded over the years, many felt they had no choice but to build without permission. If and when the demolition order came, it had the double-edged injustice of requiring that the family demolish the property themselves or else face a heavy price for an Israeli demolition team. Often demolition orders would be made for the following day. Large families were made homeless and had to desperately scramble to salvage a few belongings. Children were left traumatised.

What happened next was not part of the usual script for how these things normally played out. As the bulldozers arrived to begin demolishing his home and business, Mohammad Salahiya climbed on to the roof of his property with several large gas canisters and petrol cans, doused himself with petrol and threatened to set himself alight if the house was demolished. His children and family were with him, and others started to gather and offer their support.

He made an impassioned speech which quickly went viral on social media, saying he would rather burn the place down than face the indignity of being evicted from his own land. His house was surrounded by heavily armed IDF soldiers who watched carefully with guns poised. Over the course of the day media flooded into the area to report on events, and the international community spoke out against the action and attended the site to act as official observers.

The Salahiya family claimed that they purchased the land in the 1950s (and certainly before Israel annexed East Jerusalem in 1967), but the Jerusalem municipality disputed this, and five years before had announced their intention to build a Jewish school on the land.

Twelve hours later, long after the police had departed, Mohammad was still up on his roof. Against all odds, he had managed to defend his house for that day. People came with sleeping bags, blankets and food for the family. Paul and a few friends visited the family and said that Mohammad was almost in a daze, exhausted and shell-shocked, probably stunned by the extreme measures he had felt driven to take.

A collection of activists gathered around a fire in the garden to keep warm and several Orthodox Jews from a pro-Palestinian sect, dressed fully in black but with Palestinian scarves around their necks, sat inside the house offering their solidarity and support.

The temperature dropped to minus two degrees that night, and during the next day the family anxiously awaited their fate, but nothing happened. At 3am on Wednesday morning, the police returned and forcibly removed the family from their home before demolishing it. It was reported that the family, including a young child and elderly relatives, were beaten before being arrested and taken away.

The following morning, metal barriers had been crudely constructed to obscure the view of the rubble. At around 8am, a bulldozer returned to finish the job, and the police closed the street. What had been a family home and business was reduced to a pile of twisted metal and broken plant pots. The rain lashed down and the dark sky reflected the mood of the community in Sheikh Jarrah and across Palestine.

Demolishing property was a tactic of the occupation to displace people and whole Palestinian communities could be disbanded, and their livelihoods destroyed, without accountability. Data from the UN Office for the Coordination of Humanitarian Affairs (OCHA) showed that as of October 2024, 11,701 Palestinian structures had been demolished, displacing 18,878 people since 2004.

In the Bedouin community of Masafer Yatta over 1,000 Palestinians face eviction and the demolition of over 900 structures because they live on land that was arbitrarily designated as a firing zone by Israel during the 1980s. Attempts by the UN and the international community to prevent this from happening have slowed progress, but piece by piece it continues to be taken and whole communities displaced.

Every day, Palestinians in East Jerusalem – and across Palestine – fought against a shrinking of their territory and their personal freedoms. Land was held in the highest regard by Palestinians and many, like Mohammad Salahiya, were prepared to put their lives on the line to defend it. Demolitions were the crudest display of Palestinians being forcibly displaced by an occupying power who exerted their control in flagrant contravention of international law. Bulldozers were used as weapons of war, and the pain they inflicted was as serious as physical attacks.

All Palestinians were affected by the practical day-to-day restrictions that the occupation placed on their freedom of movement. Parts of Jerusalem, like Ali's town, lived behind the separation wall, cut off from the city. Even those who lived in Jerusalem had to navigate a complex system of restrictions about who could go where and when. This affected routine matters such as going for a walk or a run, as well as more significant issues related to accessing work and land, which often provided people's livelihood.

The checkpoint system had severed most parts of East Jerusalem from the rest of Palestine and there were numerous ways in which Palestinian land was put under threat. Within Jerusalem, the municipality ensured that areas of East Jerusalem were not invested in and lacked infrastructure. It amounted to a system of violent and bureaucratic coercion that was strangling Palestine day by day, brick by brick.

CHAPTER 6
THE OCCUPATION

During our three years in Jerusalem, there were periods of relative calm and periods of intense unrest bordering on full-scale war. Every week there were Palestinians killed by Israeli forces, and injured, arrested and imprisoned without trial. Homes and businesses were regularly demolished, fines were issued, building permits and work permits were refused, checkpoint crossings denied. People were harassed and delayed, disrespected, humiliated and dehumanised. Inexplicably, this was the level of background activity that passed for 'routine' in the Occupied Palestinian Territories.

Between 2019 and 2022 there were a handful of moments which stood out for me as being the most shocking, and where the severity of the situation led me to believe that surely this time, the change must come. This chapter looks at each of these in turn: the killing of Iyad Halaq, the battle for Sheikh Jarrah in 2021, and the killing of Shireen Abu Akleh in 2022. Each of these resonated deeply with me and made international news around the world. And yet, that hoped-for moment of change didn't arrive. When we left Jerusalem in summer 2022, it was with a heavy feeling that things were getting worse and tragically the events that have unfolded since have confirmed that.

Palestinian Lives Matter

At the end of May 2020, news and social media lit up with shock and disgust over the police brutality that led to the death of George Floyd in Minneapolis on 25th May. There were protests around the world and people rallied around the Black Lives Matter campaign. Some factions responded with claims that 'All Lives Matter', which sparked more fury from those who felt marginalised, as it failed to recognise the specific racial threats that were seen to place many people in danger. For many Palestinians this resonated deeply as all lives were not given equal chances.

Only a few days after George Floyd was killed, an innocent Palestinian man was shot and killed in the Old City of Jerusalem. He was unarmed and had learning difficulties. He was not arrested for questioning. He was not restrained. He was deemed suspicious, so he was shot several times at close range in the chest until he died.

The man was Iyad Halak, a 32-year-old from the Wadi Al-Joz neighbourhood of East Jerusalem. On Saturday 30th May he set out from his home as usual, to walk to his special educational needs school in the Old City. Suspecting him of carrying a weapon, the police called on him in Hebrew to stop. He didn't understand, and terrified, he fled. He was chased and was allegedly found cowering in an alleyway, where he was shot three times and killed.

The saddest thing about this story is that it was not unusual. Israeli police used undue force and brutality against Palestinians daily. The ongoing occupation created a conflict environment, where warfare methods could be more readily justified on a day-to-day basis. When people were injured or worse, killed, the police only needed to say that they had perceived a threat for their actions to be deemed justified.

Had it not been for Iyad's disability, which gave him an additional vulnerability, it might barely have made Israeli news let alone received any international attention. Iyad's mother was quoted as saying, 'we are convinced that those who killed him will not be punished,' and 'justice does not exist.'

Some small protests took place in Palestine and across Israel in the wake of Iyad's death and the Palestinian Lives Matter slogan gained popularity, in solidarity with the Black Lives Matter campaign. The overall reaction was muted, however, as people were afraid to come out in large numbers. They had been here before, and over 70 years of occupation had led to a weariness about the prospect of change. Unusually, the case was taken first to the Jerusalem District Court where the police officer was acquitted of manslaughter, and following appeal this decision was upheld by the Supreme Court.

The Battle for Sheikh Jarrah

In April 2021, Sheikh Jarrah was thrust into the global limelight and events nearly tipped into a full-scale war. After more than a year of Covid-19 restrictions, tensions that had lain largely dormant during 2020 boiled over in spring 2021. During Ramadan, it was customary for Muslims to travel to Jerusalem in large numbers to pray at the Al-Aqsa Mosque compound, and to celebrate in the city in ways that the police tried to limit and control.

Palestinians were well used to having all aspects of their lives controlled and restricted, but these everyday injustices became more poignant during Ramadan when they impacted on the expression of religious faith. For many Palestinians, preventing access to worship was a red line they could not tolerate.

Damascus Gate had always been a natural focal point for crowds to gather after the fast was broken in the evening, but at the start of Ramadan, which fell on 12th April, the area was fenced off by Israeli forces to prevent Palestinians from gathering there. Violent clashes occurred over several nights, with reports that far-right Jewish extremists were coming to the area to fight with Palestinians. Several videos circulated on social media of Jewish people being assaulted by Palestinians and religious tensions erupted on both sides.

During these clashes, the Israeli police liberally used tear gas, skunk spray, stun grenades and rubber-coated bullets to disperse crowds. On 22nd April alone, over 100 casualties were reported in the city. It was the worst violence that had been seen in the area for several years. The next morning, as I drove the kids to school, Sheikh Jarrah was unrecognisable to me. Huge rocks lay strewn across the roads, several skips were still smoking, and several cars had been torched or smashed in.

The putrid smell of the unique Israeli invention – skunk spray – hung heavily in the air. This secret mix, supposedly organic, could linger for months and had been used by Israeli forces as a punishment as well as a crowd dispersal technique since 2008. Online videos showed the military firing this noxious spray into the homes of Palestinians in the West Bank to make them uninhabitable.

The following day, a Friday, I took a walk near Damascus Gate. People wore face masks or covered their mouths against the strong smell of skunk spray which still hung in the air. Crowds of people, mainly men, streamed in through Damascus Gate with small prayer mats rolled up under their arms, as they headed to the Friday lunchtime prayers. There was a heavy police presence, and they watched the crowds from every vantage point.

From that point onwards, the mood on the streets changed. Israeli police were always heavily armed, and were often in full riot gear, but now they had taken up position on every street corner, with guns poised. People eyed each other suspiciously, and I felt less confident walking on the streets, afraid of being mistaken for an Israeli settler and attacked. Around this time, the epicentre of tension moved from the Old City to several streets in the heart of Sheikh Jarrah.

Back in 1956, 28 Palestinian families that had been forced to leave their homes in Jaffa had been provided with houses in Sheikh Jarrah by the United Nations Relief and Works Agency for Palestine Refugees in the Near East (UNRWA). These families now faced the imminent threat of eviction from the homes they had inhabited for over 60 years.

The legal case for their eviction hinged on the fact that they were never given owners' rights over the UNRWA housing, and Jewish families were now claiming historic rights to the land. The case had dragged on for years but had reached crunch time for six families who were nearly at the end of the legal challenge process.

The following Friday, I attended a guided walk of the area, led by a local human rights NGO and some of the residents who were facing eviction. We were told that the last time Palestinian families were evicted from this street to make way for Israeli settlers, the family had lived for six months on the pavement opposite their house. It was only the approaching winter and the threat of violence from the gun-wielding occupiers that forced them to eventually move on. We stood under the fig tree that had served as their home for half a year, awestruck at the injustice but also deeply impressed by their steadfast response.

For some time, there had been weekly protests on a Friday afternoon in Sheikh Jarrah in support of the families who faced eviction, but from April onwards these had become flashpoints for clashes with police. A friend whose apartment overlooked the street reported on 9th April that:

> As the protest moved past the entrance of the Shimon Hatsadik Tomb, two riot vans and three police cars swiftly appeared, and more than two dozen police officers and heavily armed Israel Defence Force (IDF) exited their vehicles. As the protesters turned round to walk back from the properties facing eviction, the police blocked their path. The police started to push the protesters and it quickly escalated when a police officer struck one of the protesters in the head and pushed him to the ground. He (the man who was struck) didn't look young. Another police officer threw a stun grenade into the crowd. Eight more were thrown. A second older protester was injured by a stun grenade and was bundled away from the crowd by others. After about five minutes the protesters moved peacefully away. Two ambulances arrived. A few gathered around the ambulance, possibly the injured. The protesters regrouped at their usual spot by the side of the road near the junction. Their drums and chants resumed.

From the start of May 2021, nightly protests took place in the area. Shortly after the Ramadan fast ended at around 7.30pm each evening, the siren of police cars started wailing and the loud bang of stun grenades would reverberate around the neighbourhood.

Something new was happening in Jerusalem that those who had lived through it said felt different from previous uprisings. Young people were self-organising and were taking to the streets in large numbers to call for justice. There was a vacuum of political leadership and events were being driven by the youth at a grassroots level.

Social media had moved on dramatically since the last major uprising during the Second Intifada between 2000 and 2005. Events could now be captured live on TikTok, Instagram and Twitter and streamed across the world, and the #savesheikhjarrah hashtag quickly went viral. Several young people, like the twins Mohammad and Muna El-Kurd, whose family home sat at the centre of the eviction case in Sheikh Jarrah, became local celebrities with an international social media following of millions.

During this time, the Israeli police tolerance for peaceful protest seemed to evaporate entirely and every night the protests that had started peacefully ended in reports of people being deliberately hit with stun grenades as they tried to run away and people losing their eyes to rubber bullets. Hundreds were injured and the lack of police restraint was both shocking and terrifying to us.

We were under instruction to stay indoors after *iftar* (the breaking of the fast) and from inside our apartment the sounds of sirens and exploding stun grenades reverberated around us as we obsessively trawled social media for the latest updates and live footage. A colleague who lived a few streets away had his leg burned by a stray piece of shrapnel as he was taking his binbag to the skip one evening. Our friends who lived near the epicentre of the activity saw everything unfold outside their apartment and struggled to keep their young kids away from the windows and to explain to them what they were witnessing.

Events at a political level were fuelling the tension further. The Palestinian Authority president, Mahmoud Abbas, who had served for more than 15 years, announced that he would hold the first presidential elections since 2005 in May 2021. As the date drew closer, irreconcilable issues emerged, and it was announced at the end of April that the elections would not go ahead. The thorniest issue, which Abbas cited as the reason for the cancellation, was Israel's refusal to allow the Palestinian residents of East Jerusalem to vote.

To exclude Jerusalem residents would set a precedent that East Jerusalem was no longer part of Palestine, and it was a red line for Abbas. For many Palestinians cancelling the elections was a bitter disappointment that robbed them of the hope of change. For some people, it was further proof that Israel's opposition often worked in Abbas's personal favour, and this raised questions over how hard both sides had worked to negotiate a solution.

On 7th May we drove through Sheikh Jarrah at around 7.30pm and the first people we saw were a group of young women, aged around 18, who were identically and conservatively dressed in what looked like a school uniform. They all wore white headscarves and long dresses, and they were singing together. Meanwhile, a few feet away police stood shoulder to shoulder in full riot gear. These young women and the other peaceful protesters with their placards and musical instruments shattered the image that Israel liked to perpetuate that all Palestinian protesters were violent thugs. Using violent force on gatherings like this was not only disproportionate but it highlighted the huge gulf that existed between the two sides.

The Eleven-Day War

By 10th May 2021, the violence and instability had reached a new level. Throughout the day the police had been trying to prevent Muslims from praying at the Al-Aqsa Mosque and this led to clashes within the holy compound and at several sites across the city. It was Jerusalem Day and Israel was preparing for a nationalist show of strength. The day marked the 'reunification' of Jerusalem when the East (Palestinian) side was occupied by Israel in 1967. In normal years it was a humiliating display where Israeli Nationalists were invited to march through the Old City waving flags.

I was incredulous (and more than a little afraid) that plans for the march to enter through Damascus Gate (which leads to the Muslim Quarter) and head towards the Al-Aqsa compound had been given consent to proceed by Israeli authorities despite its highly inflammatory nature. It seemed utterly inconceivable that the march could happen without putting peoples' lives at risk, and it seemed so irresponsible and unnecessary to further fuel the tensions in this way.

Streets started closing around lunchtime and we were told to collect our kids early from school – it was a Monday – and to stay indoors for the afternoon. All afternoon there were clashes and reports of escalating violence, but this had become commonplace by that stage. At 6pm, however, something entirely unexpected happened. A siren that sounded like the Shabbat siren started sounding across Jerusalem. The tone was slightly different, and it took a few seconds to realise that this was an air raid siren signalling that the city was under rocket attack. All new buildings in Israel were required to have an 'earthquake-proof' room and most older ones had identified stairwells or other safe places for emergencies. In our case, the kids' bedroom was the safest room in the apartment, and we rushed there to wait for the all-clear to be given. After a few minutes the sirens stopped, and we were allowed out again. By this stage we had come to expect the unexpected, and somehow the threat didn't feel too great as everyone knew that the Israeli Iron Dome system was world-leading at shooting missiles out of the sky.

The rockets were being fired by Hamas out of Gaza. Hamas had been the ruling political party in Gaza since they won the elections in 2006. This had caused division within Palestine as the West Bank areas outside Jerusalem were ruled by the political party Fatah. The US, EU and UK had designated Hamas as a terrorist organisation as it used violent means. This gave the international media ample grounds to justify headlines that Israel was under attack, with no regard for the context that led to such an extreme intervention.

Gaza was part of Palestine, but the geography and circumstances were very different. Gaza was a small strip of land with the Mediterranean Sea on one side, Egypt to the south and Tel Aviv only 70 kilometres to the north. Since 2007, Israel had held Gaza under blockade and all people and supplies in and out were strictly controlled, resulting in a severe humanitarian crisis. It was essentially an open-air prison where over two million people were locked into an area that was only 365 square kilometres, making it one of the most densely populated places in the world.

Israel was well trained in intercepting rocket fire and of the six rockets fired towards Jerusalem on 10th May, only one landed. It hit the nearby town of Abu Ghosh, 14 kilometres outside of Jerusalem. In the days that followed, Israel bombarded Gaza and Hamas continued to fire thousands of rockets into Israel. Tel Aviv came under frequent rocket fire and serious disruption was caused across the country.

The 'war' lasted for 11 days and in Gaza 242 Palestinians, including 66 children, were killed. At least 129 of those killed were found to be civilians. In Israel, 12 people were killed, of which two were children and all but one were civilians.

During this time, I regularly asked my Palestinian friends and colleagues how they were feeling. Inevitably, there was a range of emotions, but one of the strongest among those I spoke to was anger. They felt that Hamas's intervention had lost them the moral high ground and helped the Israeli state to justify its response. News reporting focussed on Hamas as a terrorist group and this gave weight to Israel's argument that they were acting in justifiable self-defence.

Some people I spoke to were pleased that Hamas was finally standing up for Palestinians whether they be in Gaza, the West Bank or in East Jerusalem. People were surprised that Hamas had rockets with a long enough range to reach Jerusalem, and despite reports that the rockets were not much more than glorified homemade fireworks, the attack created fear across Israel, which some Palestinians welcomed as a small compensation for the hardships they continued to suffer under Israeli occupation.

Another response was weariness, and an almost emotional inability to engage with what would come to be seen as just another twist and turn in a convoluted conflict. People's numbness to the mindless loss of life was a coping strategy developed over years and decades of suffering. Everyone I spoke to felt devastated that yet again the Palestinians in Gaza would be made to pay the highest price for Hamas's actions.

Meanwhile, in Sheikh Jarrah all law and order had unravelled. After Ramadan ended on 12th May, the protesters started gathering earlier in the day and on Friday 14th May it was reported that armed Israeli settlers were arriving by the busload in the neighbourhood and were marauding around brandishing their weapons. This was a far scarier prospect to everyone than the threat of rockets or even police brutality as the settlers had guns and were unlikely to be reprimanded for using them. In fact, most shocking of all was the prospect that the Israeli police were increasingly turning a blind eye to settler violence, which added to the lawless feel.

Despite everything that had happened, this day stands out for me as the only one where I felt genuinely afraid to walk or drive on the streets. I felt that I would be unable to protect the kids if we did encounter a settler as there was no guarantee that the police would do anything to intervene. I stayed at home and tried not to panic.

During this time, the international community was never directly targeted, but we (our family and friends) felt afraid to be out anywhere on the streets during this time for fear that our identity would be mistaken or that we'd be caught in a crossfire. The police had also started using live ammunition to disperse protest groups, and a car ramming incident in Sheikh Jarrah led to the driver being shot dead at the scene.

People became deeply depressed about the hatred that had surfaced and the deep wounds that had been allowed to fester. The situation felt out of control.

Those who hoped that President Joe Biden and the new US administration might condemn Israel's excessive use of force were disappointed. Most of my friends living in Sheikh Jarrah, some of whom worked for diplomatic missions or other NGOs, felt helpless and ashamed that their governments were not doing more. It was so painfully clear to those of us on the ground that this was not a 'fair' war, but instead the tightening noose of an occupation that politicians around the world chose not to stop.

When the ceasefire with Gaza came on 21st May it was hollow. More innocent people had been senselessly killed and Palestinians were no closer to securing their freedom. As soon as the ceasefire came into effect, the United Nations and other NGOs started pouring into Gaza to assess the damage and to coordinate humanitarian aid. The UN announced that an extra US$18 million would be made available to rebuild Gaza. Like the Gazans, the UN had been here before. Some of the projects funded by the aid money that poured in after the 2014 war had only recently been completed, and we heard that beautiful newly renovated apartment buildings fitted with solar panels and other infrastructure in Gaza had been destroyed.

My friend, who had lived in Jerusalem for many years, was in tears over the phone when she said, 'we have been here before, and we always say that we will never let it happen again, but it does.' It was not a conclusion or a satisfactory outcome, and everyone still wondered where the change would come from. If the definition of insanity was repeating the same actions over and over again and expecting different results, then it felt very apt in this case.

Civil War

An unexpected outcome of the Eleven-Day War in 2021 was that Israel felt close to civil war. As well as Palestinians in the West Bank protesting in solidarity with Gaza, people gathered in protests across Israel. Palestinians (or Arab-Israelis as they are called in Israel) make up roughly 20% of the population of Israel. People live under different circumstances, but most had been allowed to remain after the State of Israel was created in 1948 by accepting

Israeli citizenship. In theory, they should enjoy equal rights as Israeli citizens, but the reality is different, and discrimination and inequality prevail in most aspects of civil life.

Across Israel during that time social media was awash with videos of a stabbing here, a lynching there, a person shot dead, a mass riot, shops and buildings being torched, and it felt dangerously out of control. Violence was especially high around Haifa and Akko where there was a large Muslim population. As the 11 days ticked on, and Israel delayed entering into a ceasefire, there was a feeling that they were so focussed on maintaining the 'war' with Gaza that they had taken their eye off the importance of maintaining order domestically.

During this time I spoke to Nourooz who lived in the northern town of Tarshiha, not far from the Lebanese border. In 1963 it was decided that a new Jewish town of Ma'alot would be built on land there and that the two towns would merge to form Ma'alot Tarshiha. I asked Nourooz how mixed her town was in reality, and she told me that Tarshiha had remained an Arab town despite the merger decades before. Her family and neighbours shopped in Arab stores, and she used to feel quite safe at night walking her dog around the neighbourhood. That had changed dramatically over the previous weeks.

The violence that erupted across Israel had taken many people by surprise and when we spoke it was clear that she was still shaken by this. She spoke Arabic and Hebrew fluently and had very strong English. She explained that since the violence began, she had to 'think twice if I should speak Arabic,' and that she no longer felt safe on the streets. For several days her family had been too afraid to leave their house.

Reflecting on events she said she was 'shocked at the amount of hatred,' and it had left her questioning if that hatred had been lurking underneath the surface all of this time. She went on to say that it was the first time she had felt like this, and that the trouble had left a 'deep and bad scar' that would take time to heal.

Alongside a feeling of distrust towards others, the violence had reinforced the feeling that the state and the police didn't treat people fairly. Nourooz had taken part in a peaceful protest in Haifa, and similar to events in Sheikh Jarrah her experience was that the police had used disproportionate force to dispel crowds of peaceful protesters. She saw people injured and arrested and thought that the police's 'intention was to hurt.'

Nourooz ended our call by concluding that 'the apartheid, violence, occupation, terror and inequality must be acknowledged, spoken about and treated. Occupation is still treating us as numbers... Our lives have no value to them, our basic demands and rights are invisible to them. We are invisible to them. War crimes are going on for years, and no-one is doing anything to stop this.'

Nourooz was about to be married to Ahmad when we spoke, and she was planning to move to East Jerusalem to live with him and his family. As well as navigating these significant life changes, she knew that she was moving into occupied territory and this unsettled her.

Shireen

On 11th May 2022, a sombre atmosphere fell over Palestine as people woke to the news that the much-loved Al Jazeera journalist and national hero, Shireen Abu Akleh, had been shot and killed in Jenin.

Shireen had been on duty reporting on an Israeli operation in the Jenin Refugee Camp, in the northern West Bank. She was wearing a press vest when she was shot in the head. Another journalist was also shot and sustained serious injuries. In the days and months that followed people tried desperately to piece together the events of her final minutes. The commonly held belief among Palestinians, including the Palestinian president Mahmoud Abbas, was that she had been deliberately targeted for attempting to report the truth. Israeli forces denied this but four months after her death admitted that there was a 'high probability' that she had been 'accidentally hit' by Israeli fire.

There had been countless needless deaths over the years, but few shook the nation as much as Shireen's. Aged 51, she had worked for Al Jazeera since 1997 and hers was the face and the voice that had accompanied a generation of Palestinians through the hardships of the Second Intifada and beyond.

That morning, the local radio presenter struggled to report the news without breaking down in tears. In the office where I volunteered, everyone was morose. Normal business was suspended as people sadly discussed the news. 'Everyone loved her,' was the common sentiment.

Two days later, Shireen's funeral procession intended to make its way from St Joseph's Hospital – at the end of our street – towards a church in the Old City. It was a Friday afternoon and in accordance with Muslim culture, many Palestinians had turned up at the hospital grounds to pay their respects to Shireen.

Anticipating a crowd, a large number of Israeli police were deployed in full riot gear and with horses and they started restricting access to the site. Impossible rules had been imposed on the funeral gathering which sought to manipulate and control the event: no flags, no marching, no chanting.

By the time the coffin was brought out into the hospital grounds, two of the three rules were already being broken with a range of Palestinian flags on display and different songs and chanting. Emotions were running high on both sides, with the Palestinian crowd desperate to give Shireen the dignified farewell she deserved and the police increasingly anxious.

In an instant the mood flipped and the police entered the compound of the hospital and began lashing at the legs of the coffin pallbearers with their batons. The coffin swayed perilously, and onlookers watched in horror as it nearly dropped to the ground on several occasions. Miraculously the men managed to keep hold of it.

Clearly the Israeli police forces didn't see what the rest of the world saw. They didn't see the many thousands of people distraught with grief, heartbroken with loss, who came out to pay their respects, peacefully. They didn't see the right of a community, a nation, to mourn a hero.

It was remarkable that even the presence of the world's media, and the close proximity of the hospital to so many consulates, was not enough to stop the Israeli forces from deploying such unnecessary force in the cold light of day. The footage that was aired around the world that evening made for unimaginable viewing.

Shireen Abu Akleh went from being a highly effective journalist, who spent decades highlighting the injustices of the occupation, to a legend whose death itself and funeral further illustrated the shocking injustices faced by the Palestinian people.

Despite the 'high probability' that Shireen was killed by Israeli fire, the police saw no grounds to open an investigation on the matter and no-one faced criminal charges. In December 2022, Al Jazeera filed a formal request asking the International Criminal Court to investigate the case and this was opposed by the US. Two years after her death, no further action had been taken and some saw the systemic lack of accountability as paving the way for Israel to act with complete impunity.

The killing of Iyad Halak and Shireen, and the bombing of Gaza which killed 242 Palestinians during the 11-day escalation in 2021, brought the horror of the occupation into full view. This was only the tip of a deep iceberg of chilling events that occurred during the three years that we lived in Jerusalem. The UN Office for the Coordination of Humanitarian Affairs (OCHA) reported that 'measured as a monthly average, 2022 is the deadliest year for Palestinians in the West Bank since the United Nations started systematically counting fatalities in 2005.' These figures were to be hugely overtaken by the events of 2023 and 2024.

The news was overwhelming and the injustice so deeply institutionalised that horrific life-changing and life-ending events often weren't even reported. It seemed that however bad things got for the Palestinians, it was never bad enough for the international community to take a serious stance that would force Israel to review its approach. I no longer thought the problem was too complicated to be resolved; it was clear instead that there wasn't enough will to resolve it.

Israel appeared to thrive on the image that it was surrounded by enemies and was a police state out of a fundamental need for self-preservation. It would continue to ruthlessly protect its interests and creep into new territory simply because it could. The international community would object to this on paper but not in meaningful action.

When Hamas committed their atrocious attacks in Israel in October 2023 it was unexpected but tragically not surprising. The Israeli tactic of securing peace for its citizens by doubling down on weapons and walls to segregate the Palestinians had backfired catastrophically and instead the occupation of Palestine had sown the foundations for hatred and terror to be unleashed on innocent Israelis. Surely, more than ever before, the need for a lasting peace was something that extended beyond this small corner of the Middle East and was critical for the whole world.

FOLLOWING THE STAR

On 21st December 2020, the night of the winter solstice, we were treated to a very Christmassy and rare natural phenomenon: the sighting of the Star of Bethlehem. This not-seen-in-800-years spectacle involved Jupiter and Saturn aligning to create an elongated star that was thought to resemble the bright star that guided people towards Bethlehem on the first Christmas.

I bundled the kids into the car and made the short 10-minute drive up to the viewpoint on top of the Mount of Olives. There were a few people gathered there who looked to be hanging out, oblivious to the special star. A Jewish kippah-wearing family were posing for photos as they admired the city skyline and a few young Muslim women in headscarves and conservative clothing were sitting on the stone steps chatting and exchanging snacks. Jerusalem lay spread out before us. The sky was dark but a red glow still shone on the horizon, clutching on to the sun that had not long ago departed.

The skyline danced and sparkled with the gold roof of the Dome of the Rock glinting prominently. The two stars were very visible in the left side of the sky, although there was still a small distance between them.

Suddenly there was a commotion behind us as two darkly dressed young guys (each backed by a small group of friends) fronted up to each other menacingly. It wasn't clear where they were from but it looked like two gangs clashing rather than a religious fall-out. A car then came screeching to a halt near us and some of the young guys jumped in. Still with the doors open the car shot forward, nearly taking the door off on the small wall that bordered the path. They then backed into reverse as their opponents pulled out a huge metal bar and tried to hit the car with it. Suddenly on high alert, I gathered the kids close and scouted escape routes to the front of us. I knew that we weren't their target and just had to keep out of the way. The darkness helped with this and we were barely visible in the poor light.

The worst-case scenario would have been if shots were fired but thankfully it didn't come to that. Our car was stuck on the far side of the small parking lot so there was nothing to do but to wait for the gangs to depart. A bus then drew up and several of the young guys jumped on.

Crouching in the dark, my kids seemed oblivous to the danger, but I thought we had better cut the stargazing short in case further trouble followed. Driving out, I found that the road was blocked by the bus the guys had jumped on and the altercation was still unfolding. I took a different route down the hillside to get out of the way and ended up thoroughly lost and then on a big highway driving in the wrong direction.

Arriving home, I felt weary from navigating the unexpected. It was a typical anecdote which summed up what Jerusalem was like. It was beautiful with ancient and historic buildings that took your breath away. Layered on top of this was the feeling of something 'special', some cosmic power that sat above the city in the night sky creating an aura and connecting the present to the past. The people who lived there were so different from each other that each resembled a tectonic plate moving in its own direction regardless of the friction this caused. It was never still. Never predictable. The pieces of the puzzle didn't fit and things were liable to erupt at any time. Some problems were manmade and others seemed to be Jerusalem's cross to bear. Understanding Jerusalem felt like a journey of faith and endurance with no certainty that we'd reach the intended destination. Despite everything, it had us hooked.

PART 2
THE PEOPLE AND PLACES OF OCCUPIED AND HISTORIC PALESTINE

THE CHAMELEON

One Saturday, towards the end of October 2021, we found ourselves assisting a gentleman named Abu Ahmad, who had several hundred olive trees on land near Battir. His plot was outside the village, not far from the main highway from Jerusalem. When we arrived with another family, his team of assorted helpers who had been drafted in had already been working for several hours. We found a well-oiled system in place that left no time for idling, and no olive unpicked.

'*Yalla*!' Abu Ahmad shouted. 'One here! One there! You come with me!' and he set us straight to work at different stations. His approach was to prune and pick at the same time, and he used a chainsaw to bring down large branches from the tree which we then lay on the ground and hurriedly picked the olives off. They were large, deep green and sumptuous.

As we sifted through the sea of green, pulling out the leaves and small branches, a small chameleon emerged from under the weighty boughs. It was a living stick, about five centimetres long with soft, papery skin and grippy foot pads. The kids instantly adopted it, and we didn't see them again for hours after that as they took turns giving it a drink, holding it and marvelling as its skin changed colour from black to green with yellow spots.

As we worked, Abu Ahmad chatted about the price of olive oil, his seven children, and the senior position he had held at UNRWA before he retired. He was curious about the world beyond Palestine and asked questions about our homelands. During the harvest, he picked from 7am till 5pm for 21 days straight and he was glad of any help he could get. 'We are all farmers here', he said, and pointing towards another man, 'he is a bank manager but during the harvest he is a farmer.'

From the rolling fields that Abu Ahmad – and before him, his father, his grandfather, and his great-grandfather – had tended, the peaks of Jerusalem were clearly visible. The view had changed since Abu Ahmad was a child with new hilltop settlements and high-rise apartment buildings springing up to join the Jerusalem skyline. Despite these changes, he took comfort in knowing that he was tending his family land and performing a sort of birthright or ritual that had been passed down for generations.

Even with several hundred trees to his name, each olive remained precious to Abu Ahmad. After we thought we'd cleared a patch, he would send us back to search for more and inevitably there were many we'd missed first time round. His careful approach and precision came from a love and respect for the land. This deep connection to the soil was a fundamental element of being Palestinian and was something I encountered time and time again. It went some way towards explaining the sheer obstinacy of those who chose to remain in the face of such adversity.

Sitting on Abu Ahmad's land, picking his olives with the rolling hills between him and Jerusalem, another view of what it meant to be Palestinian emerged. The Palestinian spirit and sense of identity was fiercely strong, yet people's experiences were different depending on their proximity to Jerusalem, to Israeli settlements, and to the separation wall.

As we travelled around, each place we visited revealed another perspective on what it meant to be Palestinian. The tightening noose of the occupation served to isolate towns and villages from each other. This had reduced Palestine on a map to a series of disconnected blotches. The damage appeared irreversible, and each olive tree that was uprooted or structure demolished was another piece of Palestine that was being dismantled before our eyes. Between 2019 and 2022, the pace felt steady and the time remaining was hard to measure. The war with Gaza changed this drip, drip process into something far more brutal and aggressive. It was no longer inconceivable to imagine Israel occupying Gaza again and if that were achieved, who knew what would lie in store for the West Bank.

It was impossible to try and understand Jerusalem without knowing what lay beyond it and during the three years that we lived in Jerusalem, we travelled extensively across the West Bank seeing many parts of Palestine that are commonly referred to as the Occupied Palestinian Territories (OPTs). It was not a single road travelled but many individual trips, some taken repeatedly to favourite places, as the people we met and the places we visited took root in our hearts.

When we arrived in the OPTs our children were two and four, and they left aged five and seven. They remember most of the places we visited together, although perhaps through a child's lens: the best swimming places, the best ice creams and the best camel or donkey rides. These years of their childhood were filled with regular adventure and exciting memories. There were caves, river walks, rock climbing, camping, water parks, desert hikes and much more. Each season had its highlights in nature as well as culturally.

What follows in Part Two isn't standard travel-guide territory. Each place we visited showed its charming authentic character alongside the harsh realities of its current situation. Different places were inaccessible at certain times, and we were guided by local security alerts as well as the UK's foreign travel advice in terms of places to avoid. At no point did we feel unsafe taking our children to any of the places mentioned but it took a bit of local knowledge to figure out the safest routes.

During the years that we were there, we often encountered visitors who were afraid to visit East Jerusalem and the West Bank without a guided tour. This was wholly understandable but also a shame as it meant they left with a narrower view of both Israel and Palestine.

Even in peace times there were logistical challenges such as the West Jerusalem taxi drivers who wouldn't drive the 10 kilometres to Bethlehem as doing so meant crossing into the West Bank, or the Israeli hire cars that weren't insured for West Bank travel. In fact, the very mention of the West Bank could be enough to get arrivals turned back at Ben Gurion Airport and all of these factors combined to make Palestine feel like forbidden fruit.

Most tour guides wilfully offered a narrow slice of reality based on the political motives of their tour agency and this often failed to show real life for normal people. There were exceptions, however, and Green Olive tours are recommended for anyone who wishes to experience Palestine through the lens of a Palestinian tour guide.

Unwrapping Palestine, place by place and layer by layer, was something we undertook purposefully and with a slow appreciation. Even then, we could never take for granted that we'd be able to visit certain places again as Israel could turn checkpoints on and off like water in a tap. In the chapters that follow, each place had such a different feel that it was easy to forget that the West Bank is only 90 miles long and 30 miles wide, yet packed into this small and shrinking land are some of the world's greatest sites.

CHAPTER 7
BETHLEHEM

For most visitors to the Holy Land, a trip to Bethlehem is high on their list of priorities. In one day, you can tick off the main churches and feel like you have paid homage to Christ's birthplace. What most people don't see, however, is the reality of life for the many Palestinians who live in and around Bethlehem.

It is a bitter irony that Jesus, who was born in Bethlehem, brought up in Nazareth, spent time around the Sea of Galilee, was baptised in the River Jordan and then died in Jerusalem had more freedom of movement than Palestinians do today.

During the summer and autumn of 2019, I drove to Bethlehem twice a week to volunteer in the Aida Refugee Camp. Over time, I witnessed the realities of what it meant to be a third- or fourth-generation refugee living in Palestine. Several of the people I met will remain lifelong friends and I am grateful to them for the stories they shared with me. This chapter explores modern-day Bethlehem including its biblical history and the world of checkpoints and refugee camps that dominates life for many of the Palestinians who call Bethlehem home.

Crossing the Checkpoint

On a good day Bethlehem was not more than a half-hour drive from Jerusalem, but the distance travelled felt much greater than the 10 kilometres it comprised, and it felt like a different country and perhaps even a different era. Unlike Jerusalem, which was a mixed city, Bethlehem was Palestinian (in **Area A**) with Arabic as the primary language. Bethlehem and the surrounding towns of Beit Jala and Beit Sahour were Christian, but the population was predominantly Muslim, and the number of Palestinian Christians was declining.

Entering Bethlehem required crossing a checkpoint and a sign warned Israelis this came with a 'danger of death'. Crossing the checkpoint meant passing through a hole in the **separation barrier** (wall) which Israel started building in 2002 to physically segregate itself from the Palestinian Territories.

The wall, which snaked its way along the length of Palestine, was up to eight metres high and was made of ugly grey concrete. When construction started, the Second Intifada, a period of intense heightened violence, was underway and the rationale Israel gave was that the wall was needed as a temporary security measure to safeguard its citizens. Twenty years later, the wall (including both completed and planned sections) was over 700 kilometres long, despite the Green Line border between Israel and Palestine being half that length. A meandering route had been chosen for the wall which enabled Israel to further shrink Palestine. This resulted in additional land confiscations as well as cutting many thousands of people off from essential services and family.

The architecture of the occupation bred ignorance and fear between Israelis and Palestinians. Israelis were told they couldn't cross the wall, so they had no way to see reality on the other side. This helped to perpetuate the Israeli narrative that Palestinians were uncivilised and dangerous. Who were the red signs signalling 'a danger of death' there to protect? Originally, I thought they were Palestinian signs to show that Israelis weren't welcome in their territory. Later, I understood that they were to warn Israelis that the state couldn't protect them in Palestinian Territories and to strongly deter anyone from entering.

Bizarrely, even in Jerusalem where there was no wall between East and West, many in the West were completely unaware of the neighbourhoods in the East as my anonymous blogger testified.

Palestinians were only permitted to cross the wall with a permit, and these were mainly issued to workers. Every day, thousands of Palestinians crossed the checkpoints into Israel, providing a cheap and skilled 'migrant' workforce without any of the requirements of workers' rights and state protections. Many were even involved in building Israeli settlements that were taking over Palestinian land.

For some of these Palestinian workers, their journey started as early as 3am to ensure they would reach their workplace on time. The conditions in the pedestrian checkpoint were described as being unfit for animals, and hundreds of people were herded together in tiny spaces and held for long periods of time without explanation. My friend Mustafa broke his hand in the crush one morning trying to get through the narrow turnstiles. It was an undignified scrum intended to exert control and dehumanise the Palestinians who passed through. Salaries were much higher in Israel and for many it was a sacrifice worth making, even with the painfully early start and appalling treatment. Without a permit, and applications were routinely rejected without justification, Palestinians were denied all access to Jerusalem and Israel.

Despite this backdrop of suffering, Bethlehem was a charming and unassuming place. Those seeking a dusty, rural village as depicted on their Christmas cards may have been disappointed by the juice vendors, the traffic and the general hubbub that reverberated around this iconic city. It wasn't flashy or over-

View of Jerusalem from Mount Scopus

The Jerusalem skyline looking towards the Old City wall and Dome of the Rock

Damascus Gate with Ramadan lights, Old City, Jerusalem

The Western Wall, Jewish Quarter, Old City, Jerusalem

Main market street in the Muslim Quarter of the Old City

Main entrance to the Church of the Holy Sepulchre, Old City, Jerusalem

The Stone of Unction (anointing stone) inside the Church of the Holy Sepulchre

The Dome of the Rock, Al-Aqsa Mosque compound, Old City, Jerusalem

Bethlehem Old City, West Bank, Palestine

The Key of Return at Aida Refugee Camp in Bethlehem

The separation wall in Bethlehem with Banksy's *Stop and Search* artwork and portrait of Ahed Tamimi

The UNESCO World Heritage-protected terraces in Battir, West Bank, Palestine

View over Battir from the Terraces Café, West Bank, Palestine

The valley of Wadi Qelt, West Bank, Palestine

Grazing goats near St George's Monastery, Wadi Qelt

The rock bridge, part of the Wadi Qelt hiking trail

The Manara Clocktower in the Old City of Nablus, West Bank, Palestine

A derelict Palestinian home in Lifta on the outskirts of Jerusalem

The Basilica of the Annunciation in Nazareth

View towards the Al-Bahr (Sea) Mosque in Jaffa Old City

Nabi Musa, Judean Desert, West Bank, Palestine

Hiking in the hills above Sebastiya, West Bank, Palestine

commercialised, and there was a modesty in the fact that you could get a strong Arabic coffee infused with cardamom for 1 NIS (25p) a stone's throw from the Church of the Nativity where Jesus was born. Despite its sacred history it was an unpretentious place, which hadn't sold out on itself.

The birthplace of Christ, which centred around the Church of the Nativity and Manger Square, provided a serene backdrop to the town, but didn't dominate. People buzzed around living their normal lives and it felt like a 'lived-in' place rather than a showcase attraction. Bethlehem enchanted me from my first visit, and I was pleased that my volunteering gave me an excuse to return regularly.

Bringing my thoughts back to the checkpoint, I turned off the radio and concentrated as I drove slowly over the jagged metal spikes designed to slow the traffic. The checkpoint was manned by two young Israelis in full military clothing and with large rifles. There was one man and one woman, she with a thick, swishing dark ponytail, heavy make-up and long painted nails. They exuded an atmosphere of bored arrogance as they chatted and flirted.

In Israel, all 18-year-olds are required to do up to three years of military service and it is this young and heavily armed workforce who do the grunt work of maintaining the occupation, standing for hours on end in all weather conditions at checkpoints. I was sympathetic towards the situation they had grown up in, pawns in their country's political games, with little choice in whether to collaborate or swim against the tide. A few did speak out, however, and Breaking the Silence was an Israeli organisation which encouraged military veterans to expose the reality of their role in the occupation.

I was in a diplomatically registered car and the guards took no interest in me coming into Bethlehem. Their primary job was to keep Palestinians out of Israel. On the other side of the road, a string of cars waited patiently for their turn to be interrogated. This may or may not have included their car being searched, depending on the whim of the guards.

As soon as I left the checkpoint behind, the atmosphere changed. Here the separation wall was decorated with elaborate murals and slogans that reflected the mood of the town. There was a large Morgan Freeman representing Nelson Mandela, various satirical Trump slogans, several Palestinian heroes and other emotive or ironic messaging. A large mural showed Ahed Tamimi, the Palestinian teenager who, aged 16, was filmed slapping and kicking an Israeli soldier in 2017. The soldiers had entered her family home in Nabi Saleh and shot her cousin in the head. She served eight months in prison for the offence. The film went viral and she had been hailed as a hero ever since.

Ahead I saw the bright lights of the UK's famous street artist Banksy's Walled Off Hotel, which played on the dark reality of the wall. The hotel was established in 2017 to bring international attention to the absurdity of the wall and it claimed to be the hotel 'with the worst view in the world.' The hotel exuded a shabby-chic charm, and the reception area was full of taxidermy animals and original Banksy artworks. Cocktails were served from mismatched china teacups.

The hotel provided a focal point for tourists and other visitors to learn more about the occupation in a carefully curated space with its own art gallery and museum. The museum was small but punchy and I took all of our visitors there.

My friend Mustafa, who was a local tour guide, said that many local people originally saw the hotel as commercialising and glamourising their suffering. They didn't want the type of attention that it brought. After several years, however, their views had softened, and most were pragmatic that the hotel provided a useful focal point to expose the Palestinian story to time-poor tourists, while attracting people to stay in Bethlehem. The wall had created a large canvas for street art and although Palestinians could be arrested for painting on it, new and elaborate pieces cropped up regularly. In this way, the wall served as a constantly evolving storyboard which gave an insight into the psyche of the Palestinian movement at any given time.

It was an ongoing frustration for Mustafa and others that every year millions of Christians were bussed into Bethlehem on highly choreographed tours where every minute of their day was accounted for and they left without ever seeing the reality of the wall, the refugee camps or normal life for ordinary people.

Banksy had created several original art pieces on the wall itself. One of the most striking simply said 'ER, Sorry' in a royal font, familiar to Brits as Queen Elizabeth's initials which were used on postage stamps. It was a fitting reminder of the prominent role that Britain had played in determining the fate of the region.

Many Palestinians viewed the former British Foreign Secretary **Lord Balfour** as the architect of occupation. In 1917, Balfour famously wrote that he 'view[ed] with favour the establishment in Palestine of a national home for the Jewish people.' Despite assurances that 'nothing shall be done which may prejudice the civil and religious rights of existing non-Jewish communities in Palestine,' the course was set for post-World War I politics to favour the creation of the Jewish national home over protection of the native Palestinians. It also led to the UK being assigned responsibility for the administration of Palestine in the Treaty of Versailles, a period known as the British Mandate, which lasted until Israel became an independent nation state in 1948. It was clear that many blamed the British for their hasty retreat after 1948 which failed to put safeguards in place for Palestinians and meant the events of the Nakba were allowed to happen unchecked.

I turned right in front of the hotel and followed the snaking line of the wall down the hill towards Aida camp. The road was narrow with a blind corner, and I was nervous about meeting another car and having to reverse back up the track. A small group of tourists were having a guided tour of the wall, and I felt lucky as I slowly inched past them that I could return the following week and the week after that.

After two more right turns, I arrived in Aida camp and parked my car under the huge metal archway with a symbolic key on top that stretched across the entire street. To this day, many people have held on to the keys from the houses they were forced to leave in 1948 and the 'key of return' represented both their past and intended future. The Aida camp key was said to be the biggest in Palestine.

I would spend a few hours working on a project to help camp residents to enhance the tours and experiences they offered the tourist market. This was intended to generate a wider income stream for camp residents while offering tourists a different slice of Palestine such as a street art tour, a cooking class, or another cultural experience. Work on the website was nearly complete and I was happy that the project would soon be launched.

Aida Refugee Camp

Every time I visited Aida camp there was a new experience or slice of reality to glean but that was never enough to stop it feeling like an enigma to me. Aida was one of 58 recognised refugee camps that were established across Jordan, Syria, Lebanon, the West Bank and Gaza to shelter Palestinian refugees in 1948. The creation of the State of Israel in that year resulted in around 750,000 Palestinians being displaced from their homes and entire Palestinian towns and villages were either taken over or destroyed in a move that would now be called ethnic cleansing.

Experiences ranged from whole communities being forcibly removed by violent means, to people fleeing to safety and then being forbidden from returning. Israeli forces killed many of those who attempted to return to collect belongings. Many of the homes were given to Jewish immigrants, some of whom were unaware of the house's history. *The Lemon Tree* by Sandy Tolan tells a moving real-life story about a house in Ramla from both the Jewish and Palestinian perspective.

In Arabic, the events of 1947–49 were referred to as the 'Nakba' (the catastrophe) and some Palestinians I spoke to considered that it was still ongoing. In December 1948, the United Nations signed Resolution 194 which set out the principles for returning the displaced Palestinians to their homes. This resolution had neither been implemented nor rescinded, and in the absence of a conclusion, it was impossible for the Palestinian people to find closure or move forwards with their lives.

Seventy-four years later, there were now four generations of refugees living in the camps and any notion of the camps being a short-term measure had long since been dispelled. In 1949, the

United Nations established UNRWA, its Relief and Works Agency, responsible for supporting Palestinian refugees. Its mission was to help those 'who lost both home and means of livelihood as a result of the 1948 conflict.' The issues faced had largely remained the same over the years and UNRWA's mandate kept being renewed. I found it staggering that the situation had been allowed to roll on decade after decade and that even for the UN this was in the 'too hard to fix' category.

I was told that around 10 years passed before the original camp residents were willing to exchange their hastily provided canvas tents for concrete homes. They knew that accepting something akin to a real house within the camp would reduce the likelihood that they would ever be supported to leave. They wanted instead to maintain their right of return to their original villages and the homes they had been forced to abandon. It can snow in Palestine during the winter, and the many winters spent living in tents must have been unimaginably harsh.

The camp was a strange phenomenon. People lived with most of the trappings of a modern life, but they were anchored firmly to 1948 as if it was last year. There was a precariousness to the situation that prevented people from leaving or moving on, even if they could have afforded to. That is not to say that life in the camp was easy. In 2018, it was named the most tear-gassed place in the world and the Israeli police regularly raided the camp, using excessive force and tear gas to threaten and arrest people. Water and electricity were strictly controlled by Israel and were sometimes only available for a few hours a day.

UNRWA was responsible for providing basic health and education services to camp residents, but both were overstretched, especially since the Trump administration slashed the budget in 2018. Many camp residents struggled to afford the medication they required, especially for recurring conditions like diabetes. The school day was divided into a morning and an afternoon slot to accommodate the high volume of children and the rest of the time they roamed around looking for entertainment and getting under their mothers' feet.

The camp was hemmed in by the separation wall which had several watchtowers, manned by Israeli soldiers. The wall was brightly decorated with street art, much of it political, some of it amusing and other sections, such as the display of the names of the young people killed during the occupation, simply tragic.

The streets were quiet as I parked my car and headed into the Aida Youth Centre where I met Mohammad. Together with Mustafa, he had set up Volunteer Palestine in 2018. This invited people from around the world to come and live in the camp for a few weeks or months and bring their skills to support a range of projects. It had proved popular and around 300 volunteers came in each of the first two years.

Mohammad had turned 30 that year and had always lived in the camp. He was trained as a lawyer, spoke English fluently and was always smartly dressed. Before Covid-19 hit, he would visit Europe for both business and leisure at least twice a year. This wasn't the profile I was expecting from a refugee camp resident but then Palestine had redefined what it meant to be a refugee.

'*Keefik*? *Shoo Akbarik*?' 'How are you, what's new?' The strong Arabic coffee infused with cardamon was already brewing on the stove and the scent wafted through the centre. The youth centre was the main community space for camp residents and housed a school in the basement, several offices including the room used by Volunteer Palestine, and meeting rooms for all manner of community groups. The main room was bright and breezy, and people regularly wandered in for a chat or other business. On that morning, members of a women's committee sat around in a circle conducting their meeting next door.

As we sipped our hot coffee out of tiny paper cups, I enquired about events in the camp since I had last visited.

'Last night there was a raid at 3am,' Mohammad said. 'They came to arrest a 20-year-old from the camp.' I struggled to conjure an image of the fear and chaos that must accompany the night raids, while sitting in the office with the light streaming through the open window and the hum of normality ringing in my ears.

A hunched gentleman wearing an old, yet still smart, suit and the traditional Palestinian headgear (a black and white *keffiyeh* headscarf) hobbled in with the help of his walking stick. Mohammad leapt up to exchange lively greetings and pulled up a chair for him as he reached for the coffee pot. The man was one of the camp elders and proudly told me he was 90 years old. I smiled enthusiastically, faltering over the small bits of Arabic I knew.

Unable to follow the conversation, I returned to my laptop and kept typing away. Several minutes later, the gentleman's wife appeared, also smartly dressed in a full-length black Palestinian *thobe* (traditional dress) with intricate red embroidery. She also took a seat and settled in for a conversation. It was clear that the older generation was revered and respected and Mohammad dutifully played the role of the gracious host, treating them as if they were his own family.

Later, as I was leaving the centre, Mustafa came in carrying his beautiful baby girl who was around six months old. He explained that he was on duty today as his wife was making her annual trip to see her brother in jail. She could only receive a permit to travel once a year and the trip would take her all day. I was told that her brother had been in prison for 19 years after he had been arrested in 2001 during the Second Intifada period.

The baby was the apple of Mustafa's eye, and she was a lovely little thing with brown eyes, thick dark curly hair and a sweet smile. Seeing such an innocent and vulnerable child made the reports of night raids and tear gassing all the more terrifying. Even during stiflingly hot summer nights, camp residents slept with their windows closed to guard against an unexpected tear gas attack. I was told that tear gas clung to curtains and other soft furnishings for weeks afterwards, making the rooms uninhabitable.

Mustafa's mobile phone rang out and it was his mother making arrangements to take the baby that afternoon. He looked relieved. Despite his claim to be a dab hand at changing nappies, gender stereotypes were still quite entrenched in Palestine.

The tough living conditions of the camp held the community together like glue. Seeing some of these relationships up close gave me an insight into the backbone of Palestinian resilience. Many things had been taken away, including the land, but people had little choice but to get on with it and in doing so their very existence became their strongest form of resistance. I often wondered why more people didn't leave for foreign countries offering jobs and visas. Strong family ties and the bonds of community provided some of the answer, with a loyalty and a pride in Palestine also playing a role. Being Palestinian was much more than a nationality, it was a way of life, and the collective calling was stronger than individual desires. Whenever I asked someone, 'will you stay?' the answer was always firmly, 'yes.'

Whenever I was in Bethlehem, it seemed that Palestine would always be a reality. It was not something that could disappear or be made to go away.

The Old Woman and Her Olives

It was the start of October and olive-picking season in Palestine. This had huge economic significance for the many thousands of families who made their living off the land, but it was also an important cultural and historic tradition.

On one of the most memorable days that I went olive picking in the West Bank of Palestine, not a single olive was picked. I shouldn't have been too surprised as plans changed frequently. Mohammad had told me to head to the small village of Al-Walaja, not far from Bethlehem, and my first mistake was putting blind faith in my phone's map app to get me there. Driving in Israel and Palestine was a Pandora's box of surprises – on this occasion the surprise was a metal barrier blocking the road I needed to take. I cursed, and despite being tantalisingly close to my destination, turned around and re-joined the highway to take another entry road into Bethlehem.

Ignoring the 'danger to life' signs that marked out Palestinian roads, I drove into a small village praying that it would connect me with a bigger road. The streets were quiet apart from the odd stray cat or dog picking through litter at the side of the road. A few locals eyed me suspiciously but not maliciously, and I drove on. Finally, a familiar road emerged from the warren of narrow streets, and I sighed with relief to be back on track.

Arriving about 90 minutes later than planned, I was worried that the olive pickers would think me a lazy slacker for being such a late arrival. As it was, I was led into the farmer's house where everyone was sat in the lounge having their Arabic coffee with a biscuit.

'Oh, we can't pick olives today,' Mohammad translated for me. 'Not after the rain last night.' I took a seat and settled in, not sure whether to be relieved or disappointed.

This was the house of Omar Hajajeh's family, and they had been cut off completely from their village of Al-Walaja when construction of the separation wall began in 2010. The wall was built between their house and the village, and the Israeli forces had provided a tunnel to enable the family to pass under the wall to enter the village. All guests from the village had to seek advance permission to use the tunnel, and no-one, except the family members, was permitted to stay in the house overnight. Omar explained (and Mohammad translated) that many of their friends and family felt nervous about using the tunnel, and despite the family's best efforts to keep up contact with their community they had become more and more isolated over time. The conditions of their existence were so highly regulated that Omar had previously commented that animals in a zoo had better treatment than them.

Three other volunteers sat with me in Omar's front room. They were visiting from England and had founded a small UK charity which supported projects in Palestine and Pakistan. After discussions with Omar and his family a few calls were made, and the charity agreed to provide the family with six sheep. This would improve the family's self-sufficiency on the land. The four of us jabbered away in English quite happily while Mohammad exchanged news and conversation with Omar in Arabic.

Mohammad made a few phone calls and being typically sketchy with the details said that we had a few more visits to make. The other volunteers and I, suddenly finding we had an olive-free morning, were happy to be directed to whatever 'business' was needed. Leaving Omar's house the five of us piled into my car and started driving south on the road that led towards Hebron.

'We're going to see an old woman and her olives,' Mohammad said. But no, not to pick them.

'Do you know her?' we asked.

'Everyone knows of her,' he replied, but no, he hadn't met her. After a few wrong turns we drove up to where an old woman was waiting on the roadside, flanked by two younger men. She stood at the entrance to the four dunams of land that she owned and cultivated olive trees on (one dunam = one square kilometre). She greeted us with a big smile and several bunches of ripe green grapes which she immediately foisted upon us.

Despite looking at least 75 years old and hobbling as she walked, she shrugged off the offer of an arm to lean on. She wore her independence stoically despite her swollen ankles and was dressed in a traditional embroidered Palestinian *thobe*. Her teeth shone white when she spoke to us, urging us to eat more grapes with a mixture of persistence and kindness that reminded me of my own granny.

Mohammad translated the story that she told. Many years before, she had bought this land with her husband to provide for them and their son. Tragically, both her husband and son had passed away in swift succession and she was now alone and had tended the land by herself for many years. This meant travelling by bus every day from Beit Jala in Bethlehem, carrying as many two-litre plastic bottles filled with water as she could manage for her trees. Looking around, I saw that the edges of her plot were strewn with empty plastic bottles. These trees were her reason to get up every day. This was her corner of Palestine, and it was clear that she would defend it until her death. That defence was becoming more challenging, not only because of her own creeping age but because of the Israeli settlers who tried to intimidate her.

Stunned, the other volunteers and I stood humbly by, wondering where her strength to keep fighting came from. I feared I might have sold up years ago for a quiet retirement. This woman's land was her purpose and her pride, and that fuelled her strength to go on. Several more phone calls were made, and it was settled that the charity would provide her with a new water tank and the means to rebuild the perimeter wall to provide a defence against settler attacks. For a modest investment, these would provide some security and help to maintain her livelihood.

Despite the complete lack of olives that were picked that morning, I had learned more about what it meant to eke out an existence from the land than I ever imagined, and it was a humbling experience.

Backstreet Bethlehem

Over our three years in Jerusalem, we had the opportunity to visit Bethlehem many times and the novelty factor of visiting such a remarkable place never grew old. Its relaxed, low-key style made it a great place to spend time. To really know the city, however, needed a local's insight. To fill in some of these gaps, we asked our tour guide friend Mustafa for a 'backstreet tour' and left the itinerary to him.

The tour started in Beit Jala, the Christian hilltop town famous for its 'green gold' olive oil, its grapes and several beautiful gold-roofed churches. Mustafa grew up (and still lived) in the Aida Refugee Camp and as a teenager he used to walk uphill every day to attend High School in Beit Jala.

In the 19th century many Christian residents of Beit Jala emigrated to Chile, and Chile now had the largest Palestinian population outside of the Middle East. Mustafa told us he had once met a Chilean Palestinian and their Arabic was far closer to the traditional Beit Jalan dialect than that of the current inhabitants of the town. Isolated from other influences, they had preserved their mother tongue just as it once was.

Legend tells that St Nicholas spent time in Beit Jala during his pilgrimage to the Holy Land in the 4th century. He gained a reputation as a secret gift-giver and left the legacy of Santa Claus. Beit Jala was proud of its Christian history and had adopted St Nicholas as its patron saint, marking the spot where he stayed with the gold-domed Church of St Nicholas. As we walked around the steep old streets, Mustafa pointed out Ottoman and Mamluk architecture, including the large archways which used to allow camels bearing goods to walk straight into the shops.

Mustafa's main income before Covid-19 was from tourism. As we walked, we chatted about life over the past 18 months. He was an industrious guy with a young family to support and had recently worked in construction and hospitality trying to make a living. This had not been easy, and he was now working 12-hour shifts, six days a week, as a chef in a local restaurant. Despite having no prior cooking experience, he soon found himself the head chef and when we visited his restaurant a few weeks later we were presented with a hearty chicken and rice lunch that rivalled any of the local competition.

Leaving Beit Jala, we drove through the town of Al-Khader to Solomon's Pools. These three large reservoirs were built by King Herod over 2,000 years ago to channel water from the South Hebron Hills to Jerusalem and to Herod's desert fortress, Herodium, by means of an intricate aqueduct system. For years they had stood largely neglected, the subject of several failed tourism projects.

Mustafa had studied the pools in detail as part of his tourism qualification and he was knowledgeable and animated in bringing this colossal engineering project to life for us. The system stretched for around 80 kilometres and provided water to Jerusalem until as recently as the 1960s. Mustafa explained that Jerusalem was only around 50 metres lower than Bethlehem and the aqueduct dropped less than half a metre per kilometre. Some of the ancient stones that were hollowed out to channel the water still lay underneath people's houses.

Later that day, Mustafa took us to a fruit and veg seller on the roadside in Bethlehem and ushered us into the family's garden to view the ancient stones that made up part of the original aqueduct. These were a rare example of an exposed section that was still visible, running along the front of the family house. The fierce guard dog chained in the front yard deterred us from loitering too long or asking too many questions.

Our next stop on the tour was both poignant and personal. It was the end of the grape-picking season and Mustafa invited us to pick bunches of green and red grapes from the small vineyard on his family's land. The grapes were sun-ripened and dripped abundantly from the small trees. Any image of a rural idyll was more than a little tainted by the main Route 60 highway which ploughed through the middle of the family plot, bordered by a high concrete wall. The family had been left with reduced plots of land on either side of the road which made access challenging. Typically, they hadn't received any compensation from the Israeli authorities for their loss.

A large project was underway to expand the road even further, to better connect Israeli settlements with Jerusalem. Most Palestinians would not have the required permits to use the road. This was an Israeli project, on Palestinian land, to serve Israelis and further cement the position of illegal Israeli settlements. Not only was Palestinian land confiscated but their land was divided and access restricted. Watching the diggers tear up olive trees on the road to Bethlehem was painful and brought the urgency of the situation into sharp focus for me.

Our last stop was Bethlehem town centre itself for a walk around the Old City. Mustafa waved off the youngsters who were poised to pounce on us for car parking money and signalled for us to park bang in the centre of Manger Square, in a manner that only a local would feel entitled to do. As we ambled the streets it felt like he knew almost everyone, and one of his sisters popped out from inside a shop to say hello.

We were walking along the local high street which ran parallel to the tourist high street. On the tourist high street shopkeepers stood in their doorways like hawks, looking to entice people in to buy original Palestinian headscarves (*keffiyehs*) from Hebron, rugs, ceramics and other souvenirs.

Walking the tourist route was a bit like running the gauntlet and invariably involved meeting Sami. He was the larger-than-life roving café owner, who paraded his hot drinks through the Old City on a copper tray and was famous for his floral tea made with copious amounts of fresh spices. Sami didn't take 'no' for an answer and loved recounting his moment of fame when US chat show host Conan O'Brien visited Bethlehem and featured Sami on his show.

On the parallel backstreet, the shops had no signs and the customers had to actively seek out what they wanted. We peered into one shop to see two men hunkered over huge pots. The coals glowed red in a huge *taboon* clay oven where the speciality – slow-cooked lamb – was being roasted. It was then assembled in banquet-sized proportions for delivery to weddings and other feasts. Other shops and stalls sold second-hand baby items, alongside everyday goods and fresh produce. I stopped at a bakery table to buy a tray of date-stuffed biscuits. They were fresh and crumbly, with a dusting of icing sugar on top.

At the top of the town, in the heart of the Old City, the shops selling gold stood side by side. These were brightly lit, with windows crammed with ostentatious gold jewellery. Mustafa explained that when a woman married it was customary for the groom to present his bride with as much gold jewellery as the bride's family demanded. This was a form of dowry, agreed between the groom and the bride's father, and was meant to provide the new wife with a safety net should she need it. It made marriage difficult for many local young men whose wealth and earning potential was limited by the Israeli occupation.

There was a spring in Mustafa's step and a glint in his eye as he shared the secrets of the hometown he knew and loved so deeply. He was the perfect advertisement for the gritty determination that characterised Bethlehem, and we hoped he would soon have a chance to hang up his chef's apron and return to the work he was passionate about.

Christmas in Bethlehem

On the first Saturday evening in December 2020, the Christmas lights were lit in Bethlehem in a small ceremony that was streamed worldwide. Bethlehem normally attracted around two million visitors a year, but Covid-19 had hit the local economy hard, and tourists still weren't permitted into the country.

I visited Bethlehem two days before the tree lighting ceremony, which coincided with the mayor giving a press conference to launch Bethlehem's Christmas. In Manger Square the Christmas tree was up, and people buzzed around constructing a stage as several journalists filmed pieces to camera. Over Christmas, this scene would be broadcast to homes around the world as 'Christmas HQ'.

Trying to avoid tripping over sound cables, I headed along Milk Grotto Street in search of an open olive-wood shop. Despite the Christmas preparations, many of the shops had their shutters down. Towards the end of the street, I came to Christmas House, a workshop with its door slightly ajar. Inside, the owner and several others were packing up boxes for export. Without glancing up the owner said, 'the van will be here soon and the flight leaves in three hours.' Beautiful handmade olive-wood Christmas decorations were being wrapped to be flown around the world where they would take up pride of place in homes across Europe and the US.

I offered up a few words in Arabic to explain that I lived in Jerusalem. This was also a signal that I expected to pay a reasonable price, much less than the inflated tourist rates but understandably more than the local rate.

I chose an olive-wood nativity scene, with a Mary, Joseph, a shepherd and the three wise men carved out of smooth, honey-coloured olive wood. It was a thing of beauty, with each piece originally crafted, and the natural knots of the wood gave expression to the characters. To the left of the shop, visitors could observe the pieces being chipped into shape by hand in the workshop. It was a skilled and laborious job and the photographs on the wall paid homage to the older generations who had passed down the trade. Later, when I took the nativity set home, my kids were so enamoured with it that after only a few hours the Mary already had a crack through overly boisterous re-enactments. My disappointment was offset by the fact that the shopkeeper had given me two baby Jesuses and the little twins looked lovely in the crib together.

Back in the heart of Bethlehem, I moved on to an embroidery shop I had chanced upon previously which housed the Bethlehem Arab Women's Union. Tucked away on a side street close to Manger Square, it was best described as a social enterprise. The organisation paid 100 Palestinian women from surrounding villages a fair wage for embroidering goods at home which were sold in the shop. As well as creating flexible employment opportunities it also helped to keep the ancient art of Palestinian embroidery (*tatreez*) alive.

The old lady sitting behind the desk was slightly startled when I walked in. She had a warm smile and was patient in explaining the different items. She told me she had been born about 500 metres away and between her home and the shop, which was established in 1968, this was her corner of Palestine. The superior quality of the craftwork was self-evident, and the designs were both beautiful and intricate. I selected a cream-coloured table runner embroidered with a red festive pattern and some small tree decorations.

Later, I took the opportunity to visit Mohammad in Aida camp. The lockdowns had made my once-regular visits here very sporadic, and I was glad of the chance to catch up on the news as we sipped the strong Arabic coffee that was an obligatory custom. The youth centre stayed open in all seasons, but it wasn't heated and we wore our coats indoors.

The conversation took a nostalgic twist as Mohammad shared further details about the origins of the camp residents. Aida residents had come from 43 different villages located around Hebron and Jerusalem. Mohammad explained that, despite many of them never having the opportunity to visit their original villages, it was something they felt deeply connected to.

'Always the people in the camp are waiting for the moment to return,' he said. 'I believe through the narrative and the storytelling of our grandparents we are connected to the land, even if most of us have never seen it. We didn't live these stories ourselves but in our mind it's part of our memory and our life as well'.

Mohammad went on to explain that, in his imagination, the village his family is from is the opposite of the camp, with a green area, animals, people dancing *dabke* during weddings, grape vines, nice housing, good infrastructure, technology, arts, and with strong social ties among the people. The list continued as he described the idyll in his imagination.

I asked Mohammad what he thought the future held and if the refugees would still be living in the camp in another 30 years' time.

'I would like to believe it's not going to exist till that time,' he replied. 'I would like to think we are going to leave the camp and we might turn it into a museum, and each one of the houses will tell the story of the people and their suffering and hopes. I deeply believe the situation of the Palestinian refugee is going to change in the next 30 years. Oppression cannot last for ever.'

Mohammad had always been clear that many Palestinians no longer saw the two-state solution as viable. This struck me as practical, given the facts on the ground. Palestine had been chipped away at so extensively over the decades since 1948 that what remained was fragmented and continually shrinking. Forming an independent country from these disjointed villages would be near impossible. I thought back to the speckled maps that Trump had published as part of his 'Deal of the Century'.

Many Palestinians now talked about the need for human rights and equal treatment as a priority more fundamental than a country to call their own. They didn't want to live like prisoners behind walls. They deserved dignity, and to be able to preserve their culture and identity as Palestinian people under whatever political solution could deliver this.

Too often I had heard intelligent people comment that 'Israel won't go for that' in response to the suggestion that the whole territory of Israel and Palestine be amalgamated into a single state with equal rights for all. This was perceived as a threat to the Jewish way of life as it risked losing the Jewish majority and diluting the 'Jewishness' of the Jewish state. These ideas had been cemented through the Nation State Law which was passed by the Israeli Knesset (Parliament) in 2018. It stated that 'the right to exercise national self-determination in the State of Israel is unique to the Jewish people.'

If it couldn't be a one-state *or* a two-state, then some other radical solution was needed. In the wake of the war started in 2023 it was clear that returning to the status quo wouldn't be acceptable for either Palestinians or Israelis.

I left Palestine with many wonderful memories of time spent around Bethlehem and it was undeniably a travel highlight for everyone from backpackers to families. The reality, however, was that the character of Bethlehem and its very existence was under grave threat. The refugee camps were not a sustainable solution and life was lived precariously from one day or week to the next.

The checkpoints and permit system prevented many Palestinians from accessing Jerusalem, and this made life unbelievably challenging. This affected important matters like where people could work, and how they connected with their families. It also prevented simple pleasures, as with the young parents I knew who desperately wanted to take their daughter to the zoo, which was only a few miles away but on the Israeli side of the border.

Bethlehem could never be free while the Israeli occupation remained. The Holy Land that Jesus knew and travelled freely around did not exist any more. All the obstacles that made life challenging were manmade and the suffering imposed was wholly avoidable. This made the situation feel all the more frustrating and futile.

CHAPTER 8
SOUTHERN PALESTINE

Many of the Palestinian towns and villages in the countryside around Bethlehem had retained their rural and agricultural roots. Each place had its own character, and this was sometimes defined by its proximity to the Israeli occupation and the pressures that put on the town. The biggest threat they collectively faced was the encroachment of Israeli settlers. This could take the form of a few self-organised armed individuals disrupting a farmer's access to their land as well as large-scale, government-organised settlements which housed tens of thousands of people.

Battir went on to become a favourite destination of our family, and was somewhere we visited in summer as an escape from Jerusalem and in the cooler months for hiking and rock climbing. In the space of only three years, we witnessed significant changes to the landscape as a result of Israeli settlers. This chapter visits some of the places around Battir and Hebron to highlight what made them different, and the specific challenges they faced.

The Abundance of Battir

At the start of August 2020 we had the pleasure of an overnight stay at a guesthouse in the Palestinian village of Battir, only a few kilometres from Bethlehem. Battir might be one of the only places in the world that claims to have eight days in a week. Eight main families owned the agricultural land in the village and our local guide and guesthouse owner Hassan told us that 'everything in Battir is divided into eight.'

The village has a rich history with traces of its Roman and Canaanite past. The Romans built a pool to collect water from the seven natural springs that passed through the village and a channel system to irrigate the land. Over two thousand years later this system has barely changed and is still in use today. Each day, one of the eight families has priority over managing the water supply, and the water is channelled to their plot, with a fair proportion allocated to the other families. The water is measured by putting a yard stick into the well and marking out each family's daily allocation. It is archaic, yet democratic and effective.

The water channels are nothing more than stone gutters creating a network across the hillside. To change the direction of the water, the farmers simply use stones or a piece of clothing to block one water channel and divert the flow to their chosen area. I wondered why it hadn't evolved over the years into something more sophisticated than stuffing an old T-shirt into a water channel before remembering the old saying 'if it ain't broke…' Its ingenuity came from its simplicity and had resulted in thousands of years of agricultural prosperity in an otherwise dry and unforgiving land.

The area is also famous for its ancient stone terraces which allow farmable strips of land to be levelled out on a rocky hillside. The farming plots run in rows along the hillside, and each is served by the water channel running through it. The terraces received UNESCO World Heritage status in 2014.

The plentiful water supply is the key to the abundant growth of fruit and vegetables in Battir. In particular, the area is known for the *Battiri bithinjan* – aubergines. We were told that many areas claimed to offer *Battiri bithinjan* but the secret to authenticity was if there were small spikes on the green stalk of the aubergine.

Hassan promised our kids 'an adventure' rather than a walk, and that was what they got when we set out to explore the area with him. Each tree offered something different to taste, with walnuts to crack open, green beans to pick and figs, pomegranates and lemons ripening in the sun. As we walked, Hassan stopped to shout a friendly greeting to each of the farmers we passed who were tending their small plots.

The loud hee-haw of the donkey echoed around the valley long before we spotted him. He was hiding behind some luscious greenery, happily munching away and almost smiling. The kids were delighted to receive an impromptu ride on the obliging donkey's back, and they were feeling in full adventure mode by now. The donkey was rewarded with a green bean, but such was his indifference that he left it dangling out of his mouth like a crooked green cigar.

The kids were then coaxed up the rest of the hillside with the promise of a 'secret watery cave'. This was the famous Roman Bath from which the spring water could be collected. Hassan encouraged us to climb inside the dark stone structure where a few inches of icy water cooled our feet as the fresh spring water crashed down behind us. There was much shrieking and hilarity as the kids enjoyed getting thoroughly soaked. Back outside in the hot sunshine we took a cool drink from the water fountain.

As we walked back to our guesthouse, an old lady chased after us to offer us a homemade biscuit. She was welcoming and hospitable without any need for introductions to be exchanged. There was a tangible community spirit in Battir, and a hopefulness and sense of preservation and growth that was not felt in all areas of Palestine.

This had been hard fought for. In the early 2000s there was a lengthy legal battle to protest against plans for the separation wall to be built through the village. This would have been catastrophic for Battir, causing irreparable damage to the ancient terraces and effectively splitting the village in two. Hassan had worked on the campaign to have the ancient terraces listed as a UNESCO World Heritage site. When the status was granted in 2014, it proved to be a 'checkmate' move in stopping the wall from coming through the village.

We stayed at the small, beautifully restored guesthouse which Hassan ran with his sister Fattoum. There were three guest rooms, which opened out on to a pretty courtyard with numerous potted plants and artistic touches. From the rooftop, the views stretched across the valley with the railway track centrally framed as a poignant reminder of the village's proximity to Jerusalem.

That evening we sat outside under a canopy of vines, enjoying the warm air and sipping strong coffee as we chatted with our hosts about the past and their plans for the future. Battir's laid-back warmth was endearing and drew us back many times over the following years with Hassan going on to become a close family friend.

Settler Troubles

Palestine was shrinking before our eyes. Getting to know Battir better meant it was easier for us to see how things changed year-on-year with Israeli settler expansion. Every corner of the West Bank had its own problems, but we witnessed them more closely around Battir.

During autumn 2020 we had become rock climbing enthusiasts, enjoying many good weekends hanging out on the rocky cliffs around Battir. The spot overlooked the Makhrour Valley, a well-known beauty spot with a hiking path that connected Battir to Beit Jala. The limestone crags were about 10 metres high, and several climbing routes had been marked out where you could attach ropes. It was ideal for beginners as there were many natural hand- and footholds in the soft rocks. One of our favourite activities was to turn up with a mixed group of kids and adults and a picnic. Local kids and families that were passing would often stop for a chat and sometimes they asked to have a go.

The Makhrour Valley was vulnerable to settlers and land confiscations by Israel. Not long after we arrived in Jerusalem, we had enjoyed lunch with friends at the Al-Makhrour restaurant near Beit Jala. Only a few weeks later the site was demolished by Israeli bulldozers and a family lost their livelihood. The official grounds for this were usually that the owners didn't have the right permit or land rights to build a permanent structure, but the reality was that the occupation gave legal cover for Israel to take what it wanted. This was especially the case in **Area C** which, although Palestinian land, was administered by Israel.

On another occasion, we had taken a guided walk which involved olive picking and a traditional Palestinian lunch near Battir. The tour guide had built a small shelter on his own land to provide refuge from the sun and a place to prepare food and host tour groups. This included a traditional clay oven (*taboon*) which was heated by coals and used to cook aubergines for the best *baba ganoush* we had ever tasted. It was rustic and picturesque.

On returning to Battir several months later we heard that bulldozers had barged through the site, demolishing the simple structure and flattening many of the ancient olive trees in the process. In a further blow, the landowner was made to pay for the expensive demolition himself and we were told he had been left heartbroken (and penniless) by the ordeal. The destruction seemed so futile as the small structure was far from a road or other buildings and had been tastefully constructed to blend in with the natural surroundings. It felt like it was a case of Israel proving, 'we do this because we can, not because we need to.'

We were therefore very concerned to learn in November 2020 that a group of settlers had set up a small camp near the climbing rocks on the outskirts of Battir. They were armed and – it was safe to assume – volatile. We heard that when the Palestinian landowner tried to challenge them, it was he, not the settlers, who ended up being arrested. Settlers were one of the biggest threats as they were seen to be above the law and any rash violence or action they took would either not reach the Israeli courts, or if it did, would be justified as self-defence.

Overnight a family had lost access to their land and the area surrounding Battir had become more hostile and dangerous for the local community. We wanted to know if our climbing rocks were still accessible, and we set out one Sunday to attempt the same route as before. As we approached, driving along the dirt track, we saw two low-lying tents and a sheep pen that had been erected just off the road. Shepherding was an easy way to occupy land quickly as a precursor to building a permanent structure on the site. Two scruffy sofas had been placed around a campfire. A man lay sleeping on one sofa and, on the other, a guy who didn't look more than about 20 years old sat watching something on his phone. He was, presumably, the lookout and he jerked alert as we drove past and eyed us with suspicion from underneath his baseball cap.

His unease was amplified when we did a turn in the road and drove past him again several minutes later. A stone pinged off the car tyre just as we drew level with him, and the tension was palpable. He looked unsettled.

From that point onwards Hassan and a group of men from Battir organised a nightly camp out, to act as a permanent presence to prevent the settlers from claiming more land. Initially there was a feeling of camaraderie around it, but the routine became more punishing as winter dragged on. It became harder for Hassan to find a group each night who were willing to sacrifice their beds to sit out until dawn. One year later, the men were still camping out and the settlers were seeking to consolidate their position by building a permanent base. To do this they needed a new road that could be used to prevent the locals from accessing even greater sections of their land.

The protection and impunity of settlers, who could claim a stake over land and take it without consequence, drove home the injustice of the occupation. Often these land grabs were orchestrated by the State of Israel on a grander scale, in the name of infrastructure projects. A new motorway was being built to connect Jerusalem with some of the larger Israeli settlements around Hebron. Every time we drove past it on our way to Bethlehem or Battir, more of the countryside had been bulldozed over and the ancient olive trees torn up, their roots severed and replaced with tarmac. This process was irreversible.

Whether land was taken legally or illegally made little difference to the response, as the majority of the international community reacted only with softly spoken remonstrations regardless of the severity of the crimes committed. The US held the key influence and those who hoped that the Biden administration would signal change were to be disappointed as the months rolled on and the old patterns continued to repeat themselves. Meanwhile, Palestine continued to disappear piece by piece.

The Nuns of Artas

On a mild Sunday afternoon in spring we met friends at Solomon's Pools in Artas, a few kilometres southwest of Bethlehem. Arriving at the Roman reservoir pools was a rather underwhelming experience. There were no information boards to signify it was a site of interest and no obvious signs of preservation beyond the high fence which surrounded the three reservoir pools. These were the same reservoirs from Herod's time that we had visited on our tour with Mustafa.

It felt as if we were regularly tripping over King Herod's legacy in our exploration of the Holy Land. Over 2,000 years since his death, much of the awe-inspiring engineering and construction that he was famous for remained.

Herod was thought to have been born around 73BCE and reigned for 33 years before his death in 4BCE. During that time his building projects transformed the Holy Land, and in the words of our knowledgeable friend and scholar, he was 'a genius engineer, a talented diplomat and a paranoid maniac.'

Children around the world were introduced to King Herod through the Christian nativity story which relates that at the time of Jesus's birth (thought to actually be between 6 and 4 BCE), Herod was rounding up and killing all baby boys. There is debate over whether events unfolded in this way, but most historians think that Herod was certainly rash and cruel enough for there to be at least some truth in the tale.

The small car park beside the reservoirs was padlocked on our arrival, and we started our walk along a busy litter-strewn road that ran parallel to the pools. We were following a short trail outlined in the *Walking Palestine* book, but walls and structures had a habit of springing up spontaneously in West Bank areas like this, and as our sketchy start showed, the route wasn't as easy to follow as the book suggested.

Before long, however, we were climbing up among the olive and fruit trees and were on a clear track which led towards the small village of Artas. There were a few caves along this section which my son and his friend enjoyed exploring. We were gung-ho about these things, encouraging adventure and hoping that any snake or other animal that was lurking in the cave would take fright and flee long before any noisy children approached. It was only afterwards I heard that another friend had had the same idea, only to get the fright of his life when a wild dog came shooting out of the cave as he entered it, nearly bowling him over.

The name Artas is derived from *Hortus*, meaning garden or paradise in Latin and from a distance the village looked like an emerald cast into the rock. The natural springs made it a fertile area, and as we got closer neat rows of crops were visible in every shade of green. The village prided itself on its leafy green vegetables and was known for its annual lettuce festival.

The Hortus Conclusus Convent stood prominently overlooking the small village. The impressive church and convent were built in 1901 by Italian nuns, and the gleaming white facade stood out against the lush, green landscape. The name meant 'enclosed garden' and it was carefully tended by the 30 nuns from around the world who lived in the convent.

We had visited on a previous occasion and knew that the nuns were usually happy to unlock the gate to receive visitors. The Argentinian nun who came out to meet us was welcoming and happy to chat, despite the language barrier. She offered us Italian, Spanish or Arabic, none of which helped our group much, to our embarrassment. She invited us into the church and explained that there had been extended services that morning. We were the first to visit in months because of Covid-19. She missed the groups of visitors that they used to see. She had lived in the convent for 15 years and spoke passionately about the green oasis they cultivated, and the special connection of the area to the Virgin Mary.

It was an interesting example of a Christian community with strong religious ties to the Holy Land living alongside a Muslim village.

The kids had humoured our conversation with the nun, but lunch was beckoning and, leaving the convent, we drove a few miles to the legendary Jala Jungle. More than just a restaurant, this organic farm also hosted regular cultural events and parties where people camped in the extensive garden. There was a bar and inside seating area as well as tables outside in the large garden which had a shabby-chic vibe and looked out over the Makhrour Valley.

Looking again at the restaurant, I realised that the 'indoor' area was mainly constructed from a large tarpaulin that could be brought down quickly. Perhaps it was this which enabled the business to avoid a similar fate to the demolition that had brought down their neighbours' building only a short distance across the valley.

The staff were as horizontal as the venue and service was slow, but we were content to sit in the garden with golden sunshine casting a warm glow over the rolling hills across the valley. We sipped cold lemon and mint juice and the kids climbed trees. The home-cooked Palestinian food was worth waiting for when it finally arrived.

Apart from the view of the ugly separation wall, days like these were what Palestine should be about: remarkable history which dated back thousands of years, hiking through ancient olive trees and natural beauty, home-cooked local food and a warm and a welcoming culture.

Enclosed in Wadi Fukin

We had heard that Wadi Fukin was a 'nice place for a walk' and made a few enquiries which resulted in the instruction to meet a man called Ata outside the village mosque one Saturday morning in the middle of March. We thought he might point us in the direction of the walking trails, but he was generous with his time and instead gave us a fascinating tour lasting the entire morning to explain the village's troubled history.

The name Wadi Fukin comes from the Aramaic 'valley of thorns', and its predicament was starkly clear long before we arrived in the small village. As the road descended towards the village, huge Israeli settlements loomed on either side, the largest of which was Beitar Illit. The first Jewish families settled there in 1990 on land that had been confiscated from Palestinians in 1985. Rapid expansion meant that the settlement was home to 60,000 people, and it was still growing.

Multi-storey apartment blocks, all with red roofs, stood side by side on the hillside creating an impenetrable barrier. The settlement was largely populated by Haredi families and the valley floor where Wadi Fukin was situated was considered a dumping ground for their sewage and industrial waste.

Rewinding a few generations, Ata started the story, like many a Palestinian tale, in 1948 when the residents of Wadi Fukin were forcibly removed from their houses and Israel occupied the land. Many villagers ended up in the Dheisheh Refugee Camp in Bethlehem. In 1972, 24 years after their eviction, there was an unusual twist to the tale, and the residents were invited back to live in the village to make space in the Dheisheh Camp for an influx of new refugees from Gaza. Ata said that they never fully understood the reasons for this. One theory was that the Arab homes they had left needed repair by this stage and were no longer deemed attractive by Israelis. It was an astonishing example of how different villages suffered different fates in the wake of 1948. After 24 years, they must have all but given up hope for their former properties and yet perhaps their return gave hope to others, many of whom were still waiting with the keys to the houses they once left.

The village is watered by 11 natural springs and, similar to nearby Battir, there remains a system for fairly distributing the water between the farming plots. Ata told us that the village used to have 15,000 dunams of land but that had been shrunk to 800 dunams over the years following a series of land confiscations by Israel.

The land once provided excellent space for grazing sheep and there used to be around 2,000 in the village – nearly double the number of people who inhabited it. Ata doubted if there were 100 sheep now. He also talked of the natural wildlife like antelopes and gazelles that used to roam the area, but the massive construction and the subsequent destruction of natural habitats meant that they too had been lost.

As we were lamenting this, the smiling face of an older gentleman appeared from across the path waving a coffee pot in our direction.

'Ah that is Abu Omar, and we should meet him,' Ata said. 'It's not nice to refuse taking coffee.' We wandered across the road and into Abu Omar's small farm where he grew lettuces, spinach, cucumber and tomatoes.

Abu Omar had arranged some plastic chairs under the branches of a fig tree, and we sat and sipped the strong, cardamom-infused Arabic coffee. The fig tree had no leaves at that time, but Ata told us that it was a Palestinian custom that anyone passing a fig tree could help themselves to the fruits, but should not take surplus home with them. It was intended as a travellers' benefit, harking back to a reference in the Bible where Jesus picked figs from a tree.

Despite sitting in farmland with glorious spring sunshine beating down, the sense of being surrounded was oppressive. A helicopter buzzed around nearby, and the sound of Jewish prayer could be heard cascading down the hillside from Beitar Illit. Ata and Abu Omar told us that the people from the settlement weren't that violent, but it was usual for their children to throw stones and shout insults at the Palestinian residents of Wadi Fukin. They were far more concerned about the armed Israeli settlers who came from Hebron at weekends to bathe in the natural springs, as they were often violent, and sometimes prevented local farmers from accessing their land.

Huge swathes of the terrain that Abu Omar had grown up around had simply disappeared as the settlements consumed the land. Holding up a hand well-worn from a life of manual labour, he proudly told us that he had been a farmer (*fallah*) since he was five years old. The dynamite used during the construction of the settlements had caused structural damage to many of the buildings in Fukin, and unique local features such as a rock called the Time Rock had disappeared altogether. Furthermore, the loss of natural vegetation meant that there was greater soil erosion and flooding in winter.

Despite these serious challenges, the spirit of strong resistance lived on. I asked Ata if he could ever imagine leaving his village and he replied that he would stay regardless of how bad the conditions became. He talked of his father who at age 94 had never been to a dentist and 'eats lots of fats and takes lots of herbs.' This, along with a spirit of survival and preservation, was the Wadi Fukin secret to a long life.

Over the past years, Ata had established a strong connection with an American charity called the Friends of Wadi Foquin. They organised development projects and brought annual tour groups to the village as well as advocating for Wadi Fukin within the US. Over the years, the village had hosted high-profile visitors like David Cameron and Jimmy Carter, but even this political attention hadn't been enough to reverse the tide of their fortunes.

Ata continued his tour for us with a trip to see the local playground that had been built with the support of the Friends of Wadi Foquin. He also showed us the large caves which were guarded by two farmers – a brother and a sister – as their sheep and goats clambered around.

Leaving Ata, we started a short walk through the fruit trees and spring flowers. With the settlements behind us, we were suddenly transported into the serenity of the Palestinian countryside and were able to enjoy its natural beauty. This was the defining feature that should have been what Wadi Fukin was known for, but unfortunately the settlements that loomed around them threatened to suffocate the village altogether.

Feeling the Heat in Hebron

Despite it being the second largest city in the West Bank, and only 20 kilometres from Bethlehem on the main highway heading south, Google Maps couldn't calculate a route to Hebron by car or bus. Try searching from Beitar Illit to Kiryat Arba (two Israeli settlements along a similar route) and Google had no problems. In fact, almost the entire Palestinian West Bank was a blind spot for Google, and not because it hadn't been mapped. It seemed that Palestine was not something that Google liked to talk about.

Mapping problems aside, everywhere in the West Bank felt accessible to us, but Hebron had an edgy reputation which made us a little more cautious. For our first trip, we arranged for Mustafa to give us a tour. We collected him in Bethlehem, and he navigated us right into the heart of the Old City of Hebron.

Hebron is an ancient city of religious significance to Jews, Christians and Muslims who believe that Abraham designated the Cave of the Patriarchs as a burial site for the tombs of the patriarchs and their wives. For centuries small Jewish and Christian populations had lived alongside the Muslim (Palestinian) majority. In 1967, Israel occupied the city. The events that followed resulted in the important religious site, the Cave of the Patriarchs, known to Palestinians as the Ibrahimi Mosque, being divided in two to make way for a Jewish synagogue. This, and the influx of Jewish settlers to Hebron after 1967, brought a tension to the city that frequently spilled over into acts of violence on both sides.

A defining moment that sealed Hebron's fate came in 1994 when a Jewish American-Israeli, Baruch Goldstein, opened fire on Muslims who were praying during Ramadan in the Ibrahimi Mosque. He killed 29 people and injured 125. With this single act, any hopes of coexistence between Israelis and Palestinians in Hebron were extinguished. The following year, while the Oslo Accords were being agreed, the Hebron Protocol was signed, and the city was officially divided in two. The area called 'H1' was under Palestinian control and 'H2', which included all of the Old City, was placed under Israeli military control.

Mustafa outlined this troubled history for us as we approached the Old City market. Traditionally this had been a hive of commerce, but after its designation as H2 many Palestinians had been forced to abandon their homes and shops under intense pressure from the Israeli authorities. The main path through the market was quiet, and the shopkeepers who remained pounced on each passer-by with a look bordering on desperation. I felt awkward and unable to pause and browse. At one stall I stopped at, I was pressured into buying a cushion cover that I didn't really want.

Many Israeli settlers had forcibly removed Palestinians from their homes in H2 and had taken over apartments above the shops. The result created a gruesome layering of the Old City streets. A wire mesh had been placed above the shops, and below the windows from the apartments, to catch the rubbish that was thrown down by the settlers from above. We were told that although the mesh had stopped some waste and rubbish from hitting the streets below the settlers had adapted their approach and often threw liquids which could include urine or excrement. It was claustrophobic and intimidating simply to walk there.

Emerging from the market, we stood in front of the imposing structure of the Ibrahimi Mosque. Mustafa explained that we'd have to pass through a police checkpoint to enter the building and he encouraged us to do this as he waited outside. The checkpoint was imposed by Israel after the 1994 massacre to protect all citizens from acts of terror, but many suspected its real purpose was to limit Muslim worshippers' access to the mosque. It was possible for tourists to visit both the Muslim and the Jewish sides of the building and there were different prayer sections for men and women. The heavy feeling of unease I had felt since entering the city had not reduced, and I didn't loiter for long in the building.

In both the Muslim and Jewish men's sections, Paul got a closer look and explained that the tomb of Abraham was shared by both sides so that each could view it through little windows in the wall, without encountering the other side.

The Cave of the Patriarchs stood at one end of Al-Shuhada Street which Mustafa said used to be the busiest street in Hebron. It was now almost deserted, and most of the shops had closed down. We stood in the middle of the eerily quiet street, watching a few children kick a football down the middle of the road where not even a car passed by. Israeli police officers with huge weapons guarded both sides of the street.

Mustafa led us into a small café where we sat on plastic chairs, drinking mint tea and lamenting on the downfall of Hebron. The trip felt uncomfortable from start to finish and although I was glad to have seen it, it was probably one of the only places in Palestine I had no strong urge to visit again. I couldn't imagine how the Palestinian Old City residents mustered the strength to remain among such adversity.

The outskirts of Hebron told a different story altogether. Here the streets thronged with everyday Palestinian life, which spilled out noisily on to the pavements. There were countless garages fixing rust-bucket cars and a string of kebab restaurants, with smoky barbecues set up out on the street. Men, women and children, young and old, came out to buy groceries, run errands and perhaps to stop for an Arabic coffee or a quick chicken *shish*. It was as if the life and blood had trickled out of the Old City and pooled itself in the suburbs instead.

Hebron is renowned for its wide range of hand-crafted goods and I was very happy to accompany a few friends on a shopping trip one morning. Directions were given, Palestinian style, using landmarks and by passing on routes verbally.

'That's the camel meat butcher,' my friend said as she drove us past. For the avoidance of doubt, a long, severed camel's neck dangled on a hook outside the shop.

We were on our way to the leather shop called Camel, which was well known for its custom-made sandals and bags in all colours and styles.

'Umm, are they made from camel leather?' I asked the shopkeeper, unaware until that point that such a thing even existed. She assured me they were from cow's leather. Later, I wondered about this when the strong smell of the bag I purchased meant I had to open windows in my apartment for weeks afterwards.

Hebron's glass industry was famous as one of the earliest in the world, and several factories still used traditional techniques. It was over 30 degrees outside and stepping into the factory we were hit with a wall of heat from the furnaces. Several men sat in different positions, hunched over the furnaces with balls of molten glass which they spun on a long rod. After turning the molten mixture in the fire, the men removed the glass, which was still glowing hot like lava. They then blew through the pipe to give shape to the glass. It was laborious and very skilful work. As we stood marvelling at the spectacle and sweating from the intense heat, one of the workmen beckoned my son over and let him blow through the tube to form a small ball that he would shape into a glass.

The showroom next door displayed the finished products. All manner of glassware was available in different shades of green and blue, each one an original piece. Hand-painted ceramics were another Hebron speciality and as well as plates, bowls and dishes of all sizes, large items like tile tables could be commissioned at a fraction of the Jerusalem prices. Several stores offered a dizzying Aladdin's cave selection of items.

Hebron evoked the full spectrum of emotions. The Old City was shocking and tragic, the suburbs were alive and industrious. Despite not receiving many tourists, the people we met were friendly and welcoming although the city lacked some of the warmth we'd experienced in other parts of the West Bank. The occupation, and subsequent division of the city, had placed a huge amount of pressure on the Palestinians who lived there, but still the flame of their existence burned resolutely.

The influx of Israeli settlers into the Occupied Palestinian Territories had resulted in different outcomes in different places. In Hebron, this led to an artificial division of the city and an intense police and military presence which suffocated daily life for Palestinians in the Old City. In Wadi Fukin, significant land confiscations had shrunk the village to a fraction of its former self, and it lived in the shadows of the huge settlement of Beitar Illit and the direct and indirect environmental pollution that stemmed from this. In both scenarios, the Israeli occupation had physically imposed itself above the Palestinian communities.

Despite these challenges, the residents of Wadi Fukin clung to their traditional way of life and their right to remain on the land. It was a great example of the Palestinian spirit of resistance, but it also represented a place where much had already been lost from its natural character.

In August 2024, the Israeli government announced plans to build a new settlement on land belonging to Battir to help connect the large Gush Etzion settlement near Hebron with Jerusalem. It was devastating to think that the unique character of Battir was under threat, along with that of countless other towns and villages across the West Bank. The story of Artas was yet another reminder of the deep significance of the land to different religions and showed that small pockets of paradise could still be found. Everywhere I went revealed a different version of Palestine, all struggling for survival against the odds.

CHAPTER 9
DESERT DWELLING

One of the most incredible things about living in Jerusalem was that you could be dipping your toes in the Dead Sea within a half-hour's drive. To do so required descending from the city height of 765 metres to 400 metres below sea level. Leaving Jerusalem provided an instant reminder of the harsh climate and the raw beauty of the Judean Desert. It was the heart of the Holy Land with footsteps of Moses, Jesus and the disciples to retrace.

Even here, however, the dramatic landscape and rich nature were marred by the thick blanket of politics that covered everything. Palestinian land was treated as if it were in Israel, and simple activities like hiking could be dangerous because of the threat from Israeli settlers. This chapter looks at the intersection between nature and politics to reveal some of the wonder and the injustice that characterise this part of the Holy Land.

Hiking Wadi Qelt

There were many beautiful walks in Palestine, but the politics meant that routes weren't often marked, and it was a case of 'turn left at the big tree' – if the big tree was still there. *Walking Palestine* provided comprehensive route maps, but it was impossible for the book to stay ahead of the changing landscape and a route that was peaceful and accessible one year may have fallen into the hands of Israeli settlers by the next.

Paul experienced this first-hand when he and a visiting friend were accosted by an aggressive settler with a gun on a previously safe hiking route in Wadi Auja. They were skirting around the track making their way back to the car when they heard someone shouting from above. The man, who was carrying a gun, ran towards them to block off their track as he continued to shout aggressively. Despite translation difficulties, they were able to defuse the situation and make clear that they weren't a threat. They both spent several long minutes, however, thinking they might be shot, and were left shaken by the experience.

Wadi Qelt was known as the pearl of the Palestinian walks. It ran for around 20 kilometres from Jerusalem down to Jericho, descending around 1,000 metres as it went. There were several points of interest along the way which made obvious markers for dividing the route into smaller sections.

'Wadi' is the Arabic word for valley, and these were normally dry riverbeds for most of the year which gushed with water after the winter rains. In one section of Wadi Qelt, there were pools deep enough to dive head-first into the cold water from surrounding rocks. One Saturday, we encountered Israeli kids there who had walked down from the nearby hilltop settlement to cool off in the deep pool and they encouraged us to take the plunge. In another section the path criss-crossed over the streams, offering a watery hike that included traversing over a rock bridge that gave the illusion of dangling on a precipice and made for dramatic photographs.

The water sustained a wide array of animals and vegetation and as well as the familiar sights of rock hyraxes (squat, cat-sized animals) and ibexes, there were often circling birds of prey, frogs, reptiles and other wildlife to meet. On several occasions, we arrived in Wadi Qelt to be greeted by the racket of animated frog calls reverberating across the valley. On another walk Paul rescued a sheep that was stuck on a rocky ledge with no sign of the rest of the flock in sight. Nature was always around and it was a green paradise in the midst of a desert landscape.

Wadi Qelt was in Area C land which meant that it was part of the Palestinian West Bank but was placed under Israeli military control by the Oslo Accords agreement of 1993. Area C comprised 61% of the West Bank and the intention (according to the Accords) was that over time it would be transferred back to the Palestinian Authority. Over 30 years later, not only had this process not begun but Israel had instead continued to build settlements and other infrastructure on Area C land. This made it almost impossible to conceive that Israel would ever hand it over.

This complicated arrangement meant that, despite it being Palestinian land, Israel could prevent Palestinians from building and controlled access to parts of the site. For example, the top section of Wadi Qelt had been deemed an Israeli National Park which required ticketed access. The middle and lower sections were wilder, and anyone could turn up and walk there.

On 27th December 2020, at 5pm, Israel started its second full Covid-19 lockdown. In order to squeeze as much out of our last day of freedom as possible, we made plans with several other families to hike a nine-kilometre section of the Wadi Qelt trail.

We drove down the bumpy road to the old Ottoman house, one of the marker points part-way along the route. There were a few moments where all four wheels of the car weren't on the ground at the same time, much to the horror of our friend in the car behind who had white knuckles by the time she arrived. A few Bedouin families lived around the Ottoman house, but any prior grandeur had fallen away over the years and goats and sheep appeared to have the run of the place.

Our route took us on a narrow path which was mainly flat and ran alongside the ancient Roman aqueduct. Our destination, nine kilometres away, was St George's Monastery. As we set off the sun was already high in the sky and it was warm for December. The air was still, except for birdsong.

As we clung to the steep cliffs, we admired the goats traversing the rocky canyons with ease. In one part of the aqueduct, we saw the small body of a young goat that had fallen into the water and died. Paul grabbed a big stick and was able to pull it on to dry land. Further along, we all stopped to marvel at a large crab – about a palm's size – hiding behind a rock in the aqueduct water. We had stumbled upon freshwater crabs on other walks, but it remained a mystery as to how they had come to settle in such lofty and unlikely locations.

The kids' enthusiasm waxed and waned and there were regular treat stops, water stops, wee stops, and getting stones out of shoes stops. But overall, they loved it and were carried along by the gang, albeit slowly, and with the 5pm deadline looming large.

We were all relieved to finally see St George's Monastery emerging like a mirage out of the rocks. This ancient site hailed from the 5th century and was still inhabited by Greek Orthodox monks. On a previous visit, I had found them to be very hospitable, offering juice for thirsty travellers and sweets for the kids.

Sadly, on that day the gates were firmly padlocked, and we ended our hike with a steep clamber up and up and up to the road above St George's. Several young Bedouin guys who were hoping to exploit any weary travellers foisted a (very welcome) fresh juice on us and a (not so welcome) scarf. Their main income was made offering donkey rides to tourists down and more importantly, up, the steep slope to the monastery. It had been a fantastic day out and at only a 30-minute drive from Jerusalem this hike packed a punch on accessibility, adventure and natural beauty.

Desert Adventures at Nabi Musa

Nabi Musa was situated in the Judean Desert, a few kilometres away from Wadi Qelt and about two thirds of the way between Jerusalem and Jericho. The site is said to contain the tomb of Moses, and despite this being a point of dispute it has remained a holy place for Christians, Muslims and Jews.

Its rugged and isolated beauty made it one of my favourite places and it was somewhere we were repeatedly drawn back to. At the start of June 2020, I invited a group of friends to join us there for a birthday barbecue.

The short drive from Jerusalem to Nabi Musa was my hands-down favourite journey, perhaps in the entire world. As soon as you joined the highway leaving Jerusalem, you passed through a tunnel underneath the Mount of Olives. When you emerged, you were in another world. Small Bedouin encampments dotted the hillsides, and it was common to see shepherds herding their sheep and goats across the valley. There were donkeys and camels on the horizon, and all the props of a biblical scene and a simpler existence were here.

The desert wasn't composed of silky sand dunes, it was rockier and grittier. A ripple of golden, wind-blasted hills stretched into the horizon with edges as sharp as glass. With certain twists of the road, you could catch a glimpse of the Dead Sea sparkling on the horizon and on the far side of the banks lay Jordan. The desert landscape changed throughout the year and in spring after the rains a thin covering of grass coated the hillsides, transferring them into emerald beauties before they surrendered to the summer's heat leaving them dusty and dry. The light was always pure and golden and the air dry.

Travelling along this road your foot stayed on the brake as you headed down, down below sea level, down into the middle of the Earth, the temperature creeping upwards. It was common for the area around the Dead Sea and Jericho to be 10 degrees hotter than in Jerusalem and the drive only took 30 minutes. The temperature gauge kept creeping up – 35, 36, 37 degrees.

'I'm driving slowly to stop it going up any faster,' Paul said in jest, but we both knew it was futile.

Blink and you would miss the brown sign indicating the turn-off for Nabi Musa. As we left the highway and rounded the corner, the low, sandy coloured structure of Nabi Musa revealed itself with its smooth, white-topped domes. We had visited once, months before. The mosque itself was modest, with visitors only allowed to peer through the window at the tomb inside. It was the rolling hills of the desert landscape beyond that pulled us in.

We drove past Nabi Musa and officially went 'off road', bumping along the steep and rocky track that led up the hillside. We parked up and both jumped out to survey the location. The dry heat swallowed us whole and the wind, like a hairdryer on full blast, puffed my dress up like a parachute. There was no shade, and the cliff edge was steep. This was not to be our spot.

Driving back down the track, now with our first guests in tow, we parked up by a small, abandoned structure with a domed roof.

'There is shade here and good rocks to sit on,' we enthusiastically said, '... but WHAT is that pile of fur?' Gingerly, we realised that the fur pile had recently been a camel. Ominous dark blood stains marked the entrance to the hut.

'Hmm, I'm not sure we want to eat our dinner next to a dead camel,' our friend reasonably pointed out. By the time we noticed the splodges of fat we had parked beside, it was time to make a hasty retreat. Admitting defeat for a second time we drove down the hill in search of a sacrifice-free, shaded spot to set up our base. The price to pay was losing the views from the exposed hilltop which stretched out to the Dead Sea and Jericho.

Finally, not far from the road, we stopped again. It was still hot, but it was approaching 5pm and the sky was taking on the colourful palette of the setting sun. Its rays had given up their fight and were no longer oppressive.

The kids scampered off, delighted to be a little pack of six ranging in ages from three to nine. They started to dig for treasure and dinosaur bones and fossils, their imaginations fully inflated by the magical setting. We lit the barbecue and watched the flames lick up within a few minutes. As 6pm came, and with it a trickle of cars appeared and headed up the hill beyond us.

As the sun set, we noticed a huge moon had started to rise from over the horizon. It was a pale silver and perfectly round. From our position below sea level it took on gigantic proportions. Hurriedly, we clambered up the hillside to get a better look.

'The moon, the moon, come look at the moon!' we shouted. We hadn't known that it was a full moon night and started snapping photos that had no hope of capturing the beauty of the moment. It felt like the icing on the cake of an already memorable evening.

From the top of the hillside a piece of discarded metal caught someone's eye. The kids ran over and were amused to find an abandoned ironing board. It felt as out of place as could be but added a surreal element to the fun.

The light dipped lower and lower until we were in darkness apart from the silver beam from the rising moon. Further up the hillside, a shadow darted across the horizon, and we saw the bushy tailed and pointed ear silhouette of a desert fox.

This had been the spot. The desert had relented its heat to reveal its treasures, in a site close to where Jesus and Moses had walked. Back in the cars and we were all home within 20 minutes. It was a privilege of Jerusalem life that such a stark landscape lay so close to the city. We put our tired, dusty and ketchup-stained children to bed and started looking at the calendar for the date of the next full moon. The sky had our interest now.

Under the Night Sky

In August we were back in the same spot around Nabi Musa, this time for an overnight stay. The annual Perseid meteor shower was taking place and we were invited to join a gang of friends to lie underneath the stars in search of this natural wonder.

As well as holding the tomb of Moses, the site had been a stopping point for travellers for thousands of years. The caravanserai surrounding the tomb had recently been restored simply and beautifully to showcase the original architecture and stonework.

We walked for about 10 minutes up the rocky path behind Nabi Musa to find a dark vantage point from which to start our stargazing. There was palpable excitement in the air as we all found a corner of the large rug to lie down on. Eyes fixed upwards, we waited for the show to start. Almost immediately, a bright ball shot across the sky leaving a shimmering trail in its wake. I gasped, amazed at the brightness and speed with which it had travelled.

There was a mixture of wonder from those who saw it and annoyance from those who hadn't yet settled into place. And then we waited and waited. The kids grew impatient and there was the rustling of crisp packets and the giggle of jokes.

'There! Over there! Ah, it's gone.' The energy ebbed and flowed with real and imagined shooting star sightings. Over the next few hours, the lucky ones saw more than 20 meteors with one or two spectacular highlights.

There was something very calming about looking up rather than down, and it seemed that the sky over the Holy Land was almost as lively as the ground with regular astronomical displays visible throughout the year.

That night we baked. The temperature remained over 30 degrees and the air was thick and still with no hint of a breeze. Some members of our group dragged their mattresses outside to continue stargazing as they tried to doze off under the energetic sky.

It was a short and uncomfortable night, but worth it to wake up in Nabi Musa to see the pink glow of dawn over the desert landscape. I thought about the lives of the Bedouin communities struggling for survival. Our Palestinian friend, Samaher, said that you couldn't talk about East Jerusalem without referring to the Bedouin. Her knowledge came from a combination of working on Bedouin issues as well as her own personal research. She told me what she knew.

The Bedouin were a group of Arab, originally nomadic, peoples who had historically inhabited desert regions in North Africa, the

Arabian Peninsula, Iraq and the Levant. The English word Bedouin came from the Arabic *Badawi*, meaning 'desert dweller'.

Most of the East Jerusalem Bedouin communities were located just a few kilometres east of Jerusalem on the hilly landscape that sloped steeply towards the Jordan Valley and the Dead Sea. The communities were small and scattered, and even within a single community houses were spread out.

The Bedouin lifestyle relied on raising animals that grazed on pasture lands. Their livestock needed vast areas of land for grazing, and it was normal for shepherds to roam over a large distance. Samaher told me that the East Jerusalem Bedouin suffered from political and cultural marginalisation. They faced endless challenges such as water scarcity and a lack of schools and other forms of infrastructure. In addition, they were not allowed to build or graze their livestock and their land was often confiscated when the Israeli military moved in. In some places Bedouin children were chased and taunted by Israeli settlers and many Bedouin parents no longer sent their children to school, choosing to home school them instead.

Samaher had worked on projects with the Bedouin and found them to be incredibly kind people, hospitable and proud of their heritage. She said that a guest of a Bedouin family would typically enjoy a meal of *mansaf* (a lamb, yogurt and rice speciality) and Arabic coffee or Bedouin tea around the campfire. A spoken agreement and a handshake meant far more in their culture than written contracts. All they asked was to be left to their chosen way of life, and they rewarded respect with respect.

Driving back to Jerusalem before 8am, and with the temperature already near 30 degrees, I thought of our air-conditioned apartment, the shower I would have and our well-stocked fridge, with the guilt of someone who could barely conceive of a nomadic existence. I admired the simplicity of the Bedouin life, led entirely on the land, and I hoped that they would be protected and allowed to remain as an important part of Palestinian culture and heritage.

The Baptism

It was just after 8am one hot Sunday morning that we pulled out of our driveway and spotted our friend Ahmad from the bookshop who was delivering the daily newspapers. We explained that we had important business baptising our friend's baby at Qasr Al-Yahud.

'Is it being born in the river?' Ahmad asked. 'I've heard of some people doing that.' An already unusual morning got a little bit stranger as we tried to imagine someone giving birth in the murky waters of the River Jordan with two sets of border guards overlooking the site.

Qasr Al-Yahud, the 'Baptism Site', was where John was said to have baptised Jesus. It was only a few miles from Jericho and a 30-minute drive from Jerusalem. Its religious history was already weighty enough without the additional burden of politics which added a macabre drama to the site.

Similar to Wadi Qelt, the area was part of Palestinian Area C but was being managed by Israel as a national park, and from the site Israeli police patrolled the border with Jordan. As we turned off the main road the desert stretched for miles on either side, barren except for a few date palm trees. Several small churches lined the route. It was only during 2020 that the site was finally cleared of the hundreds of landmines that had lain dormant since the 1967 war, and although the landmine signs were gone the area didn't invite aimless wandering around.

The Baptism Site was a curious place. The river was less than 10 metres wide, flowing gently and heavy with a clay-like mud that gave it a café latte colour. One riverbank belonged to Palestine and the other to Jordan. On each side, wooden platforms had been built to allow visitors access to the river to immerse themselves in the holy water in a ritual re-enactment of John's baptism of Jesus.

A frayed rope ran down the middle of the river marking out the international border. On both sides border police guards stood in dark combat uniforms with heavy boots and long rifles to prevent anyone from making the short swim across the border. The symmetry of the site was unnerving, and it felt absurd that an international border was being policed with guns on a site of such religious significance.

We had visited once before, in 2019, when religious groups poured into the site daily and brought with them a fervour that was intoxicating. We had watched as an African group, dressed in white smocks with red crosses, sang gospel songs and prayed together. Some cheered while others wept. Everyone who submerged themselves in the water looked deeply moved by the experience.

The baptism of our friends' baby girl was to be a symbolic gesture and they had invited a few families to join them for the ceremony. We enthusiastically purchased the large white smocks with large red crosses from the gift shop which were the customary costume for anyone wishing to enter the water. Standing on the riverbank we sang a song, followed by a Bible reading, and we then waded into the water to wet the baby's head. The water was cool and welcoming. Temperatures in the Jordan Valley frequently rise above 40 degrees, and it was already in the mid-30s before nine in the morning.

It was a joyous event, full of love and goodwill for the baby. Like so many places in the Holy Land the site had a certain gravitas that was utterly at odds with political systems based on division and hatred. The Baptism Site was close to Jericho, and we continued the celebration with lunch and a swim. It was a memorable day and another reminder of the many religious wonders of the Holy Land.

Jericho had several claims to fame and a few notable sights which we explored over several visits. It was the oldest continuously inhabited city in the world, and it was the lowest city on the planet. History dated Jericho's earliest settlement to 11,000 years ago (9000BCE) and it lay 258 metres below sea level in a dramatic location on the flat plain to the west of the River Jordan, and below the Mount of Temptation.

It was possible to take a cable car up the Mount of Temptation to visit the monastery, which marked the spot where Jesus was thought to have endured 40 days of fasting before he was visited by the Devil. The date palms of Jericho stretched out across the valley floor from this elevated point. Jericho dates are arguably the best in the world. Whether owing to the inordinate amount of searing sunshine they receive, or the fertile soil near the Dead Sea, the dates are large and succulent.

The 8th-century remains of Hisham's Palace, with its beautifully restored intricate mosaic flooring, gave a hint at the grandeur of Jericho in centuries, and perhaps millennia, before. Those days were gone, however, and despite its historic and religious credentials, Jericho left me feeling somewhat flat.

The grid of streets that made up the city centre seemed to lack heart. Perhaps it was due to the oppressive heat that baked the city from May to October.

For this reason, many people (including us) knew Jericho for its choice of waterparks and there were several with ageing slides to choose from, along with hotels with nice pools or private villas. Many wealthy Palestinians kept holiday homes around Jericho, and I was told it wasn't policed very closely and could be a magnet for drugs and other crime. A stone's throw from Jerusalem, its dramatic scenery and relaxed vibe made it feel like a world apart from the pressures of the city and every time we visited there was something new to discover.

National(ism) Parks

During our first year in Jerusalem, we shunned Israeli national parks as being a symbol of the occupation. It was certainly true that converting land into nature reserves safeguarded it for Israel and prevented Palestinians from using the land.

Israel had an extensive network of over 70 national parks and heritage sites which were administered by the Israel Nature and Parks Authority. The sites covered a range of places of historic interest as well as natural beauty spots and hiking routes. They were well maintained and always offered good maps and facilities. The problem was that as well as being spread across Israel, many of the parks (such as Wadi Qelt and the Baptism Site) were in Area C of Palestine. This normalised the occupation as it treated Palestinian land the same as Israeli land. Visitors, who had to pay their entry fee to the Israeli Parks Authority on a site that was branded the same as countless other sites in Israel, would be forgiven for thinking they *were* in Israel. I was often confused by this.

On several occasions, different people had told us that, after 1948, Israel had planted many trees that weren't indigenous to the region, such as pines, to grow quickly and obscure what remained of the Palestinian villages that had been forced out. It was said that as well as growing densely together, pines grew deep roots which destroyed the foundations of the old Palestinian houses. It seemed that even something as inherently good as tree-planting could come with darker connotations in Israel.

Our unofficial boycott of the national parks ended abruptly during Covid-19. The West Bank was closed for many months and the national parks offered one of the only escapes into the countryside. I'm disappointed to say, we sold out. The national parks had a monopoly on some incredible historic and natural sites and the allure was too strong. I fiercely held out against buying an annual pass for the parks as that would be endorsing them, and instead was the fool that gave them even more money over the course of the year by visiting more sites than we planned.

At the start of August, Paul had an unexpected bank holiday, and we decided to visit the nature reserve of Ein Prat. It was another example of a site in Area C that was managed by the Israeli Parks Authority. It formed the top section of the Wadi Qelt valley, generally considered to be Palestine's best hiking trail. The park felt particularly controversial territory to visit, as you had to pass through an illegal Israeli settlement to reach it. Accessing the road down to the park meant passing a yellow barrier gate which was manned by a casually dressed man in a T-shirt and jeans with a huge gun who made us slow down and declare our intentions. This was yet another way that Israel controlled access to the site, along with the pre-booking system which had been introduced during Covid-19.

Despite these barriers, the beauty of the spot attracted Palestinians as well as Israelis. Later that day, we met two Palestinian guys lounging in the river, who said it had taken them three attempts to access the park. Showing their ID card at the entrance gate could be enough for them to be sent away, even if they had an advance booking. They had persevered as they loved the spot and considered it their right to enjoy it. They exuded the excited euphoria of those who had beaten the system. It was a small victory on land they should enjoy free access to.

A stream meandered through Ein Prat, providing a focal point for families of all shapes and sizes to cool off in. The water was only a few inches deep in places, but it was nearly waist height in other sections. Looking around I saw that swimwear wasn't de rigueur unless you were a small child. I had observed previously that both Israeli and Palestinian women either didn't go in for swimwear, or it closely resembled everyday clothes. I was wearing a skirt and T-shirt and resolved to get both wet.

After only a few minutes we spotted a huge green toad hiding in the reeds and stopped to admire it. It seemed like this was going to be a watery adventure, so instead of walking along the path to the deeper sections of the river we decided to wade through the stream instead. We probably only covered a distance of a few hundred metres, but the kids had an absolute blast as they clambered over rocks and swam through the different pools.

Taking the river route gave us more time to observe the wide variety of people who had collected in and around the water. Several groups of young Israeli girls wallowed in the water as they chatted. Beneath the branches of a low-hanging tree a young Orthodox Jewish couple (presumably married) sat with their prayer books as the tassels of his white shirt dangled in the water. Muslim families gathered around big picnic rugs as the children waded in the stream. Next, we came to the Palestinian guys we had met who had fought for entry. They had settled in a spot with enough drinks and snacks to spend the day there. They joked and laughed, making the most of their short holiday.

It was a soggy car journey home, but the outside temperature was still sizzling, and the ice cream shop was closed, so nobody minded the wet clothes. I still had mixed feelings about enjoying beauty spots that had been politicised and where access wasn't free to everyone. The injustice of it tarnished even the best of experiences.

Was I in Israel or Palestine? I was never more confused than in the area around the Dead Sea and Judean Desert. If somewhere looked and felt like Israel, if Israelis lived there, if Israel managed the land, then one by one people started to believe it *was* Israel. This was what occupation looked like in many parts of Area C in the Palestinian West Bank. The indigenous Palestinian communities such as the Bedouin were being forced out and made to feel like imposters on their own land. Simple activities like hiking, which anywhere else in the world are accessible to everyone, were controlled by Israel and denied to many people. It was hard not to conclude that trees and nature were being deployed as weapons in a highly sophisticated war of attrition against Palestinians.

CHAPTER 10
CITIES AND SAINTS

The diversity and complexity of Palestine never failed to amaze me, and each village, town and city that we visited had a strong sense of its own identity. Ramallah had been a small village which grew into a new city in the 1990s when Yasser Arafat made it the administrative hub of the Palestinian Authority. Money had poured in from international aid and from the diaspora, and it had expanded quickly. Its modernity felt at odds with the traditional Palestinian way of life. In contrast, Nablus had been inhabited since Roman times and offered an unfussy version of Palestine. Small villages like Aboud pinned their identity on their religious heritage, and the Saints of Aboud were referred to as if they were neighbours or church elders still living among the community.

All three of these places were part of the Palestinian West Bank and represented modern Palestine. Towns and cities thrive on commerce, and I've included the story of two Palestinian breweries to demonstrate the potential, yet limitations, West Bank businesses faced. These limitations stifled the growth and prosperity of Palestine as a whole and may in part explain why people felt rooted firmly to history rather than the uncertain future.

Smelling the Air in Nablus

The main road, Route 60, from Jerusalem to Nablus cuts through the heart of the West Bank. The road twists with the contours of the rolling West Bank hills and the sky feels big and open. The skylines of Jerusalem, Ramallah and even Tel Aviv can be seen on a clear day. Route 60 is a shared road which means that both Israeli and Palestinian cars are allowed to use it. Different coloured number plates make it easy for police and checkpoint officials to distinguish between Israeli (yellow-plated) and Palestinian (green-plated) registered cars.

Along Route 60 there are turn-offs for both Israeli settlements and Palestinian villages. As the road approaches Huwara, a tension point arises. This is a Palestinian village which has grown into a town, around four miles south of Nablus. Passing through it, I had enjoyed its Palestinian sweets (similar to baklava) and its *manaqish* (*zaatar* and white cheese-topped breads hot from the oven). There was also the usual array of fruit and vegetable stalls, car repair shops, overflowing bins, stray dogs, people on their way to the mosque and the general hubbub that we often found in Palestinian towns. Sometimes when we drove through Huwara, especially on a Friday afternoon, there were Israeli armoured vehicles and soldiers with large machine guns positioned along the main street of the town. We didn't witness any direct confrontations but there was often a palpable tension in the air and a huge amount of history and hardship that we would never understand.

Entering Nablus, it felt as if we were leaving the visible signs of the occupation behind. We never saw Israeli police in the heart of Nablus and because it wasn't geared towards tourists, the version of Palestine that it served up always felt undiluted and unpolished. During 2022 (and into 2023 after we left), Nablus became a hotspot for confrontations between Israeli military and Palestinians, and even before the 2023 war with Gaza, the UK Foreign Office advised against all but essential travel to Nablus. This was really sad as Nablus had so much to offer visitors during more peaceful times.

'Soap, *knafeh*, cafés... that's Nablus,' said our tour guide for the day, lining up the places he would take us. It was a drizzly Saturday in January, and we had come with several other families for an insider tour of Nablus. In keeping with the generous spirit of Nablus, we were to be guided by not one but two Nablusi guys, coincidentally both called Moath, who had offered to show us the sights.

Nablus was established by the Romans in 72CE and was named Flavia Neapolis. It is situated in a valley, between the looming shadows of Mount Gerizim on one side and Mount Ebal on the other. The mountains give the city a feeling of privacy and spaciousness, away from Israeli settlements.

Nablus has an old-city charm, bursting with curiosities. From our first visit, we experienced the warmth and hospitality of Nablusi citizens. On one occasion my daughter was being potty trained, and the panicked opening line of 'please can we use your toilet?' led to several interesting encounters with strangers. Before we knew it we were being led into a Sufi community centre, offered strong coffee and given the chance to have a go at beating a very large ceremonial drum (Sufism is a branch of Islam which focusses on Islamic spirituality and ritualism).

The two Sufis then insisted we follow them for a guided tour of an apartment they were renovating. They seemed genuinely proud of their craftmanship, and delighted to have the chance to show it off to us. We took a few minutes making appropriate 'ooh' and 'aah' noises and thanked them again for their bathroom facilities.

Nablus exuded a 'no frills', well-worn ambiance. There weren't too many sights for visitors to trouble themselves with, so instead of feeling as if you were on a tourist merry-go-round, visitors could relax into a casual exploration and spend time doing what Nablus did best – food, drink and curiosities. That's not to say that Nablus wasn't steeped in history, as it was surrounded by some fascinating ancient sites to rival any other part of the Holy Land.

The Moaths told us that the current Old City was built in the Ottoman era and the 'real' Old City, which could be found at Tel Balata, dated to around 400BCE. We'd stopped at Tel Balata before and had been underwhelmed by the neglected archaeological site which anyone could clamber over without the need of an entry ticket. Burnt embers and empty bottles suggested that young people brought some life to the site in the evenings but during the day it was deserted and almost derelict.

Looking into many of the shops in Nablus Old City, you'd be forgiven for thinking they hadn't changed a bit since Ottoman times and holding on to ancient crafts and techniques was something Nablus was proud of. In one of the famous soap factories the owner told us that the factory was 850 years old and that they 'would lose the spiritual side' if they moved to a new location. Ancient urns and tools demonstrated how the process had remained unchanged over many years. In a solid testimony to the quality of their soap, the owner syringed some olive oil out of a barrel and invited us to taste it. There were no chemicals, just high-grade natural products.

When a young man wheeled his rickety wooden cart past, we peered in to try and identify the offering. It was a wobbly set-milk pudding with honey on top and for two NIS (45p) it stopped us in our tracks for five minutes as we passed the spoon between us. A few locals gathered around the cart to chat and eat the mid-afternoon dessert.

Nablus is a foodie place. The absence of gaudy tourist tat means that the markets are dedicated to local products for local people.

There are spices and dried fruits galore, nuts, sweets, coffee, herbs, meat... the full Palestinian larder. Every time we visited Nablus, we left with a new food obsession. One time it was *sahlab*, a thick, gloopy, rose-water-flavoured milky drink that came as a powder and rivalled hot chocolate on a cold winter's day.

On this occasion, it was a dusty red spice exotically named 'Gazan thyme'. Thyme was big in Palestine as it was the main ingredient in *zaatar* (a ground mix of dried thyme and sesame seeds). The Gazan thyme was gently spiced, salty, sweet and versatile. The Moaths told us that the spice shop was the oldest and the best, and it was a real Aladdin's cave of curiosities.

Inside the shop huge sacks of freshly ground herbs and spices rested on the floor. Their colours were lurid, and a sweet smell tickled our noses. Customers trickled in with a solemnity like they were visiting an apothecary, and some handed over lists as if giving a prescription to the chemist. The shopkeeper carefully weighed and measured the goods on large copper scales before wrapping them securely in small bags. There was a respectful sanctity which gave a calm order to the proceedings.

Specifically, Nablus was famous for its *knafeh* – a sweet and syrupy dish with lots of oozing melted white cheese. It was popular across Palestine, but locals said the Nablusi version was the original and the best. We learned that it was invented by a rich gentleman who wanted 'something heavy' to eat after a day of fasting during Ramadan. *Knafeh* was part of everyday life in Nablus and around 50 men jostled to get to the front of the busiest *knafeh* place. I wasn't sure if ordering *knafeh* was considered men's work in Nablus, but the women and children stood back. It was a classic 'no frills' Nablus spectacle. On one side of the alleyway several men were constructing fresh *knafeh* on enormous, round, silver trays. Once ready, the tray was held overhead and precariously carried across the street to the service side of the business where it was divided into brick-sized portions and served on polystyrene plates to the assembled crowd. People then hovered on street corners, or crouched on pavements, to enjoy the warm, syrupy dessert, eaten with plastic forks.

In the warren that made up the Old City, the shops were like small caves carved into the wall. There was the ironmonger, the baker, the butcher, the spice shops, the pet shop, the chicken shop, and so it went on. In Arabic, to go and visit somewhere was often translated as 'to smell the air' and this felt fitting in Nablus with so many competing smells, both aromatic and pungent. It was a true assault on the senses.

The chicken shop consisted of small cages stacked on top of each other and in summer the smell of hot feathers was sickly and overpowering. When a chicken was purchased, the shop keeper would throw open the cage and grab a bird by the neck. He would then walk the bare length of his shop to the back wall where, out of sight, a sharp axe was presumably brought down on the chicken's neck.

Outside the butcher's shop, the head of the latest carcass was hung on display. Walking past, we gaped at the long pale, pink tongue of a cow which lolled grotesquely out of its mouth. The glazed eyes looked out from under tufts of black hair, smeared with blood. As I peered into a plastic box at the butcher's stall, a pair of teeth smiled back. It wasn't clear if they came from a goat or a lamb's head, but I could barely imagine the culinary end they would meet. The next bucket was filled with intestines so white they gleamed in the sun. There was a complete absence of pretence, which was refreshing.

It was common to see a camp bed set up inside a shop where the owner lived and worked. Often faded photographs with curling edges hung on the wall. These showed the generations who had tended the business before the current owner. Proud men stared back with dark hair, bushy moustaches and the brown, pressed clothing of a vintage era. Often these family photographs stood alongside one of the young Yasser Arafat, and in the most prized versions sometimes the family members would be standing alongside Yasser himself. There didn't seem to be any edges between work and life, and ambling along the street felt like peering into the soul of Nablus.

There was no chance of us blending in, but despite our obvious foreignness, people were friendly and shouted out warm greetings unrelated to the goods they were peddling. We pottered around happily, picking up pieces here and there. Freshly ground coffee, a bag full of cinnamon sticks, Nablusi soap, pencils for school. Paul went for a cut-throat barbershop 20 NIS (£4) haircut and fell a little bit more in love with the city. Dicing with backstreet barbers was a hobby of his but we went too far on a subsequent trip when we let another Nablusi barber loose on our daughter's beautiful curls. Several years later, the mention of the Nablus barber still strikes fear in her heart.

When in Nablus, it was possible to visit the community of Samaritans who lived on Mount Gerizim, perched on a hill overlooking the city. They were the only group to have dual Israeli and Palestinian citizenship and sat as a unique ethno-religious community between the two sides. The Samaritans had diverged from Judaism and believed that they practised the original pure form of the religion. Mount Gerizim was more holy for them than Temple Mount in Jerusalem. The community of Samaritans numbered only 800, with half living on Mount Gerizim and half in Holon, south of Tel Aviv.

On a visit to the gated community, we were given a tour of the museum. The female tour guide explained that preserving and growing the community was their top priority, and that the small numbers and rejection of inter-faith marriages had led to a limited gene pool. To address this, women had been found in Ukraine and Russia who were willing to marry Samaritan men and convert fully to the Samaritan way of life. In this way, the population was slowly increasing year-on-year. It was an interesting insight into another group, deeply connected to the history of the Holy Land and struggling to maintain the purity of their existence.

Back in Jerusalem, Mahmoud from the bookshop laughed when we told him how much we'd paid for parking in Nablus city centre. These businesses operated on the basis of one or two young guys spending the day shuffling many cars around a tiny space, a bit like a game of Tetris. You had to hand over the keys and leave your car in their hands. Mahmoud told us that next time the phrase we needed was, '*ana mish kharouf* (I'm not a sheep) – or in other words, you can take advantage of me a little but don't completely take me for a ride.

A Home Visit in Ramallah

September had started and we spent most of the first weekend in Ramallah. We had visited on many occasions before, but I still didn't feel I understood the spirit of Ramallah or where its heart was. It was originally a small farming village but expanded rapidly after the Oslo Peace Accords in 1993 when Yasser Arafat made it his residence and the home of the newly formed Palestinian Authority. For me, Ramallah represented a hazy memory of austere news footage during the early 2000s of a political conflict that seemed both distant and impenetrable.

Before he died under suspicious circumstances in 2004, Arafat lived for two years under siege by the Israeli military who surrounded his compound. The site was now part of an informative museum where you could visit the mausoleum of Arafat along with the living and working quarters where he spent his final years. Across Palestine, it was common to find official photographs of Arafat in offices and other spaces and he remained a hugely popular icon. Some Palestinians viewed Arafat as a hero; others felt he had sold out on a free Palestine by signing the Oslo Accords. To this day, his signature black-and-white checked *keffiyeh* is worn by all generations of Palestinians and is a symbol of resistance.

After the signing of the Oslo Accords foreign investment poured into Ramallah at a dizzying rate. As the base for the Palestinian Authority it became a de facto capital city while the preferred capital of Jerusalem remained beyond reach. Downtown Ramallah had high-rise buildings and a polished veneer. For every beat-up rust-bucket car there was likely to be a flash Mercedes cruising past. For every humble falafel stand there was a newly opened coffee bar or a trendy shisha lounge.

It was difficult to see past the gloss to the lives of the real Palestinians who call Ramallah home. We were lucky to visit several people in their family homes in and around Ramallah and this helped to colour in some of the details, although quite how representative they were was questionable.

One Saturday, we were invited to dinner with one of Paul's work associates, Omar. I was sceptical, as the last time someone from a partner organisation invited us for dinner it had resulted in a year's worth of hassle where our host expected preferential treatment while at the helm of a sinking project. The hostess on that occasion had gone to great lengths making hundreds of tightly stuffed and rolled vine leaves which would have taken hours to make. It had been an enjoyable afternoon, but I resented the barely concealed motive.

Over several weeks, Paul had been hosted at both of Omar's separate residences and he waxed lyrical about what a good friend and fascinating individual Omar was, causing me to agree to the dinner. As a teenager during the First Intifada, Omar had spent over five years in an Israeli jail where he was badly beaten by the prison guards. He used the time to learn Hebrew fluently and left prison with a determination to work with – rather than against – Israelis to broker deals for his community. Despite the harsh treatment, he was one of the lucky ones, and he left with his sharp intelligence intact.

The reason Omar had two residences was that he had two separate wives and families. Polygamy is allowed under Muslim law, but it is no longer common practice. In Omar's case, his first wife was ill and presumed dying when he married his second wife, only for the first to make an unexpected recovery. For someone of his standing who could afford to keep two households the arrangement seemed to work well.

Ramallah was still a rabbit warren of roads for us, and we arrived a little late and apologetic. The house sat on the outskirts of a village overlooking Ramallah and had been recently built to impress. Imposing columns stood like guards at the entrance gate.

Omar came out to meet us wearing a well-worn T-shirt, flip flops and a large smile.

It immediately put me at ease that he didn't expect any formalities. His wife, Fatima, was conservatively dressed in Islamic style with a full-length dress and head scarf. She also greeted us warmly, but the language barrier prevented us from bridging the distance between us. She had a wry smile that suggested a good sense of humour and I was sorry that I could not converse with her more freely.

Their only son was seven years old and he was friendly and kind. He was happy to share his elaborate toys and immediately let my son have a go on his motorised quad bike, before offering to take both our kids on a tour of the garden and to meet the kitten he was looking after. He seemed happy to have some young company and the kids brushed the language barrier aside with a childish ease that the adults struggled to replicate.

Fatima invited me on a tour of the house which was a Palestinian custom that didn't seem to be reserved for grand abodes like theirs. Stepping inside the front door, we saw that the salon room was ornate and decorative. A large chandelier hung from the ceiling which was two storeys high. A spiral staircase stood proudly in the middle of the room reminiscent of a Beverly Hills-style mansion. I admired the views from the different upstairs bedrooms and made suitable 'wow, *kbeer*, *jameela*' noises of approval.

We then settled outside for a barbecue involving a generous array of meats, salads and fresh bread. Omar darted between the table and the barbecue with an ever-wider selection of skewers and juicy morsels. It was another Palestinian custom to provide enough food for a banquet and we had to protest strongly to stop more meats from being loaded on to our plates.

Later, as the men inspected the new chicken coop which was being built by several workmen that evening, I followed the kids into the house. We had brought his son a very bouncy ball as a small present and I was alarmed to find it ricocheting around the lounge, dangerously close to the chandelier. Just as I was wondering if I should call time on the game, I noticed that Fatima had pulled out a prayer mat and was completing her evening prayers on one side of the room that was obscured by the columns. I ushered the kids back out to the garden to give her some privacy.

Their son was returning to school the following morning after a long summer holiday, which had been extended due to Covid-19, and we were careful not to overstay our welcome. When we were leaving, I regretted that we wouldn't be able to repay the favour and invite the family over for dinner at ours.

Ramallah was only 15 kilometres from Jerusalem, but as West Bank Palestinians they didn't have a permit to cross over into Israel and that meant they couldn't visit us in Jerusalem. For all the wealth and status that they appeared to have, freedom of movement could not be bought, and the thorn of the regime wounded everyone indiscriminately.

The following morning we were on the road to Ramallah again, this time to hang out at the trendy Snobar. It was tucked away on a Ramallah hillside and was completely hidden from the road. Descending the wooden stairs into the venue you entered into a green and chic oasis. There was a generous scattering of cushions creating private seating areas among the decorative hanging bicycles and potted plants. It was quirky and relaxing with a great restaurant, bar and a large swimming pool where people came to spend a lazy afternoon.

We had arranged to meet several families there and before long there was a pool-party atmosphere in full swing. Food and drinks were delivered, the guys had a beer, music bounced around us and the sun beat down on the freezing cold water of the deep pool. I had not been expecting to find a holiday resort in Ramallah and although it didn't feel like an authentic version of the city, the hipster vibe was an escape from the pressures of Jerusalem.

In the car on the way home, my three-year-old daughter asked, 'are we Palestinian?' We explained that we weren't. She took this on board and a few minutes later said, 'I just heard a Palestinian,' when she meant the call to prayer. It was sweet that she was trying to make sense of her surroundings, and we could all relate to the difficulties of that, regardless of age. Palestine looked different from every angle we viewed it and was many things for many people.

The Saints of Aboud

Arriving in the small West Bank town of Aboud, with zero expectations about what we might find, I was unaware that I was about to be charmed by this historically rich Christian town. Despite being called the Holy Land on account of Jesus's birth, life and death in these parts, there were alarmingly few Christians still living in Palestine.

It is estimated that Palestinian Christians make up fewer than 2% of the West Bank population and fewer than 1% of the population of Jerusalem and Gaza. In 2017, estimates suggested there were only 47,000 Palestinian Christians left in the Holy Land, with most having emigrated due to a variety of religious, political, social and economic challenges.

Before 1948, many Jerusalem Christians lived in the west of the city. When they were displaced during the Nakba, many struggled to find employment during the 1950s. Palestinian Christians used to monopolise the tourism industry and established connections with Western countries to lead tours and pilgrimages. As Israel tightened the noose of the occupation, it became harder for Palestinians to continue this trade. Many had chosen to study abroad or emigrate with their families. The wall and permit system also isolated Christian communities from each other, which made it harder for those remaining to stay connected to their identity as Palestinian Christians.

Our local corner shop owner, who had olive trees in Aboud, encouraged us to visit and gave us the phone number of a man called Victor to call when we reached the village. Arrangements were made, and when we pulled into Aboud one Saturday morning the smartly dressed gentleman who greeted us turned out to be no less than the Mayor of Aboud. Victor proudly told us that Aboud had the third oldest church after the Church of the Nativity in Bethlehem (339CE) and the Holy Sepulchre (335CE) in Jerusalem. He also noted the church in Burqin as part of this original set.

The story was that St Helena (mother of the Roman Emperor Constantine who allowed Christianity to be practised freely after the year 313CE) travelled to the Holy Land in the year 324CE in search of the Holy Sepulchre (Jesus's tomb). On her journey, she sought to follow in Jesus's footsteps, doing good deeds and founding several churches on holy sites along the way. Aboud was one such place that Jesus was said to have passed through, and St Helena founded the first of many churches there.

Victor disappeared into a house opposite the church to collect the key from the family entrusted with the honour of holding it. We had already been introduced to several generations of the family as they inquisitively eyed us up the moment we strolled into their street. The village was relaxed yet dignified. The faded murals of Jesus and other biblical scenes were tasteful rather than tatty.

The key that arrived was a true relic made of solid metal and was around 15 centimetres long. It was not the sort of thing you casually carried around in your pocket. Victor opened the doors of the Church of the Virgin Mary, and we stepped inside the holy space. It was clear there had been much investment in maintaining and restoring the church over the years, and this had achieved the delicate balance of celebrating the original features while keeping its vibrant colours and a rich, cosy feel. It felt almost luxurious without being decadent.

The parishioners were particularly proud of an ancient tile in Aramaic script which was still visible within the church. Its discovery in the 20th century gave weight to the evidence that the church pre-dated Crusader times. Many of the ancient stone columns were thought to be original, and great care had been taken to bolster them in a way that allowed them to take pride of place within the structure of the church.

The population of Aboud was around 2,200, half of whom were Christian, and half Muslim. Victor told us it was a peaceful union between these two religions. The tour of the holy riches of Aboud continued, and Victor bundled us into his saloon car to drive us to the Orthodox Monastery of St Barbara. We felt deep in Palestine and yet from these hills, on the outskirts of Aboud, the skyscrapers of Tel Aviv and the glint of the ocean behind were clearly visible which was disorientating.

The story of St Barbara was more elaborate than the site itself. Legend tells that Barbara lived in the 3rd century and was imprisoned by her father in a tower to protect her from outside influences. Despite this, she declared herself a Christian (still considered a new and controversial religion at the time) and her father tried to kill her. She escaped from the tower, deploying a series of miracles, and took refuge in a small cave near Aboud. Her father caught up with her and beheaded her with his own hands, only to be struck by lightning and killed himself.

Since that day, Barbara became known as St Barbara, or the Great Martyr Barbara, and she is celebrated in many countries around the world on 4th December. In Aboud, her day of remembrance is 17th December and Victor emphatically invited us to join the procession and services that would mark the day the following month. He explained that the celebrations would be led by the Scouts and Girl Guides who played traditional Palestinian folk songs and Christmas carols, accompanied by bagpipes and drums. The villagers proceeded with this musical accompaniment from the village up to Barbara's tomb. Prayers would then be said outside the tomb and candles lit.

The small caves where Barbara hid were open to tourists, but a local guide was recommended to bring the site to life. The gates looked like they languished largely closed despite the new approach road built recently with foreign investment. Victor didn't miss a trick in highlighting the number of important sites that still 'needed a project,' and even pre-Covid I doubted that Aboud had featured on many tourist itineraries despite being charming and historically rich. Passing another locked gate, Victor told us that a new guesthouse would open soon.

'It's nearly finished. I will call you when it opens,' he said, as we hoped it would see the light of day.

It was a hot day, despite being November, and our impromptu tour ended at the Zarqa spring at the far end of Wadi Limone, a well-known hiking hotspot. Several families picnicked by the spring as the kids splashed in the cool water and dangled their heads in to drink from the fountain.

Having heard that Aboud's olive oil was some of the best in Palestine (a much-contested category), we stopped at a village shop to buy an enormous vat of fresh-pressed oil. Two sons and their mother ran the shop and they were quick to tell us how tough life was for Christians in Aboud, and how everyone left or was being pushed out. It was a good reminder that what many Palestinians needed wasn't another guesthouse, or a paved road for tour buses to swoop in and out on, but a protected homeland and equal human rights.

Intrigued by the celebration, Paul returned to Aboud to attend the Barbara Day procession the following month. He said that this consisted of a large crowd of several hundred people making the walk to the memorial site before gathering at the village hall to hear young people sing and dance the traditional *dabke*. There was a festival atmosphere and the traditional 'Barbara cake', made with dried fruit and nuts, was handed out in white plastic bowls with sweets sprinkled on top. It was heartening to see that, despite the challenges faced by Christians in Palestine, St Barbara's legacy still held the power to unite people on this small hilltop town in Palestine and around the world.

Palestinian Breweries

If you wanted to drink local beer in Palestine, the choice was between Shepherds or Taybeh. They both tasted good and came from tenacious small family businesses.

The conservative and predominantly Muslim population of Palestine meant that beer was not part of the culture. There was a local market in Christian areas and among internationals, however, and both breweries also exported their goods internationally.

One Saturday we made an unexpected tour of Shepherds Brewery in the town of Birzeit, 10 kilometres north of Ramallah. We had been visiting friends who lived there and before lunch (more of a feast really), we went on a stroll through Birzeit's picturesque old town and down towards the brewery.

It was a bottling day and the manager Alaa, a friend of our friend, agreed to let us step inside the small factory to see the production line in full swing. It was a satisfyingly efficient process. First the brown glass bottles rolled along the conveyor belt to be filled. Then, just as the beer was starting to bubble up into the neck of the bottle, they were capped. They were then rolled around the corner, where the bottles were dried before the labels were stuck on.

Alaa had first got his taste for beer, and learned about home brewing, while at university in the UK. After graduating, he had been inspired to start the brewery in his hometown of Birzeit and Shepherds started trading in July 2015. They had since gone from strength to strength, and the brand was very prominent, especially around Bethlehem.

Stepping into the shop at the front of the factory was a bit like visiting a traditional English pub and Alaa looked at ease behind the bar as he offered up samples of the new winter ale. The Christmas tree made from beer bottles gave a festive glow to the room as we merrily stacked up beers and local wine to take home. It was great to see a local business thriving despite the challenges faced.

The other Palestinian brewery, Taybeh, also knew how to welcome visitors. We had visited several times, including for their Oktoberfest in 2019. When the brewery was founded in 1994 it was the first in the Middle East. Madees, the daughter of the founder, was the driving force behind daily operations. When we arrived, she welcomed us in for a chat about brewing in Palestine, to sample the beers on offer and for a tour of the equipment.

Madees explained the immense challenges that the occupation posed on the export of their beer. Despite the difficulties, it was a story of resilience and resistance and when we met the brewery was exporting its beer to ten countries around the world.

Madees explained the logistics involved in this. 'We have to get the permit first from Israel to send our beer to the port (Haifa or Ashdod),' she told me. 'Once we get the permit, we are not allowed to load containers on site at the brewery and so we have to find a Palestinian truck driver and an Israeli truck driver on the other side waiting to pick up the beer. What should take two hours driving from Taybeh to Haifa port takes us three days for the beer if things move smoothly.'

Madees went on to explain why they persevered in such difficult circumstances.

'It's very important to us, regardless of the challenges and difficulties we face, to export our products. This is our form of resistance to the occupation, and we continue to do business and grow locally and internationally.' Madees then said that her family strongly believed that, in order to build the State of Palestine and the economy, Palestinians needed to invest their money, knowledge and experience in the country to avoid being at the mercy of investment from foreign governments.

It was also a way to project an alternative image of Palestine to a foreign audience. Madees described how internationals did not know that Palestinians have a micro-brewery, drink alcohol and even have an Oktoberfest. 'When they see Taybeh in Europe for example, this intrigues them in wanting to know more about Taybeh beer, Palestine and the occupation,' she explained.

Taybeh had recently sent their first shipment of beer to Jordan. This was a proud moment for Madees and her family.

'Imagine, after twenty-six years we were finally able to send the beer to our neighbours! After entering Jordan, I hope this will be our gateway to other Arab countries. And possibly to the Far East,' she concluded.

It was especially difficult to succeed as a business under the conditions of occupation, and support for local businesses like Taybeh and Shepherds was critical if they were to be able to grow and inspire other businesses in Palestine.

Palestine was a treasure trove of riches and yet it didn't hold its own purse strings. Each place we visited had unique and wonderful things to offer but the occupation served to stifle industry and create an instability that deterred many people from visiting. We viewed Nablus as 'authentic', but did we mean stuck in the past? How different would Palestine be if businesses were supported to innovate and export their goods? Taybeh and Shepherds survived against the odds, but the challenges faced were too overwhelming for most businesses to overcome.

Similarly, would Palestinian Christians be thriving as an integral part of Palestine if it weren't for the harsh realities of life under the occupation? Ramallah as the seat of the Palestinian Authority was frozen in time, with a president and powers that were not equipped to deal with the modern reality. Palestine had so much historic and religious richness to offer the world, yet ongoing instability meant not all areas were accessible to foreign visitors. This left Palestine with the dual curse of not always being able to welcome people to see it first-hand and with severe difficulties in exporting Palestinian produce to the world.

CHAPTER 11
OFF THE BEATEN TRACK

The entire Palestinian West Bank from the south of Hebron to the north of Jenin was little more than 90 miles long and 30 miles wide. Getting truly lost and finding wilderness was something we constantly aspired to, and we felt closest to this when we travelled north of Nablus. Each trip included in this section was an adventure that left a deep impression on us. Sometimes it was the generosity of the people we met, the glimpse we got into village life, or the rhythms of agriculture. Above all, we felt furthest from the occupation on these trips and the places we visited allowed us to colour in more detail about both what Palestine was like, and also what it could be if given the conditions to thrive.

Nisf Jubeil

Around 20 minutes north of Nablus lay the quaint little village of Nisf Jubeil, perched on a steep rocky hillside. Along with Battir, it was our favourite place to retreat to and be swallowed up by Palestinian village life. When we arrived on our second visit, a group of older men were sitting on plastic chairs in the narrow street in front of their house, exactly as they had been on our first visit several months before. A few kids played around them as the adults smoked, chatted and drank coffee. Spotting an opportunity to make a few shekels, one of the older kids offered to run and fetch their donkey to give our kids a ride on. They were pleased to take up the offer, and were ceremoniously paraded along the short street on the donkey's back for a few minutes.

Several hills surrounded the valley, and a large Palestinian flag stood proudly on the neighbouring hill. There were several walking trails leading off from our guesthouse and within a few minutes of dumping our bags we were climbing up through the olive trees to get a better view across the valley. An older man dressed in a smart suit and *keffiyeh* passed us and stopped to ask where we were from. We exchanged pleasantries as he chided us for only having two children. He was the proud father of eight sons and one daughter, and it was clear he thought us lazy for not going the extra mile.

The sun was starting to dip and cast a warm, golden glow over the purple jacaranda and laden pomegranate trees. A friendly-faced donkey peered out from behind the tree it was tethered to, and we stopped to say hello. The sun became pinker as it set lower, and we wished we had longer to explore before darkness fell.

The three-room Mosaic guesthouse was run by a man called Rami. The family room, which was essentially a cave with exposed rocks and a section of glass flooring, added to the rustic ambiance. Rami had a warm smile and a round face. I suspected he would be a quiet man even without the language barrier between us. As we sat outside in the pretty white stone courtyard with lights twinkling around us, Rami ferried a wide range of little dishes and plates of delicious local food from the kitchen to the table. The garden was well tended and provided fresh herbs, including mint for the sweet tea.

Almost all the food Rami gave us was local produce, and when it was in season each crop was pickled, pressed or preserved to provide a year-long supply. Even those with very modest incomes could eat well in Palestine as there was never any shortage of olives, oil, dates, raisins, honey, jams, *zaatar* or lemons along with the fresh fruit and vegetables of the season. Rami's mum's homemade *labneh* balls (a soft cheese) were especially good, with a strong, tangy kick of flavour.

As we lay ensconced in our cave room at night, the murmur from the men on the street wafted in through the open windows. The darkness was absolute, and sleep came easily, except for the time that the whole village raucously celebrated a wedding into the small hours.

In the mornings, we awoke to the rural sounds of cocks crowing and donkeys heehawing as they lumbered to their work. The rising sun lifted animal smells into the air. Ambling through the village before breakfast, we passed several young boys who were hurtling down the steep slopes of the valley on their makeshift go-karts. When we passed the donkey from the night before, the owner emerged from behind a gate and leapt into a waiting car. 'Take him, take him for a walk,' he said. We untied the donkey's rope but he dug his heels in and refused to budge.

No trip to Nisf Jubeil was complete without visiting the workshop which employed local women to produce hand-painted ceramics. These were sold in several places across Palestine including in Sunbula, the Fairtrade shop in Sheikh Jarrah. Six women sat around a large workbench, their covered heads bent over plates and bowls which gently spun as their paintbrushes added intricate detail to their designs. I chose a set of olive painted plates, the same that Rami used in his guesthouse, hoping that some of the wisdom of Palestinian cooking would rub off on me. Nisf Jubeil never failed to serve us with a laid-back slice of Palestine that felt restorative, and we loved it.

Encounters in Sebastiya

In the middle of November we travelled to Sebastiya, a small historic town north of Nablus and only a few miles from Nisf Jubeil. It is an archaeological haven with evidence of a history stretching back at least 3,000 years to Canaanite times. It also played a significant role during Israelite, Hellenistic, Herodian, Roman and Byzantine times and visitors can explore the impressive remains from the Roman town. Sebastiya's other claim to fame is as the burial place of St John the Baptist. His tomb is within the Nabi Yahya Mosque which was converted from a Crusader church by Salah Ad-Din (Saladin) in 1187.

The religious and historic weight of the town makes it popular with Christian, Muslim and history-loving tourists, but Covid meant we only ever saw it deadly quiet. We had ticked the main sights off on a previous visit and had returned for the hiking trails. As we arrived in the small town the only signs of life were a few older gentlemen hunched over their backgammon boards in the community centre which took pride of place in the central square.

We were staying for two nights at a small guesthouse with six rooms and were delighted to find upon arrival that our friends from Jerusalem were the only other customers for the weekend. Abu Ahmad, the proprietor, was a generous host who treated us like long-lost friends. After serving tea, he pulled down his family photograph albums and settled into sharing tales of travellers and times gone by.

The guesthouse was set in the top floor of an old Arab palace and had an understated grandeur with high-domed ceilings and many archways. Abu Ahmad told us that a women's cooperative ran their businesses from the ground floor, aided by the support of several European donors. A long list of plaques from over the years showed that foreign investment had played a big part in the upkeep of the building.

After a traditional dinner of *maqloubeh*, the famous Levantine upside-down dish, we put the kids to bed and then fell into the trap of keeping quiet for them and ending up asleep ourselves before 10 o'clock. Perhaps it was the deep sleep we enjoyed in Palestine that always refreshed us, and even the persistent cry of the dawn call to prayer didn't disturb us.

The next morning, breakfast involved a lavish spread of fresh falafel, pitta breads, hummus, eggs and stuffed pastries as well as some vegetables and other jams and dips. It was a feast so soon after the large dinner, and for this reason most Palestinians didn't contemplate breakfast until at least 10 or 11am.

Feeling well set up for a day in the countryside, we set off on foot to explore. There were several circular trails that started from the town. These led into the surrounding hilltops and offered spectacular views for miles around. The path we took followed the Haroon spring and within a few minutes of leaving the town we were in the middle of a green oasis. The trees were laden with the last of the season's figs, large ripe pomegranates and lemons starting to turn yellow. The sheer size of the trees told that they had been there for a very long time. The olive trees were gnarled and twisted, their branches bare, having been stripped of their fruit over the past month.

As the path started to climb, we passed through a small village of several large houses. Two boys eyed us suspiciously as they led their huge sheep through the street. We were enthusiastic with our '*Merhabas*' and this seemed to satisfy them that we weren't posing a threat. We trailed after them, with the large sheep, all grinning white teeth, lumbering between us.

Further on, a man came running out of his house to speak to us.

'Where are you going? Why? There is nothing up there!' We did our best in broken Arabic to reassure him that we were just walking. Walking for the sake of it wasn't very Palestinian, and the lockdowns and lack of tourists meant that fewer foreigners than ever were passing his door.

He wasn't about to let the opportunity pass and invited us in for coffee. I looked at Paul, raising my eyebrows slightly. Without either of us uttering a word we exchanged a conversation we often had in these situations. Me: 'do we really have to go into this random guy's house and make small talk and waste our time?' Him: 'you never know, it could be interesting. Sometimes you have to give people a chance.'

So, in we trailed, kicking off our shoes at the door and sitting on the man's sofa. Orders were barked to his wife in the kitchen to make some tea and several children of varying ages grinned expectantly at us. I thought it was strange when he asked what was in our rucksack, and the conversation really started to take a turn for the worse when he enquired about the contents of Paul's pockets. When he started asking for 'dollarette' we stood to leave, just at the moment the tea tray finally appeared. Unsure whether to stay or go, we awkwardly settled in to try and drink the hot tea quickly before beating a hasty retreat.

On this occasion, it didn't work out, but I still admired Paul's willingness to be a 'yes' man. More often than not, this had opened the door to interesting encounters in Palestine and in other places we had travelled.

Resuming the walk, the kids were distracted now by rock-hopping on the steep ascent to the top of the hill. They bounded up, trying to avoid scratches from the sharp thorns and squashing the pretty pink wildflowers that poked out from between the rocks.

At the top stood the ruins of Maqam Sheikh Sha'leh. The *maqam* appeared to be a building marking a site of religious significance which had been used as a burial site. None of the locals we asked were able to give a clear explanation of it and it was now abandoned and open to the elements. The kids loved exploring the secret staircase and hidden rooms and from the flat rooftop you could see out towards Haifa and the coast looking west, and over towards Mount Gerizim and Nablus looking south. Along with the views, we soaked up the solitude of the place.

Swimming at Al-Badhan

A friend let us into the secret that the small town of al-Badhan was a popular holiday destination for Palestinians from across the West Bank. Deciding to give it a try, we had the surreal experience of boarding Palestine's only aeroplane on the journey there. After the year 2000 the Palestinian airport near Jerusalem was closed and West Bank Palestinians could only fly out of Jordan. The airports in Gaza were also closed after 2004.

In a bizarre tale, in 1999 twin brothers from Nablus bought a disused Boeing 747 for $100,000 and paid $50,000 to transport it by road from Israel to the West Bank. The project had stuttered and stalled for different reasons over the years and for two decades the plane sat abandoned on a roadside between Nablus and the al-Badhan valley. In 2021, the project was finally completed and the renovated aeroplane, gutted of its seating, was opened as a café. With its tail painted in Palestinian colours it made for a quirky attraction and we stopped by to take a few photos and board Palestine's only aircraft. The middle-aged twins, who were dressed identically in brightly coloured shorts, polo shirts and golf socks were on site to welcome visitors, answer questions and grill meats to serve. They didn't speak any English so we couldn't ask the many questions that arose from their eccentric story.

Continuing, the road dipped down to the wadi of al-Badhan which had several fresh springs running through it. A range of swimming resorts (several with amusement parks) had been built along the village's main road to provide easy access to the water. Arriving felt like time-warping back to a 1970s seaside resort. Several shops were piled high with rubber rings and plastic swimming aids in all colours and sizes. The road signs advertising the resorts were sun-faded and drained of colour. Rusty Ferris wheels and the metal arms of other rides jutted out, their days of motion long behind them. We might have kept driving if it hadn't been for a promise made to the kids that their patience on a hike would be rewarded with submersion in water of one sort or another.

Several pairs of eyes followed us as we walked in and tried to decipher the Arabic signs pointing towards the various attractions. It became apparent that there were different swimming pools for men and women, with children able to visit either. We took a kid each and headed off in separate directions to find our respective pools. After stumbling around in the vast garden area for some time I finally found the well-concealed entrance to the women's swimming area.

Four or five women sat chatting amicably at the entrance as they guarded the site. They were friendly and patient with my broken Arabic, explaining that we needed to buy a head covering to enter the pool. After paying the tourist rate for a cotton cap, we went in to get changed.

The women in the water were conservatively dressed and I was very relieved that I had anticipated this and had packed shorts and a sports top for swimming.

'Is that your PE clothes?' my daughter asked. After I had wrestled the cotton swimming hat on to her head, and secured my own, we were ready to go.

Having a young child with me was a sure-fire way to appear unthreatening and the women sitting around the pool smiled and greeted us. Not wanting to attract undue attention, I slid into the icy waters without a fuss.

In the pool, women splashed around with their children, and there was a fun, holiday atmosphere. A few young girls swam over to exchange greetings with us and practise the few words of English they had learned at school. Several of the women wore large inflatable life rings around their waists and I realised that they couldn't swim. The Israeli occupation had denied many Palestinians access to the coast, and swimming pools were not that common, so it stood to reason that few had learned to swim.

It was a refreshing dip but the cold water, sourced directly from the spring and unheated, meant that we didn't stay in the water that long. Leaving the pool, we reunited with the boys and sat for a few minutes taking in the unique scene.

There were lots of small channels of water trickling down the slope of the resort. These were wide enough for plastic tables and chairs to be set up in the stream. Each family had bagged a spot and sat around the table with their feet submerged in the cold water up to ankle level. Most groups had brought picnics or even barbecues and some were enjoying shisha pipes.

Each small group comprised a mix of generations. Palestinian grannies had slid off their leather sandals, lifted their traditional *thobe* dresses a few centimetres and were cooling their feet in the water. For many, I imagined, this was the closest thing they would get to a 'day at the beach.' A canopy of vines provided shade overhead and with the water gently flowing past, it looked a blissful way to spend an afternoon.

A small boy came over to us and offered a plate of hummus. We looked up and his mother waved a greeting from a few tables away. Next the boy came with some pickles. Then some cucumbers. Then some bread. Then some more hummus. I walked over to say hello and to thank the lady for her generosity. She was about my age and didn't wear a headscarf. Her food offerings had been a conversation starter, and very politely she asked if we were Israeli. She was very interested in where we were from, and how we had come to find ourselves in al-Badhan. The hospitality was remarkable, and I was embarrassed to realise that our own picnic had consisted of four meagre sandwiches – already eaten – and a few other trimmings, now much depleted. To repay the favour we offered the last of our Jericho dates and bought her kids ice creams.

On the way home, we decided to stop in Rawabi. This was a newly built Palestinian town which had divided opinion, with some people referring to it as the 'Palestinian settlement'. For some, it provided the opportunity to live in spacious newly built apartment blocks in the middle of a conveniently appointed town with ample parking and affordable prices. Others, however, saw it as a 'sell out', as secret deals had supposedly been struck with Israeli authorities to allow its construction and it resembled the illegal Israeli settlements that dominated the Palestinian hilltops.

We were intrigued and parked up for a wander around and a spot of lunch. Sitting outside a café in the centre of town, we could easily have been in an upmarket corner of London, Paris or New York. The modern plaza was surrounded by eye-wateringly expensive designer shops and the eating options centred on elaborate coffees, skinny sandwiches and wraps that could only be ordered using a QR scanner. It was probably the least Palestinian place we had been, but I could still see the attraction for some.

Rawabi had been built on the confidence that, once people saw it, they would want to live there. The town felt quiet and only partially occupied but a shopkeeper told us that everything had been sold and that new apartment blocks were being built to meet the demand. It was an experiment in town planning, and only time would tell how successful it would be and what it meant for the future landscape of Palestine. In one day, we had travelled to a Palestine of both past and future. The old Palestine felt more connected to notions of family and community, and that was a defining feature that we continued to find across Palestine and hoped would continue. It remained to be seen if there was an appetite for the easy-living version of a modern Palestine that Rawabi offered.

Spring in Zababdeh

Spring was the best hiking season in Palestine as the wildflowers came out in abundance and the temperatures were moderate. We had missed the entire spring of 2020 due to Covid-19 restrictions so by spring 2021 we had a full itinerary of trips planned.

That was how we found ourselves on a busy street in the small, northerly town of Zababdeh on a Sunday morning in February. A man waved frantically from the kerb, and we stopped to let our guide, Mohammad, jump into the car. At over half an hour later than planned we were bordering on rude, but he smiled broadly and dismissed our apologies.

Zababdeh lies 15 kilometres southeast of Jenin and is approximately a 45-minute drive from Nablus. Often in Palestine there was a feeling of being hemmed in, with settlements and other signs of the occupation crowding the space. The area around Zababdeh made Palestine feel big, surrounded on all sides by rolling hills and valleys which connected the different towns and villages. Israel felt like another country away, and the scenery was not tainted by the architecture of the occupation.

Zababdeh is a picturesque town which was new by Palestinian standards. It had been founded in 1834 by Greek Orthodox Christians and the population was now two-thirds Christian and one-third Muslim. The local sites looked interesting, but we left the town almost instantly to reach the start of our walk some 10 kilometres from Zababdeh.

We were walking with another family and had warned Mohammad that despite our enthusiasm, progress would be slow with five children ranging in age from four months to seven years. He reassured us that there were pick-up points on the route should we need to use them, which was a good thing as we were to later find out.

Setting out we were immediately plunged into a sea of green with every shade imaginable bouncing back on our eyes. The sun was high in the sky and the valley was lush. Nearby a young boy used an old scythe to chop some greenery which he placed in his donkey's saddle bags.

Spring flowers had started to dot the landscape with flashes of red and yellow, but Mohammad told us that the start of March was the best time to come as the irises were in full bloom then. He was incredibly knowledgeable about the plants and animals we encountered. A cat-like noise was an owl. A spider-like web contained a ball of wriggling baby caterpillars. These were spread along the route and although not poisonous, I dreaded stepping on one by mistake.

Sitting under a large olive tree for shade, we paused for a break and chatted. We were Mohammad's first walking tour since Covid-19. One day he had been guiding a group when he received a call from the police to say that things were shutting down immediately and he would be jailed if he continued walking. He explained that it would take him two hours to bring his group of Canadians to a road where they could be picked up, and this was permitted.

Arriving back at his village near Jenin, later that day, Mohammad entered a 17-day precautionary quarantine. Rumours were rife that he had Covid-19 (he didn't), and that as a tour guide, he was culpable for bringing it into the country. He said with sorrow that these views had affected him and his family a lot over the past year.

We asked if he had taken Palestinian groups out between the lockdowns. He smiled wryly and explained that 'they always want to go in groups of at least a hundred people.' He said that an arrangement with a few people might lead to many more turning up, and that details on the distance to be covered and the appropriate clothing would not be passed on.

'Why did you not tell me?' a young woman dressed for the town would say when faced with a difficult path.

'Because I didn't invite you!' Mohammad would respond.

Large groups were challenging for him to manage and could have a negative impact on the environment. A sprawling group led to people being spread out over large distances, which delayed everyone and could be dangerous if people weren't dressed properly. Suddenly we didn't feel so bad about our five kids dragging their heels a little.

At lunch time we stopped, and Mohammad expertly lit a fire and pulled out a frying pan to cook a *shakshuka* on. This was a popular Palestinian dish with eggs cooked in a tomato sauce and eaten with bread. There was tea with sage afterwards and the chance to rest and take in the beautiful scenery.

By 4.30pm the sun was starting to dip and the shortest legs were wearying. We took Mohammad up on the offer of completing the final two kilometres back to Zababdeh by taxi. It had taken us a ridiculously long time with the kids to cover around eight kilometres but dawdling along had given us more time to notice the wildlife and to absorb the natural beauty of the area.

It was only when we hiked that we got to leave the manmade structures behind and see what the land of Palestine was naturally like. If we were lucky enough to walk somewhere with no views of Israeli settlements or the separation wall, it was easy to believe we had slipped back in time to a pre-industrial age where nature reigned supreme. In these areas it wasn't difficult to see where the Palestinians' love and respect for the land came from.

Tobacco Picking in Zabuba

On our way to Zabuba, the most northerly village in Palestine, I vowed that we would never return. We were already running late before we got lost following the woefully bad navigation app. We had scratched the car turning an impossibly tight corner through narrow streets and we were bickering and in a bad mood. Then we arrived and were given such a warm welcome that all my irritation instantly evaporated.

Our tour guide for the day was Mohammad, who had previously taken us around Zababdeh. On this occasion, we had come to his home village to learn more about Palestine's tobacco-growing industry. On arrival, we were ushered into a sheltered area where chairs had been assembled around the coffee pot. Along with biscuits and sweets, cubes of homemade jam were offered on cocktail sticks.

Mohammad said that Zabuba was famous for its tobacco leaves as the chalky soil gave a light taste to the leaves that those in the know could distinguish.

'We are professional smokers,' he said laughing, handing round the tobacco seeds that were usually planted in the spring. An older gentleman nodded. He had been 12 when he started smoking and had clocked up 50 years of experience already.

Much to the delight of our kids, and the other family with us, our transport for the day was to be a tractor-drawn trailer. A friendly young man called Tamer was introduced as the tractor driver and it was his family's fields that we were off to see. Tamer was a vet by profession, but Mohammad told us that even people with important jobs still had to help with tending the family land.

As the tractor rumbled along, Mohammad chatted with us about family life in rural Palestine. He told us that Tamer, who was 31, was engaged to be married that summer. Mohammad said that he had warned Tamer that he needed to finish building his house before getting engaged.

'If you ask to marry someone, the first question the family will ask is if you own your own house,' he told us. Speaking from experience, Mohammad warned that another reason for completing the house before the engagement was that 'if not, the girl will want to choose everything, and it will be very slow.' Mohammad explained that if you passed the test of having a house, then the girl's family would want to come and see it before they agreed to the marriage. Despite having just met Tamer, we were invited to attend his wedding. It was normal for the whole town or village to be invited to weddings and this sometimes meant that there were over one thousand guests.

Mohammad said that families worked together as a single financial unit and the annual income from tobacco and other produce would be invested in those who needed money for study or home building or improvements. Mohammad started planning his own house aged 18, and it took him 12 years to complete it.

Meanwhile, the tractor had been bumping along past verdant fields of tobacco, cucumbers, sesame, chickpeas and watermelon. In some of the fields workers hunched over the crop, methodically working along the lines to pick small cucumbers. It was a perfect rural scene, apart from the tall electric wire fence which stood several hundred metres away, chopping the land in two, with a concrete watchtower at one end.

Mohammad told us that the fence around Zabuba was one of the earliest parts of the Israeli separation barrier to be built in the year 2002, and that it instantly cut many people off from their places of work. The only silver lining to this, he said, was that 'many people went back to their land.' This had also been the case during Covid-19 and cultivating fields that had been left fallow had created more sense of community and a collective ownership and pride in the land.

We hopped off the tractor and started trying to make ourselves useful by picking the first leaves of tobacco. The plants were surprisingly bushy with lush, green leaves like giant lettuces growing in neat rows. We were told that the first, outer leaves were the best quality but that these were mixed with leaves from the second and third pick to make a well-rounded cigarette.

I had refused the rubber gloves Mohammad offered us, and before long my hands were coated in a sticky black glue like the thick sap from a tree. It dawned on me that this was the tar that normally ended up in a smoker's lungs and made smoking so dangerous.

We picked leaves for around an hour and the large sack started to fill up. We joked that someone would need to come and tidy up the plants we had missed or messed up. Jumping back on the tractor we trundled past more fields, and Mohammad jumped down regularly to offer us fresh samples.

At one stop, it was chickpeas growing on vine-like tendrils. These were peeled like peapods to reveal one or two green chickpeas inside. They tasted fresh and sweet. A little further along, we were invited to pick green peppers from low-hanging plants. Mohammad then boarded the tractor with two huge fresh watermelons under his arms and offered them to us. There was a sense that the land was bountiful, and that people could take what they needed without damaging the supply.

Leaving the field behind, the tractor trundled along until it stopped outside several houses with a barn to the back, where the dried leaves were taken to be made into cigarettes. Earlier in Zabuba, we had seen the freshly picked leaves strung up in rows to be dried for 20 days before they were transported to this barn. An ancient cutting machine was demonstrated, and piles of tobacco lay on the ground like hay, waiting to be stuffed into the cigarette papers. A fresh smell, like tea leaves, hung in the air.

When we left, Mohammad declared that it was finally lunchtime.

'We will eat at my place,' he told us. We didn't want to impose on his family, but he insisted, casually dropping in that 'today is my daughter's birthday, she is one today.' His apartment was part of a wider set of connected houses where his extended family lived. He took us into his lounge area and offered us drinks as we cooed over the birthday girl. The kids were given large party hats and balloons and we joined in for an enthusiastic singing of Happy Birthday in both Arabic and English.

His wife had a delicate face and a youthful energy. She was friendly and hospitable as she darted around her kitchen preparing a generous lunch for us, which Mohammad's elderly mother joined us for. Despite my limited Arabic the old woman talked incessantly, pointing outside the windows to things she wanted us to see. Nodding and smiling went a long way.

On that day we were treated to much more than a tour. It was a unique experience to see not only Mohammad's home village, and the rituals of the agricultural life that sustained the community, but also the warmth of his family home.

This was the Palestine we loved. Away from tourists, and largely away from the Israeli police and the military, there was space to just be. The places we visited were connected to nature and the land whether through old traditions and farming techniques or village life. It was sometimes possible to forget about the occupation for a few hours, and to simply enjoy the wonderful landscapes and generous hospitality of the people we met. It was far from a free Palestine, but these trips made it much easier to conjure up an image about what a free Palestine could look like and it was a special thing to behold.

CHAPTER 12
HISTORIC PALESTINE

Before the creation of Israel in 1948, all the territory now known as Israel and the Occupied Palestinian Territories was simply called Palestine. In using the term 'historic Palestine' I want to highlight several places within Israel which continue to have particular significance for Palestinians.

There are different reasons for this – places like Lifta that are no longer inhabited, places which represent commerce and access to the sea, such as Jaffa, Haifa and Akko, and places of religious importance, like Nazareth. Then there are places like Umm Al-Fahm which show the contrast between Arab-Israeli towns and other parts of Israel, and the Negev, where Bedouin communities struggle for survival.

Many Palestinians that we met in Jerusalem and across Palestine had stories about homes that their families were forced to abandon in 1948. There was a deep nostalgia for the past, and a feeling that the injustice of the Nakba still needed to be righted. Palestinians with Jerusalemite status are free to travel around Israel as they wished, and for some, regular trips to Jaffa or their original home villages were performed as a frequent pilgrimage. Most West Bank Palestinians were denied access to Israel, however, including East Jerusalem, and they could only dream about what the places that made up historic Palestine were like.

Part of what it meant to be Palestinian remained in these places after 1948, and this chapter explores the prominent towns of historic Palestine I visited to see what remains of their past and describes my search for signs of peaceful coexistence.

The Ghosts of Lifta

As you approach Jerusalem on the main highway from Tel Aviv, Lifta lurks like a ghost town on the hillside. It is a prominent reminder of the Nakba and the events of 1947–49.

Lifta is unique in that many of the original houses are still standing. Of the estimated 600 villages that were depopulated of their Palestinian residents during 1948–49, most were destroyed altogether, or like Ein Karem and Ein Hod, were repopulated with Jewish families.

On a Saturday morning in spring, we were joined by a large group of friends for a guided walking tour of Lifta. Our guide was from Zochrot, an Israeli NGO organisation aimed at sharing information about the Nakba, and the Palestinian right of return, with Israelis in Hebrew. This was unusual as Palestinians spoke and wrote about the Nakba in Arabic or English and Israel did not recognise the history in the same way. Zochrot's mission, in their own words, was to 'promote accountability for the Nakba among the Jewish public of Israel and the implementation of the Right of Return of Palestinian refugees.'

The first striking thing was that our meeting point was a petrol station near the central bus station in Jerusalem. We had been to Lifta several times before, and it always involved a short motorway journey that gave the impression of leaving the city behind. We were told that the reality was that Lifta used to extend much further into the city centre, and it had only been a short distance for locals to bring their produce for sale at the central Mahane Yehuda market.

Tucked in behind the main road, an unmarked path weaved its way down the steep hillside towards the abandoned village. Tall cactus plants, fig trees and green almond trees lined the scenic route. We had heard before that where you found cactus plants, there was a high chance that Palestinians used to live there. These plants often formed the outer protective fence of a village and being a stubborn plant would often remain even when villages had been destroyed, providing a tell-tale sign of a place's history.

At the bottom of the path we came to the freshwater spring which fed three pools. Our guide, Umar, told us that the water used to be evenly distributed between the different family plots of land, similar to the system used in Battir. The freshwater pools had different purposes for cleaning people, houses, then animals, in that order of priority. These days the spring was a popular bathing spot in the summer and several families, both Jewish and Muslim, had gathered with picnics on the day we visited.

Our route led us past the mosque, which was believed to date from the 13th century, during the time of Salah Ad-Din's army. Some graffiti marked the walls and there was broken glass where an art project had been attempted and later vandalised. Umar said that it was now the site of frequent parties, and he was visibly moved by the desecration of this holy site, commenting that the 'situation is really painful for a holy place.'

We moved on to see a building with high ceilings and arched windows that had served as the village's olive press. Umar told us that there had been several olive presses in the village and that this indicated a prosperous community. He painted a picture of a thriving community before 1947, and we were interested to hear how the events of those years had changed the fate of Lifta so profoundly.

The Israeli narrative around many events during 1948 was that the Palestinian families had voluntarily left their houses. In explaining how the events of 1947 and 1948 unfolded in Lifta, Umar stressed that it was a gradual expulsion. First one person was murdered, then a coffee shop was attacked, killing six people. Every week there was a fresh attack where people were shot at by **Zionist** militia forces. Families didn't feel safe any more and some people started to leave, mainly for East Jerusalem or Ramallah. Initially, each family kept one young man in their house to protect it and, lowering his eyes, he went on. 'The result was very sad, and they didn't manage,' Umar said.

For many residents of Lifta, the final straw came on 9th April 1948, when the village of Deir Yassin, a short distance away from Lifta on the opposite hillside, was violently attacked by Zionist paramilitary groups. What ensued was nothing short of a massacre, and over a hundred people were killed, many of whom were reportedly in their own homes at the time. It was a horrifying example of ethnic cleansing. The elderly, women and children were not spared, and the brutality of the event sent shockwaves of terror throughout other Palestinian villages. Umar explained that the mentality at the time was 'we will not wait for our massacre.' It was striking that all these events preceded the creation of Israel in May 1948.

This provided some context to explain why the villagers of Lifta felt they had no choice other than to leave. But why had their houses not been destroyed as had happened in other areas? Several possible explanations were offered for this. Initially the large and attractive houses served a useful purpose in housing Jewish immigrants. Ownership of the houses was never transferred to these families, however, and many of them accepted the offer of better accommodation in the early 1970s. By this time many of the Lifta houses had fallen into a state of disrepair and needed renovation.

Once the houses had been vacated, instead of being demolished round holes were drilled in the middle of their roofs to make them uninhabitable to illegal squatters. One theory was that the authorities wanted the houses to appear to collapse naturally. Quality Palestinian craftmanship meant that they still stood resolutely and most can still be entered even after over 40 years of exposure to the elements.

Another theory was that by leaving Lifta standing and uninhabited it reinforced the narrative that Palestinians had voluntarily left their homes and that these, and other homes like them, had not been destroyed by the Israeli state. After 1948, many Palestinians were injured or killed attempting to return to their homes to either collect items or tend to their land and the Israeli authorities made it clear that returning was not possible.

For years, Lifta had remained untouched, and it was a painful symbol of the Nakba for many people. Change was afoot, however, and a new sign pointed to the Lifta Boutique Hotel & Spa. This was a luxury venture charging exorbitant rates for its location and facilities. We wondered what story the proprietors told their guests about the history of the village and the reason for its derelict condition.

Several plans had emerged over the years to clear the site, but these always faced strong opposition. The future of Lifta remained uncertain and the hotel was perhaps an ominous sign that further development was inevitable. No trace of Deir Yassin remained, not even on a map. Lifta was a constant reminder to Palestinians of the horror of the Nakba years and what had been lost. Its presence served as a memorial to those less fortunate, who had been both physically and geographically erased.

Mary of Nazareth

Visiting Nazareth felt like going on a pilgrimage, and that is exactly what it was. Famous as the birthplace of Mary, and the childhood home of Jesus, the town was steeped in Christian history. Nazareth was a classic example of what was known in Palestine as 'a "48" town'. The residents were predominantly Arabs, and it was intended to be part of the future Palestinian state in the UN 1947 Partition Plan. It was seized by Israel during the 1948 conflict, but the Arab residents (a high proportion of whom were Christian) were not forcibly removed but instead allowed to stay and eventually to gain Arab-Israeli status. Some called it 'the Arab capital of Israel'.

To this day, many Palestinians use **'48'** as a place name for anywhere that is considered part of historic Palestine. This leads to phrases like 'it's in 48' or 'I'm going to 48'. This not only makes clear that Palestinians feel a strong affinity to a place as a part of historic Palestine, but it also gives them a way of refusing to recognise present-day Israel. Since 1948, the Christian population of Nazareth has greatly reduced, and Muslims now make up the largest percentage of the population. In theory Jews, Muslims and Christians now live together in the city, but it is difficult to tell how harmonious this arrangement is in practice.

Arriving in Nazareth, we stumbled straight into Abu Ashraf's famous restaurant which presented itself like a ramshackle museum. A vast collection of coffeepots, jugs, trays and other antique items hung from the walls and roof, creating a cluttered cavern. Rushing over to greet us, the owner made us welcome but insisted that photographs were strictly prohibited. We ordered a selection of Arab dishes for lunch and were talked into a plate of Abu Ashraf's signature dish – small syrupy pancakes stuffed with walnuts called *katiyef*. Usually these were a Ramadan speciality, but Abu Ashraf served them up fresh all year round. It was a cold January day, and we welcomed the warm, syrupy little parcels.

I wanted to stay somewhere that had original character and the Fauzi Azar Inn promised to provide it. It was in the heart of the Old City and was a beautiful Ottoman-era building set around a pretty courtyard. It had high ceilings and arched doorways with several grand entertaining rooms. We had a basic yet elegant family room, but the inn also offered bunk rooms for young backpackers seeking a more traditional hostel.

The inn had a fascinating history. It had been an Arab family home which fell into disrepair and sat vacant for many years. A young Israeli wanted to open a guesthouse in Nazareth, and he approached the family to seek their permission to work together on renovating the property. The family were highly sceptical about working with an Israeli and felt that to sell the property to him would dishonour their father and grandfather's name. They didn't see the attraction of Nazareth as a tourist destination and considered the Old City to be dirty and dangerous.

The Israeli guy had charm, vision and perseverance, however, and he slowly won them over. This resulted in a strong partnership which closely involved the original family and led to the restoration and preservation of the building with respect to its heritage. Through a collaboration with a hostel in Jerusalem, they secured a steady stream of tourists who were helping to inject fresh life and energy into the Old City. This was an encouraging story of the sort of mutually beneficial arrangements that were possible if political differences could be set aside.

The main attraction in Nazareth is the Basilica of the Annunciation where the Angel Gabriel is said to have told Mary that she would bear the Son of God. The church itself is a wonderful mix of modernist architecture and ancient stone. The Upper Basilica Dome which dominates the skyline was built in the 1960s, but within the church the Grotto of the Annunciation covers the spot thought to have been Mary's actual home.

A stone's throw away stands the modest St Joseph's Church which marks where Joseph's carpentry workshop was thought to have stood. It was quite something to step inside the scenes of the Bible like this, and when we visited the Basilica was airy, spacious and accommodating to visitors. There was a casual accessibility that felt refreshing.

The mosaics in the grounds of the Basilica were an unexpected highlight. Nations from around the world had been invited to gift a long and narrow mosaic portrait of Mary and Jesus in their national style. The result was eclectic and entertaining, with Mary adorned in all manner of gowns and costumes from kimonos to harem pants as well as more traditional garments. It was a unifying and celebratory display of Christianity from around the world.

That afternoon we climbed the steep path beyond the Old City in the hope of visiting the Church of Jesus the Adolescent. I desperately wanted to see evidence of young Jesus as a teenager as those years seemed overlooked, but it was not to be. We got lost, the walk was too long and we called it off when we found a *knafeh* shop offering strong coffee and (more) syrupy puddings to perk up the kids.

There were further culinary delights in store that evening when we stumbled upon Alreda for dinner. On entering, it had the atmosphere of a gentrified pub where everyone knew each other, and older men gathered to play board games as they smoked. The atmosphere was warm, and the staff were attentive. The menu described itself as Arab fusion and it was perfect for the kids, offering juicy beef sausages and pizzas with exotic toppings as well as traditional Palestinian casseroles and other dishes.

The Nazareth that we experienced was charming and welcoming to both Arabic and Hebrew speakers. To the untrained eye it looked like a good example of coexistence, but I suspected that behind the scenes Arab-Israelis did not enjoy the same rights and freedoms as other Israelis. They had paid a high price to achieve their hybrid status, and only they could say if they considered it worth the sacrifice.

Juicy Jaffa

On a lazy summer's day, we mobilised ourselves for a late afternoon trip to the picturesque town of Jaffa. Despite having lived in Jerusalem for well over a year by that stage this was only our second visit to Jaffa, and we had spent even less time in the neighbouring metropolis of Tel Aviv, which we usually used as a parking spot and not much more.

Jaffa is an ancient port town that has been inhabited for thousands of years and is mentioned several times in the Bible. It lies on the Mediterranean Sea and has always held great strategic importance as the primary arrival and departure point for historic Palestine. Jaffa Gate in the Old City of Jerusalem points towards Jaffa and is the entry point into Jerusalem for visitors arriving from overseas.

The town took on greater prominence during the 19th century as the international export of goods boomed. Jaffa was famous for its Jaffa oranges which had a thick skin that made them ideal for export. It was from this great industry that the much-loved British Jaffa Cake came into existence.

As the population of Jaffa grew, a new suburb was founded in 1909. This expanded quickly to accommodate the steady influx of Jewish immigrants from Eastern Europe and over time became the separate city of Tel Aviv. Before 1948, the population of Jaffa was predominantly Muslim but there had always been Jewish and Christian communities present. This led to the 1947 UN Partition Plan advising that Jaffa should be part of the Palestinian state. This was hotly contested as Jaffa held strategic importance as a key port in close proximity to Tel Aviv. In 1948, Israel stormed Jaffa and forcibly removed the majority of the Arab residents. Those who remained were largely confined to the Ajami neighbourhood to the south of the city where they were strictly controlled. This wound had never healed, and many Palestinians consider Jaffa their ancestral home and a stolen jewel.

Standing proudly in the northern end of Jaffa is the iconic clocktower which the Ottomans built here and in several other Palestinian towns in the early 20th century. Jaffa is still characterised by its Ottoman and Arab architecture which is in stark contrast to the modernist feel of Tel Aviv where high-rise quirky designs and Bauhaus buildings reign supreme.

The afternoon was hot, and the streets were quiet as we ambled along the narrow, winding streets of Jaffa's Old City. We peered into the windows of closed jewellery shops and art galleries and felt disappointed that there was little evidence of their Arab past. The posters on shop windows were all in Hebrew. We bought arty postcards in one place and oversized ice creams in another to placate the kids.

The market area was slightly livelier. This was normally a fun and quirky neighbourhood, jam-packed with record shops, vintage clothing, antiques, bric-a-brac and trendier, more upmarket boutiques. The shops sold a mix of hippy-style clothing, with flowing fabrics in all patterns, and trendy beachwear. The residents exuded a sun-kissed 'beach to bar' vibe. The atmosphere was youthful and fun. There were traces of Arabic, but Hebrew was the dominant language and there was little to evoke the Palestinian Jaffa of the past. Several shops were already packing up for the day as the afternoon edged towards evening and we decided to take a quick dip in the sea before dinner.

Despite the sun starting to set, the air was thicker and more humid than it had been in Jerusalem, and we hoped to catch the sea breeze. In the harbour area a few men sat hunched over their fish stalls, selling the last of the catch of the day.

Most sun worshippers gravitated to the beaches of Tel Aviv where the contrast with conservative Jerusalem was eye-popping. Skimpy swimwear adorned bronzed bodies, often accessorised with a tiny dog as people power walked, jogged, danced and did yoga with zeal. The games of beach volleyball were particularly competitive and often drew a crowd of observers.

We were seeking a lower-key affair, and instead chose to follow the promenade south for a kilometre until we came to Ajami beach. It was immediately obvious that this attracted a very different, far more modest and overtly religious clientele than the hipster Tel Aviv beaches.

There were more families, and they came with several generations in tow, big picnic baskets and a more relaxed atmosphere than the uptight health fanatics of the Tel Aviv beaches. Swimwear and normal clothes were interchangeable, with both modestly dressed Jewish and Muslim people paddling in the sea. We did a typically British complicated towel dance to get changed and then waded into the warm, refreshing water.

For most Palestinians, the beach is a pipe dream. The coast used to be a big part of Palestine from Gaza up to Akko, with many people having a soft spot for Jaffa. Many Palestinians cherish memories from childhood weekends and holidays spent at the sea, or these memories are passed down from the older generations as a lost part of Palestine. Palestinians no longer have any access to the sea (if you exclude Gaza which is under Israeli military blockade).

The sun was nearly setting by now and the sea breeze felt cool on our skin. We dressed, and with hair caked in salt, walked the short distance to the Kerem Street branch of the Old Man and the Sea. The fish restaurant has legendary status and people come from far and wide to enjoy it. We chose a table outside and ordered a large jug of lemon and mint juice as we selected our fish.

Selecting a fish from the menu was enough to trigger an onslaught of copious small dips and salads to arrive. Three waiters dished out the little bowls as if dealing a pack of cards. By the time they were finished we had no less than 23 small dishes teetering on the table. These delicious morsels, some spicy, some creamy, some crunchy, were a feast for the eyes and the palate.

Jaffa, which was once the jewel in the crown of Palestine, was an example of a '48 town' which now felt very Israeli and had lost a lot of its original character. Despite this, in the architecture and the stones of the town there were shadows of its former elegance, and the role it played in Palestinian history. It still thronged with life, but the real challenge would be for it to find a way to assimilate its past and its present.

Coexistence in Haifa

I went to Haifa hoping that it would be all about the food, and it was, but there was more to be found in this relaxed and artsy city. After Jerusalem and Tel Aviv, Haifa is Israel's third largest city. Its renowned port has given it an industrial image, and although this is still prominent, it was clear that the city had benefitted from a revamp and an injection of investment over the past decades. The result was lots of focal points to interest tourists.

Many Jewish immigrants to Israel arrived in Haifa, and by 1939 they had already overtaken the Muslim and Christian populations. Haifa was designated as part of the Jewish state in the UN Partition Plan, which led to violence during 1948. Many of the Arab residents were either forced to leave or chose to do so and they now comprise around a quarter of the population of Haifa.

The centrepiece of Haifa is the impressive Baha'i gardens, also known as 'the hanging gardens of Haifa' which sweep down the hillside for 19 terraces, and a reported 1,500 steps. With two kids in tow, I was not overly disappointed that they were closed on the day we visited. Instead, we enjoyed the great views of the site from the German Colony area which was at the foot of the gardens. The colony area was established in 1868 when a group of German Templars (Protestant Christians) moved to the Holy Land and formed communities in Jaffa and Jerusalem as well as in Haifa. They built homes in the farmhouse style they were accustomed to, and these gave the area a European feel that felt at odds with the rest of the city.

The area was jam-packed with restaurants, cafés and ice cream bars. Most had nice outdoor seating areas set back from the street with twinkling lights and quirky décor creating a convivial atmosphere. It was still 'coat weather' in the evenings but we were happy to dine outside.

Of the restaurants we tried, Fattoush stood out for its stylish ambiance and excellent Middle Eastern menu which included a wide range of Palestinian and Lebanese favourites. It was the sort of place where it was worth over-ordering plates to share, especially salads and starters, until the table was full.

Another food highlight for me was a very unassuming Arab bakery near our guesthouse, which sold excellent freshly baked pastries in the morning. These are common across Israel and Palestine, with sweet and savoury pastries in a range of different shapes and sizes available. The triangular, spinach-filled *fatayer* in Haifa stood out above the rest for their zesty taste and crumbly thin pastry.

In search of more culinary highlights, we took a walk through the meandering streets of Wadi Nisnas. This was a Christian-Arab neighbourhood, with a focus on good honest cooking. On one street, two falafel restaurants faced another falafel restaurant and a hummus place with no apparent need to worry about the competition. People queued for the fresh sandwiches then huddled outside on the pavement to eat them.

There was an array of other shops selling herbs, coffee, baklava-type sweets and treats and – only seen in Christian areas – pork shops with dried and cured meats. There was also very good street food, with several tables lining the main thoroughfare offering a 'fill a plate' option. The stall we settled on offered rice dishes, stuffed vine leaves, cheese-filled breads, several vegetable sides, a chickpea stew and an attitude that you needed to sample everything.

In between eating, we ticked off some of the main tourist sites such as the cable car which runs from the beach up to the Stella Maris Monastery, the science museum and one of the local national parks. Sadly, when we visited, the beaches around Haifa were still suffering the after-effects of an oil spill along the Israeli coast. Clumps of black tar hid underneath the sand, and without us noticing we suddenly had it on our hands and shoes. Across the bay the ancient, fortressed town of Akko was visible.

Haifa is often cited as a successful example of Jewish and Arab communities living side by side. The atmosphere was certainly relaxed when we visited, with shopkeepers flitting between Hebrew and Arabic without the suspicion that hung in the air in Jerusalem. There also wasn't the pretence of Tel Aviv, with its catwalk-like promenade for the fit and the beautiful. I suspected, however, that harmony was a veneer that had been painted on to Haifa and that beneath the surface things weren't as rosy for the Arab citizens as the city authorities would have you believe. This later proved true. During the escalated tensions of 2021, Haifa became one of the leading areas of unrest within Israel.

Driving back, we stopped off in the small town of Jizr Az-Zarqa. This was the only coastal village outside of Gaza that had a predominantly Arab population. The single-way tunnel under the main road which connected the village to the rest of Israel was the first sign that it was considered a Palestinian place.

Despite being one of the poorest towns in Israel it had a nice atmosphere, and the beach area was quaint with fishermen sorting out their large nets and a few ramshackle huts offering fresh fish and other food. It felt like a forgotten place, and it was worth a visit to see another example of the contrasting fates of different areas that sat side by side, supposedly in the same country.

Similar to Nazareth, there was a lot to like about Haifa, but it was difficult to tell if the Arab citizens who lived there felt that they were part of a two-tier system. Some people held it up as a possible model of coexistence and I desperately wanted to believe that was possible.

Defending Akko

Akko, Akka or Acre has attracted many names for itself over its long history. Known as the capital of the Crusader Kingdom it looks every part the medieval fortress city, but has been continually inhabited since around 3000BCE, making it one of the oldest cities in the world.

The centre of Akko was pedestrianised and accessing the Old City meant first battling the crowds to find somewhere to park along the sea wall before entering the maze of narrow streets.

Our second visit to Akko coincided with the end of Ramadan, a Christian parade and Israel's Independence Day so the town was in full celebratory mode, accommodating the mix of cultures and religions from those who claimed Akko as their own.

Akko has been shaped by each of the empires who passed through it over the centuries including the Romans, Crusaders, Mamelukes, Byzantines, Ottomans and finally the British. It is not short on history, and this has earned the Old City UNESCO World Heritage status.

In 1947 the UN Partition Plan for Palestine intended that Akko should become part of the Palestinian state, but the town was captured by Israel in 1948 and three quarters of the Arab residents were forcibly displaced. Despite this, the Old City maintains an Arab presence and the Arab population is now estimated to be around a third of the total. This is high for an Israeli city but low compared to pre-1948 demographics.

We were staying at the restored Ottoman guesthouse Arabesque which, despite its name, was owned by a US father-son team. Their project had parallels to the Fauzi Azar Inn in Nazareth, in that the owners had won over the neighbours and sensitively restored a dilapidated old building, transforming it into a coveted haven for tourists which effortlessly combines original features with modern luxury. As well as sumptuous rooms, the space offers a quiet courtyard to escape the bustling Akko streets.

Akko was a place to get lost in. It is said that most places could be reached within five minutes on foot, but the compact geography didn't help me to get my bearings. The circular layout of the city, however, meant that if you just kept walking, you'd end up back where you started before long.

The stone streets were narrow and dirty in places. In summer, there was a smell of garbage and stray cats picked through the rubbish. There was an authenticity to the Old City market, which was like Nablus but with a greater expectation of tourist footfall.

At the harbour, the steep stone walls stood around 10 metres high. It is a local custom for people (normally teenage boys) to jump off into the sea and this provides a regular spectacle for tourists. We sat on the thick stone walls and watched a group of young guys take turns at launching themselves off the wall into the waves below. They passed a Palestinian flag between them, creating a colourful parachute which billowed behind the jumper.

Palestinian flags are often not tolerated by Israeli police and people can be arrested or attacked for carrying them, so it was a doubly bold move. In the sea below, several speedboats with music blaring zoomed around, creating waves and offering a slightly hair-raising thrill for tourists. Health and safety weren't words that carried much weight here.

Akko is famous for its fresh fish and its hummus. For fish, Uri Buri, the eccentric Israeli chef, was the best of the best. We had visited for dinner previously and it was one of the finest tasting menus we'd ever had. The restaurant was simply decorated, with the sunset taking centre stage over the bay, and the food was interesting and delicate. During the violence that erupted in 2021, the restaurant was burned down but it was renovated and reopened within the year.

The Said restaurant in Akko, a less refined affair, was an essential stop for breakfast or lunch. Their famous hummus was served on huge individual plates with bread and pickles. There was no menu, the only choice being whether to have the hummus smooth, with chickpeas, or with beans on top. The establishment did a roaring trade, with people queuing outside for tables at peak times, and the simplicity of the business model was genius.

As darkness fell, the lights of Haifa were visible across the bay. These two cities are neighbours, or even sisters, and yet they feel very different. Akko continues to cling to its heritage while Haifa has embraced modernity. Both sit somewhere on the spectrum between Israel and Palestine.

Kindness in Umm Al-Fahm

Looking to grab a quick lunch on a Saturday – Shabbat – in Israel led us into the Arab town of Umm Al-Fahm, where we were greeted with unexpected hospitality. I didn't know anything about Umm Al-Fahm before we went other than that it 'had a bad press', and I was glad I saved the Googling until after our short visit.

On the map, Umm Al-Fahm lies very close to the motorway, and being an Arab town, it felt like a safe bet for a quick falafel sandwich. The map was deceptive, however, and we were soon twisting and winding our way up the steep road into the Fahm hills.

Umm Al-Fahm with its population of 55,000 was bigger than we expected and comprised a rabbit's warren of streets. If the narrow streets were part of a one-way system, we weren't in on it. Eventually, we came to a halt in an unofficial parking spot in one of the winding streets on the outskirts of the town centre.

The plan had been to 'grab and go', but as we entered the café a man sprung up and moved his two young sons, both in crisp white karate outfits, to a smaller table to accommodate us, and the café owner started assembling small plates on the table. It was clear that this would be a sit-in affair.

We ordered falafel sandwiches and were encouraged to select salads and other accoutrements from another counter. The food was good and the service efficient. Strong Arabic coffee was served. By this time, karate dad had finished eating and before leaving he came over to say, 'no money, it's done.'

He didn't know where we were from, hadn't spoken to us, and yet had paid for our lunch. It was touching and baffling in equal measure. The awkward ritual of refusing as well as accepting at the same time followed and left us feeling like we'd missed the opportunity to show our gratitude. It was a highly unexpected and extremely gracious act of kindness.

After karate dad left with the kids, we asked the café owner 'why?' and received a shrug of the shoulders and the wise words that 'Allah decides these things.' The conversation then led to where the best viewpoint in Umm Al-Fahm was and the second act of kindness of the day.

As we got up to leave, a tiny man appeared in the shop's entrance, and we were told that he would take us to the viewpoint. We could do nothing but accept, and he jumped into the front of the car. A few women, in long dark dresses and headscarves, stood huddled in their doorways chatting and casting unsure looks about the arrangement.

'Left, right, *dogarie, dogarie*,' (straight on). We were led back through the narrow, twisting streets and even higher up the hillside to the top of Mount Iskander. The tiny man had slightly greying hair (one of the only signs he wasn't in fact a child) and a thick padded jacket despite the heat. His smile was generous, and he acted as if being whisked away by foreigners was all in a day's work. He beckoned us to stop next to a building site where the viewpoint was partially obstructed, but nevertheless we admired the West Bank stretching out below us with views across to Jenin. We returned the man to the town centre and offered him a small tip which he firmly refused.

The proximity of Umm Al-Fahm to Jenin, and the supposed close links between the towns – one in Israel, the other in occupied Palestine – is part of the reason for Umm Al-Fahm's bad reputation. Whether by flaw or design, Umm Al-Fahm is one of the places where the separation wall is not entirely secure, and people and goods can circumvent the checkpoints to pass between Israel and Palestine.

Over the years there had been various political scandals involving Hamas, and regular accusations that the town was a hotbed for Islamic fundamentalism. In March 2022, two young men from the town travelled to Hadera in Israel where they killed two Israeli border guards. They had pledged their allegiance to ISIS and this incident, and the huge fallout from it, hung heavily over the town.

From its hillside location, Umm Al-Fahm teeters somewhere between Israel and Palestine. In 1949, its leaders pledged allegiance to the State of Israel and its citizens took Arab-Israeli status. Despite a strong allegiance with the Palestinian cause, there was outrage in 2004 when Israel proposed that Umm Al-Fahm and two other Arab towns that form 'the triangle' could become part of a land swap in a future deal with Palestine. Many residents spoke out against the plan and said they felt insulted that their Arab-Israeli citizenship could be stripped from them. Presumably, despite the many challenges faced, their lives were still easier on the Israeli side of the fence.

We were sorry not to have more time in which to visit the Umm Al-Fahm art gallery and we left with more questions than when we arrived. We hadn't asked anything of Umm Al-Fahm, yet the hospitality of the people left a lasting impression that made it worthy of further exploration and required an open mind to consider the unique challenges faced by this community.

Survival in the Negev

As soon as the weather started to cool in the autumn, we took advantage of the chance to explore the Negev Desert area in the south of Israel (called the *Naqab* in Arabic). Surprisingly, it covers around 55% of the country and yet it is home to fewer than 10% of the population. Deserts are not known for being hospitable and the

Negev is no exception: temperatures are extreme, water is scarce, and the rocky landscape is challenging.

As we drove south on Route 40, the trees started to fade away and were replaced by thorny tufts and gnarly shrubs. The Negev serves as a huge backyard to Israel and the barren landscape was dotted with ugly industrial structures and military training camps, tucked away from everyday sight. For miles we were blinded by the brightest light emanating from an incredibly tall structure which we discovered was the Ashalim solar power station. There was a futuristic feel about the place that was unnerving.

The vastness of the land was perhaps the most striking thing about the Negev. My friend Mohammad once said he had been shocked on a trip to the north of Israel to see how much space there was. He had assumed that Israel was full and that was why they were forced to expand into the West Bank. He would have been horrified to see the huge uninhabited expanses of land that characterised the Negev. Despite the abundance of land, Israel was unwilling to recognise the many Bedouin villages that housed around 160,000 people across the Negev. It wasn't a question of capacity but rather a determination to force Palestinians off the land.

Large Bedouin camps had been erected close to the roadside, and I tried to catch a glimpse of what life was like for these communities as we drove past. Goats, sheep and camels wandered around children playing in the dust. Various ancient vans and car parts littered the site. The word 'ramshackle' came to mind, and I wondered if this was a life choice or a consequence of the fact that all permanent structures risked being torn down.

Bedouin life hadn't always been as precarious as this. The nomadic Nabataeans established a vast desert caravan route in the

3rd and 4th centuries BCE which connected Arabia to the empires of Greece and Rome. Petra in Jordan was one of their most impressive cities, and across the Negev the remains of Avdat, Mamshit and Shivta left an insight into a prior age of grandeur.

We visited the city of Avdat, 650 metres above sea level, and marvelled at the views across the deep valley. This was close to the Avdat National Park, an Israeli park, which offered a slice of the dramatic landscapes and abundant wildlife that made the Negev so breathtakingly beautiful. Within minutes of arriving, we were walking on a rough path surrounded by high rocky cliffs. On one side a family of ibex clung to the rocks as they gnawed on thorny bushes. I bent down to pick something up and came eye to eye with a huge iguana-sized lizard peering out from underneath a bush.

The sun was beating down and we walked slowly, enjoying the stunning scenery and looking for insects and creatures. Dragonflies the size of small birds darted around in an array of rainbow colours. A park warden prevented us from going into the natural spring to cool off, and instead we sat at the side watching as a large crab scuttled around in the shallow waters.

Later that day, we climbed up to the viewpoint at Mitzpe Ramon and looked down over the awe-inspiring scenery of the Makhtesh Ramon crater. At nine kilometres wide and 40 kilometres long this was often referred to as Israel's Grand Canyon and it was a sight to behold.

We were staying in a kibbutz, and I was fascinated to learn more about this curious Israeli phenomenon. The first kibbutz was founded in 1909, and their heyday was in the 1960s with many Europeans and socialist sympathisers coming to volunteer in kibbutzim. There are still around 270 kibbutzim across Israel, and although things have changed significantly they still carry a leftist hippy reputation.

Most are small communities, dedicated to agriculture and communal living. We had driven past many previously, and from the perimeter they were usually protected like fortresses with yellow metal gates and strict access control.

In the evening, we were surprised to see that Arabic was the main language among the other guests. One man told us that he was from Hebron, but he stayed on the kibbutz during the week and travelled home at weekends. It wasn't clear if he was employed on the kibbutz or was using it as affordable accommodation, but it was another side to the hidden economy of Palestinian workers.

Life in the desert entails battling for survival against a harsh climate and limited resources. Summer is long, and daily temperatures often exceed 40 degrees with 50 degrees not unheard of. The kibbutz had invested heavily in ecological technologies to make the most of its limited resources.

As we were leaving, we chatted to a young female member of staff. She told us she had opted to come to the kibbutz instead of serving in the military. Lamenting the fact that Israel still had compulsory military service for young people she shrugged and said, 'small country, lots of enemies.' I didn't press her on who those enemies were. It was interesting that even someone who didn't want to participate in military duties themselves still saw the need for them. The perception of being continually under attack appeared to be deeply ingrained in the Israeli psyche.

Sadly, this came to pass in October 2023 when Hamas militants burst out of Gaza and carried out multiple attacks on kibbutzim members from around a dozen different communities in the northwestern Negev area near the Gaza border. The death toll exceeded 1,100, and images of whole communities wiped out by brutal attacks shocked the world. The notion that Israel, a highly militarised state, could protect its citizens with walls, barriers and brute force was shattered.

The Negev remains largely undeveloped and despite the harsh climate, it is a valuable resource. It is the only part of the Holy Land that feels genuinely spacious enough to accommodate different communities – both Israeli and Bedouin – living alongside each other, but the political situation made peaceful coexistence feel even more utopian and remote than ever.

Travelling around historic Palestine it was easy to see why many Palestinians mourned what was lost to them. Some people still clung to the 1947 UN Partition Plan as being the blueprint for the two-state solution that would bring peace to the region. It was very difficult to see, with over 70 years of history under the bridge, how that was realistic. During this time, several generations of Israelis had put down roots, and the towns and cities – part of the Israeli state – were their home. Many of the places that had been left in 1948 no longer existed or had been reduced to a pile of overgrown rubble.

There were small shimmers of hope in places like Haifa, Nazareth and Akko where it seemed like coexistence might be a viable future, but the events of 2023–24 showed that tentative periods of calm could be shattered without notice, and the damage took years to repair. The reality was that the Palestinians who chose to remain in Israel, by accepting Arab-Israeli status, were not given equal rights under Israeli law and this continued to fuel inequalities and tensions within communities.

It felt like an apartheid system was in place, and until Israel was held accountable for this, it was difficult to see how any lasting peace or stability could be brokered that would allow for coexistence to thrive.

WRAPPING UP

Unwrapping Palestine, and Israel with it, changed my world view forever. There was nothing harmonious about what we found, and each fragment of reality jostled awkwardly within an incongruous whole. When we left Jerusalem in July 2022, it was with a heavy feeling that things would get worse before they got better. There was little hope, and that made it difficult to leave the people we'd come to know and care about.

The diversity of the people who call Jerusalem home should be something that enriches the city. Instead of bringing people together, however, it appeared that the different religions were pitted against each other and often competed over the same religious sites – in extreme cases, such as in Hebron, splitting them down the middle. The religious similarities were buried in favour of highlighting the differences, and the result was that different communities either didn't mix or they clashed, often violently.

Examples of peaceful coexistence were hard to find. Yet it hadn't always been like this, and older generations spoke of Jews, Christians and Muslims living alongside each other without religion being the defining characteristic of an individual or family.

Israel's occupation of the West Bank (including East Jerusalem), and its policy of further encroachment on Palestinian Territories, perpetuated a system that committed grave human rights abuses and an intolerable oppression of the three million West Bank Palestinians.

It was clear to anyone who spent time in Palestine that the Israeli occupation used unnecessary force on Palestinians, and this led to deaths, injuries (many of them life-changing), ritual humiliation, harassment, fear and severe disruption to everyday life. At a land level, the occupation took the form of demolitions, confiscations, refusing building permits, and the building of illegal settlements. Freedom of movement was controlled by the separation wall, checkpoints and a complicated permit system that prevented many Palestinians from accessing Israel. When these measures were combined with a justice system that was designed to favour Israelis and provide impunity for Israeli settlers the result was the toxic suffocation of all Palestinian rights and freedoms. This was the ugly face of occupation that I witnessed.

Whether you called it racism, discrimination, apartheid or inequality, the facts seemed clear that international law was being flagrantly contravened in multiple ways. Several high-profile reports by Human Rights Watch (2021) and Amnesty International (2022) presented years of meticulously researched evidence to justify the claim that Israel was an apartheid state. Yet, arguing the semantics of apartheid did nothing to reduce the level of persecution and oppression that was commonplace across Israel and the Occupied Palestinian Territories.

The International Criminal Court's case to investigate war crimes committed against Palestinians had made little progress since it launched in 2019, and it wasn't clear that any change would follow the ICJ's ruling in July 2024 that the occupation of the West Bank and Gaza was illegal. This hinged on the argument that Israel had not fulfilled its responsibilities as an occupying power. Despite the wealth of evidence being offered, it appeared that the international community was still unwilling to confront Israel and to decisively push for peace and accountability for what was taking place.

During my time in Jerusalem, I often wondered about the level of awareness that the average Israeli had about Palestine. Great effort was taken to ensure that most Israelis would never need to cross a checkpoint nor see the separation barrier, let alone meet the people who lived behind it, and it didn't feature highly as an election issue in Israel. It wasn't clear if control of the media and public narrative were so good that Israelis were sheltered from the reality of life in Palestine, or if they simply didn't care.

Clinging on to what remains of Palestine is an urgent and all-encompassing struggle for many Palestinians. We had heard people, especially the younger generation, say they no longer cared what it was called. They would sacrifice their dreams of an independent Palestine if it meant being able to stay on their land and live in peace with equal rights to Israelis.

Thoughts of peace and equality felt particularly remote following the events of October 2023. I had seen with my own eyes the spirit of Palestine and travelling around Nablus, Ramallah, Bethlehem and the villages in between, I found a unique place with a thriving culture, a strong identity, and a deep connection to the land. I was continually impressed to meet people who lived for their family and their land, and under the wide blue sky of Palestine it was easy to believe that this was enough. People received us warmly into their homes and the stories they told were filled with love and hope amidst lives overshadowed by pain and suffering.

A new story is needed. A story where Mohammad and Mustafa don't live their whole lives in a refugee camp. Where Hassan didn't have to camp out overnight to stop his land being stolen. Where Ali could travel to work directly rather than taking indirect routes across checkpoints. The war that started in 2023 felt like a

WRAPPING UP

watershed moment. In the months following October 2023, and during 2024, people around the world cried, and protested. They wrote to politicians, and they begged for a new world order where Palestinian lives were valued as equal to Israeli lives – and indeed all lives around the world.

The walls and double standards need to fall if Palestine and Israel are to have any sort of future that isn't built upon blood and retaliation.

Change won't come from the political order. It needs to come from people around the world uniting to say *'khallas'* ('enough' or 'it's done') to the occupation and the loss of innocent life – on both sides. Our humanity unites us, and as humans we have to demand better. We have to use our voices, our votes and our passion as if the mothers, brothers, children and family being killed are our own. History will judge us for our inaction as well as our actions. Both Israel and Palestine and the many inhabitants of the Holy Land deserve their security and the conditions to thrive. That shouldn't be the pipe dream of the naïve, but the reality we help to shape.

The End

READER'S GUIDE

This book assumes no prior knowledge of Jerusalem, Israel and Palestine. Below are some words and terms in alphabetical order that appear throughout the book. These are my explanations, in 'jargon-free' language rather than official definitions.

'1948' places – This is used by Palestinians to refer to places that were part of Palestine before the creation of Israel in 1948. Most 1948 places have a large Arab population who were forcibly displaced during 1947–49. Towns and cities such as Akko, Nazareth and Umm Al-Fahm continue to have a large Arab-Israeli population. Some Palestinians use the term '1948 land' to refer to all of Israel.

Areas A, B and C – The Oslo Accords divided Palestine into different administrative areas. Area A (18%), where the Palestinian Authority (PA) administers civil and security matters; Area B (22%), where the PA administers only civil matters; and Area C (60%) where Israel maintains full control. The plan was that control of Area C would be gradually passed over to the PA but instead Israel has consolidated their control over Area C by building extensive settlements for Israelis to live in and supporting infrastructure.

British Mandate – In December 1917 Jerusalem was occupied by British and Allied forces under the command of General Allenby and the occupation of Palestine by the British was complete by 1918. At the end of World War I the League of Nations agreed that Britain should rule Palestine under a mandate to protect both the native peoples and the interests of the international community.

Following the Balfour Declaration, the mandate was also to promote the creation of a home for the Jewish people in Palestine. The British Mandate took effect officially from 1923 and lasted until 1948. Any successes in establishing an effective administration during this time were overshadowed by Britain's failure to prepare for the peaceful handover of power to both sides.

Checkpoints – In 2020, OCHA reported that Israel had 593 checkpoints and road blocks across the West Bank. These control the movement of people and goods into Israel, which Israel claims is necessary to provide security. Checkpoints are manned by armed Israeli military personnel who can search people and vehicles and refuse entry without reason. They are a place of danger and harassment for Palestinians, many of whom need to cross checkpoints daily for work or family reasons. They also prevent the import and export of Palestinian goods which stifles the economy.

Creation of Israel – In the late 19th century, the Zionist movement gained popularity in its calls for the creation of a nation state for the Jewish people. Following World War I and during the British Mandate period, plans were made for Israel to be established in Palestine.

World War II and the horrific events of the Holocaust gave greater impetus to the argument that the Jewish people needed a country to call their own. The United Nations, newly formed in 1945, was tasked with developing a partition plan which would separate Palestine into two separate states for the Arab and Jewish populations. This plan included withdrawal of the British forces.

The plan was adopted by the UN in November 1947. Israel was established on 14th May 1948 with David Ben Gurion as its first prime minister. The British forces withdrew without having prepared any sort of handover and with ill-managed violence between Jews and Arabs which laid the foundations for the Nakba.

East and West Jerusalem – West Jerusalem is defined as the part of the city that was separated in 1949 when the Armistice Agreement left Israel in control of the western part and Jordan in control of the eastern part, including the Old City. Israel captured all of Jerusalem in 1967 and annexed it to the State of Israel. Although governed by a single municipality, policing and services are different. These days West Jerusalem has a distinctly Israeli/Jewish feel and East Jerusalem is the Palestinian (Muslim/Christian/Arabic-speaking) part of Jerusalem. Palestinians consider East Jerusalem to be the capital city of a future Palestinian state. There is a growing number of Israeli settlers living in East Jerusalem and it includes a number of suburbs that are now physically separated from the rest of East Jerusalem by the separation wall.

Gaza – Gaza is a small strip of land that lies on the Mediterranean Sea and borders Egypt to the south and Israel to the north and east. It is home to over two million Palestinians. Gaza has been under a full blockade since 2007 which means that Israel controls the entry and exit of people and goods into Gaza. It has long been considered a humanitarian crisis and the world's largest open-air prison. On 7th October 2023 Hamas militants broke out of Gaza, killing 1,100 Israelis and sparking an intense bombardment of Gaza which killed over 40,000 Palestinian civilians in the first year of war.

Green Line – The Green Line is the invisible border that separates Israel from the Occupied Palestinian Territories. The line was agreed during the 1949 Armistice Agreement between Jordan and Israel. In central Jerusalem, it is an unmarked border with the tramline following one section of the line between East and West Jerusalem and there are no checkpoints dividing it.

Historic Palestine – This term is sometimes used to describe all of the territory that now comprises Israel and the Occupied Palestinian Territories (before the creation of Israel in 1948). It is also known by both sides as the land 'between the river and the sea', referring to the River Jordan and the Mediterranean Sea. I have used it to identify places in modern-day Israel that are of historic significance to Palestinians.

Holy Land – This term is used to describe the entirety of Israel, Palestine and parts of Jordan which are of religious significance to all Abrahamic faiths – Christianity, Islam and Judaism. The most prominent Holy Land sites stretch from the Sea of Galilee in the north of Israel, down through the River Jordan to Jericho and onwards to Jerusalem, Bethlehem and Hebron.

Intifadas – The **First Intifada** was a period of Palestinian sustained resistance to the occupation between 1987–93. During these six years around 1,200 Palestinians were killed by Israeli forces who were criticised for using disproportionate lethal force. Non-violent resistance included a boycott of Israeli goods and a refusal of many Palestinians to work in Israel. The **Second Intifada** took place between 2000–05. It was a period of violence which was characterised by Palestinian suicide bombing attacks in Israel and Israeli reprisals and collective punishment. During these five years, an estimated 3,000 Palestinians and 1,000 Israelis were killed; and an estimated 119,000 Palestinians were detained, many of them teenagers who could be held for years without trial.

Israel –
Population: 10 million (as of end of 2024).
Main religions: Jewish (75%), Muslim (18%), Christian (2%).
Primary language: Hebrew.

The State of Israel gained its independence in 1948 (see **Creation of Israel**). Israel is a Jewish state and as such it is able to legislate in favour of Jewish people and preserving Israel's Jewish heritage. Where Israel is mentioned in the text this refers to state governance and authorities rather than the Israeli or Jewish people.

Lord Balfour – In 1917 Lord Balfour, the British foreign secretary, made a declaration stating that he 'view[ed] with favour the establishment in Palestine of a national home for the Jewish people.' Britain had supported Arab forces to bring an end to the Ottoman rule of Palestine and Britain had made contradictory promises and commitments regarding the future of the land. Balfour and the British government were accused of not doing enough to protect either the indigenous Palestinian people or the Jewish people in the years leading up to and immediately following the creation of Israel in 1948. Lord Balfour is often unfavourably remembered as the 'architect' of occupation.

Nakba/ Naqba – This is a Palestinian word which means 'catastrophe' in Arabic. It is used to refer to the events during 1948–49 when an estimated 750,000 Palestinians were forcibly displaced from their homes leading to many deaths. These events occurred during the creation of the State of Israel. Many Palestinians were forced to flee and ended up in Gaza, the West Bank, Jordan, Lebanon and Syria. Israel's policy of forcing them to leave helped to expand the territorial boundaries of Israel and minimise its non-Jewish population. With few exceptions, the Palestinians were not permitted to return.

Occupation – International law considers Israel to be the occupying power in Gaza and the West Bank, including East Jerusalem. The International Court of Justice has said this occupation is illegal. Since 1967, the occupation has placed all Palestinians under Israeli military rule, which has denied them the right to exercise the freedoms citizens normally enjoy, such as freedom of movement and equal treatment in legislation.

Occupied Palestinian Territories (OPTs) –
Population: 5 million (2 million in Gaza, 3 million in the West Bank).
Main religions: Muslim (98%), Christian (2%)
Primary language: Arabic

This term is often used to refer to Palestine as it recognises the ongoing Israeli occupation as a barrier to an independent Palestinian state. Israel occupied the West Bank (including East Jerusalem) and Gaza in 1967 and has not withdrawn from these territories despite repeated calls from the UN and other bodies that it must do so or be in contravention of international law, which the UN International Court of Justice (ICJ) has now said it is.

Old City – The Old City of Jerusalem is one square kilometre in size and is home to the Western Wall, the foundations of which are believed to have been the Jewish Holy Temple (on the spot that Jews refer to as the Temple Mount), the Muslim Al-Haram Al-Sharif (the Al-Aqsa Mosque compound including the Dome of the Rock, Islam's third holiest site – sitting right above the foundations of the old Jewish Temple) and the Church of the Holy Sepulchre where Jesus was said to have been crucified and buried. It is a commercial as well as residential area and is divided into what is now known as the Muslim, Christian, Jewish and Armenian Quarters. Seven gates lead into the Old City and it is largely pedestrianised. Israel occupied it in 1967 and it became part of Israel under Israeli law and part of the Occupied Palestinian Territories under international law.

Oslo Accords – Following the violence and turmoil of the intifada years, peace talks were held to seek a resolution to the conflict. The result was a set of agreements between the Government of Israel and the Palestine Liberation Organisation. The First Oslo Accord was signed in Washington in 1993 and enabled the creation of the Palestinian Authority, with limited powers of governance over parts of the West Bank and Gaza. The Oslo Accords divided Palestine into Areas A, B and C with the intention that all areas would be placed under Palestinian control five years later. Over 30 years on, Israel has expanded its control of Palestinian land.

Ottoman rule – Palestine was part of the Ottoman Empire for 400 years between 1516 until the British took over in 1917. During this time the Ottomans were known for their oppressive rule and heavy taxation as well as significant building projects. During the rule of Suleiman the Magnificent in the 16th century, the Old City walls and the Dome of the Rock were restored.

Palestine – Before the creation of Israel in 1948, all the land belonging to modern-day Israel and occupied Palestine was referred to as Palestine. It had been ruled by the Ottomans for 400 years and the British for over 20 years so there was no experience of an independent Palestinian state. Prior to the creation of Israel in 1948 the United Nations proposed a partition plan that would create a Palestinian state alongside the new State of Israel, but this did not happen. The majority of UN members have recognised Palestine as an independent state but the UK, US, Germany, France, Canada, Australia, Japan and other Western powers do not recognise it as such, arguing that it does not have control over its borders, economy and security and it is under Israeli military occupation. Palestine is often referred to as the 'Occupied Palestinian Territories' and refers to the West Bank (including East Jerusalem) and Gaza.

Palestinian Authority – Established in 1994 following the Oslo Accords, the Palestinian Authority (PA) ruled over the West Bank and Gaza until 2006 when Hamas took control of Gaza. Based in Ramallah, the PA was led by Yasser Arafat until his death in 2004. Since 2005 the PA has been ruled by Mahmoud Abbas (Abu Mazen). Abbas has been criticised for his authoritarian leadership, for not holding presidential elections since 2005, for corruption and, by many, for compromising the goal of independence by collaborating with Israel on its occupation. The PA has very limited powers and as such can only perform some of the functions of an independent state.

Refugee camp – Following the Nakba and the displacement of Palestinians from their homes in 1948, the United Nations established 58 recognised refugee camps across Jordan, Syria, Lebanon, the West Bank and Gaza. These were intended to be temporary, but they are still in place and the United Nations still provides some essential services in refugee camps through the United Nations Relief and Works Agency for Palestine Refugees (UNRWA).

Religions are born – When Jesus started spreading the Christian message, Judaism had been around for an estimated 1,500 years. The First Jewish Temple was destroyed in 586BCE and the Second Temple was destroyed by the Romans in 70CE. It was only in 313CE when the Roman Emperor Constantine converted to Christianity that it became permissible to start building churches. The Church of the Holy Sepulchre (335CE) and the Church of the Nativity (339CE) are two of the earliest surviving churches in the world. Islam was founded in the year 610CE. Construction of the Dome of the Rock started in 685CE following the Arab Conquest of Jerusalem by the Caliph Omar and it was opened in 692CE, marking the spot where the Prophet Muhammad ascended to heaven. This is said to be the same spot (Mount Moriah) where the Prophet Abraham was tested by God and the First and Second Jewish Temples stood.

Roman times – The Romans controlled Palestine from around 63BCE with the infamous King Herod ruling a state in Palestine (Judea from 37BCE). He was a talented diplomat as well as a ruthless ruler accused of mass killings and brutality. He is credited with grandiose building projects such as restoring the Second Temple, and building Herodium, Masada and an impressive aqueduct system. He was king at the time of Jesus's birth and was said to have murdered baby boys to protect his authority.

Salah Ad-Din – In 1187 Salah Ad-Din (commonly referred to as Saladin in the West) captured Jerusalem from the Christian Crusaders and it fell under Islamic control shortly afterwards. He allowed Jews to resettle in the city and is known by Muslims as a hero who saved Jerusalem. Salah Ad-Din Street in East Jerusalem is one of the main commercial avenues leading to the Old City.

Separation wall/barrier – Israel began construction of the separation barrier ('the wall') in 2002 when the Second Intifada was at its height, claiming that it was a necessary temporary security measure. The wall is twice the length of the Green Line that divides Israel and Palestine and has been used to confiscate further land from Palestine. In many places the wall runs through the middle of villages and has cut Palestinians off from Jerusalem. The most famous section of the wall in Bethlehem has become a global icon of the occupation. It is also known as the separation – or apartheid – fence, barrier or wall. In 2004 the ICJ ruled that the wall was illegal.

Settlements – Illegal Israeli settlements are areas where Israelis have built homes in parts of Palestine that were occupied after

1967. Since the early 1970s settlement building has been a strategic tactic of successive Israeli governments to expand the State of Israel. Settlements are usually gated communities which are heavily protected. They are often established on confiscated Palestinian land and as well as fragmenting Palestine they undermine both the idea and the practical implementation of a two-state solution. Settlements enjoy the full protection of the State of Israel, which has built extensive infrastructure to accommodate them.

Settlers – Settlers are Israeli people who choose to live in Israeli settlements. Some people choose to live in settlements for practical reasons including state subsidies and incentives, while others are motivated by ideological reasons, such as seeking to expand the State of Israel. Most settlers live in properly planned and developed towns with good infrastructure and transport connections. A smaller number establish outpost settlements by forcibly taking Palestinian land. Settlers in these smaller outposts often use violence to terrorise and intimidate local Palestinians, destroying land and property to coerce them to leave. Settlers are seen as having impunity as they are rarely prosecuted for crimes, including the killing of Palestinians.

Sheikh Jarrah – This Palestinian neighbourhood in East Jerusalem lies one kilometre outside the Old City. It is mostly home to elite Palestinian families and many of the foreign consulates and NGOs. It made headlines in 2021 for the violence that erupted in the wake of several eviction cases which were served against Palestinians by Israeli settlers seeking to claim the area.

Six-Day War – In 1967 Israel occupied areas of Palestine, Syria and Egypt during the Six-Day War. Israeli forces drove Jordan out of East Jerusalem and the West Bank. Israel captured the Golan Heights area from Syria and the Gaza Strip and Sinai from Egypt. Israel still occupies these, along with the West Bank including East Jerusalem. Despite repeated calls from the UN for Israel to respect pre-1967 borders, Israel continues to build on occupied land and considers Jerusalem to be the undivided capital of Israel.

West Bank – The West Bank is a stretch of hilly territory to the west of the River Jordan and to the east of the plains of Israel by the Mediterranean Sea. It was named the West Bank when Jordan annexed the territory between 1948 and 1967. Jordan then saw itself as made up of an East Bank and a West Bank. It was occupied by Israeli military forces in 1967, and divided into Areas A, B, and C after the Oslo Accords in 1993. Around three million Palestinians live there, but so too do hundreds of thousands of Israeli settlers, with the support of the State of Israel. The West Bank includes East Jerusalem with the Old City at its heart.

Zionism – Zionism was founded as a political movement at the end of the 19th century to help establish a Jewish homeland in what was then Palestine under Ottoman rule. There is no single vision that unites Zionism, and having established Israel in 1948, strands of Zionism vary in their views on how the homeland should be consolidated. Some Zionists advocate that Israel extends to all of historic Palestine, while others would like to reach a territorial accommodation with Palestinians.

ACKNOWLEDGEMENTS

This book is dedicated to the friends we made in Palestine who shared their family homes, their stories, their home cooking and their time with us so that we could start to understand what it means to be Palestinian. All of the characters and their stories are true but some of their names have been changed in the text to protect their identities. For that reason, I'm not going to list them all here, but they know who they are.

It has been a real pleasure working with the team at Bradt who have been professional and enthusiastic about the project throughout. Sincere thanks to Adrian Phillips, Anna Moores, Claire Strange, Neil Matthews, Ian Spick and David McCutcheon. A special thanks to Gail Simmons who expertly and patiently guided me through the editing process and to my friend Martin Sterling for his unofficial editorial support.

My heartfelt thanks go to Thiru Abeyewardene for allowing me to use her wonderful Jerusalem artwork on the cover and in the book but more than that for being the best Sheikh Jarrah neighbour we could ever have hoped for.

Unwrapping Palestine was not a solitary journey, and many dear friends have unnamed cameo roles in the book. I hope they will enjoy spotting themselves in the text while understanding why I've made Palestine itself the leading character.

Finally, to my husband whose love of the Middle East has been contagious. You have inspired and challenged me, been a critical reader and a constant supporter. I couldn't have done it without you.

Free Palestine.